POLITICAL ECONOMY, CAPITALISM, AND POPULAR CULTURE

POLITICAL ECONOMY, CAPITALISM, AND POPULAR CULTURE

Ronnie D. Lipschutz

WILLOW INTERNATIONAL LIBRARY

ROWMAN & LITTLEFIELD PUBLISHERS, INC.

Lanham • Boulder • New York • Toronto • Plymouth, UK

Published by Rowman & Littlefield Publishers, Inc.
A wholly owned subsidiary of The Rowman & Littlefield Publishing Group, Inc.
4501 Forbes Boulevard, Suite 200, Lanham, Maryland 20706
http://www.rowmanlittlefield.com

Estover Road, Plymouth PL6 7PY, United Kingdom

British Library Cataloguing in Publication Information Available

Library of Congress Cataloging-in-Publication Data
Lipschutz, Ronnie D.
   Political economy, capitalism, and popular culture / Ronnie D. Lipschutz.
   p.   cm.
   Includes index.
   ISBN 978-0-7425-5650-8 (hbk. : alk. paper) — ISBN 978-0-7425-5651-5 (pbk. : alk. paper) — ISBN 978-0-7425-6788-7 (electronic)
   1. Economics—Sociological aspects. 2. Capitalism—Social aspects. 3. Capitalism and mass media. 4. Popular culture—Economic aspects. I. Title.
   HM548.L56 2010
   306.3'42—dc22

2009029801

Printed in the United States of America

You are a slave, Neo. Like everyone else, you were born into bondage, born inside a prison that you cannot smell, taste, or touch. A prison for your mind. Unfortunately, no one can be told what the Matrix is. You have to see it for yourself. . . . This is your last chance. After this, there is no turning back.

—Morpheus, in "The Matrix," 1999*

---

*After requesting permission from Warner Brothers to reproduce the entirety of Morpheus's first exchange with Neo, I was told, "Please be advised that Warner Bros. cannot grant permission to use the dialogue from the film due to certain obligations, which are confidential in nature." Hmm. . . . The exchange can be found at www.whysanity.net/monos/matrix3.html (accessed June 25, 2009), and the complete film script is available at www.imsdb.com/scripts/Matrix,-The.html (accessed June 25, 2009).

Contents

Acknowledgments

T HIS BOOK REFLECTS A LIFELONG IMMERSION in novels and films, especially those having to do with worlds and times other than those in which I have lived. At one time, my interest in these texts was largely restricted to those moments when I had both the money and the time to pursue and peruse them; as I proceeded through graduate school and into professional and academic life, there seemed to be less and less time or money, not to mention the apparent irrelevance of films and novels to my research and writing on global politics. It came as something of a shock of delight, then, when I came to recognize, during the 1990s (and after exposure to constructivism, postmodernism, and poststructuralism), that both politics and political economy not only played a role in the composition of works of popular culture but were also embedded in and reflected by those selfsame works. My first published effort in this direction was, consequently, *Cold War Fantasies: Film, Fiction, and Foreign Policy* (2001), the outgrowth of an undergraduate seminar in which I tried to use films and novels to illuminate the Cold War, which by 1995 was already becoming ancient history. The book appeared not long before the attacks of September 11, 2001, and although still in print, it fell victim to the vicissitudes of global politics.

The book you hold in your hands is farther ranging and much more focused on contemporary matters than *Cold War Fantasies*. Nonetheless, it, too, is premised on the idea that we can see much more in popular novels and films than appears on the page or the screen and that, sometimes, we need to peer through those barriers in order to understand what might "really" be going on, behind the scenes, as it were. You will discover that several chapters have had earlier lives as articles or chapters in other volumes, but a good deal of the material has been written specifically for this book. I hope it proves not only a good read but also an informative one.

While many people, as always, contributed to the making of this book, the final version is my responsibility alone. Nonetheless, among those I want to thank, in particular, are Aida Hozic, Corina McKendry, Mary Wieland, Mary Ann Tétreault, Jutta Weldes, various anonymous reviewers for journals, Susan McEachern, and the editorial staff at Rowman & Littlefield.

Portions of chapter 3 have appeared in Ronnie D. Lipschutz, "'Soylent Green . . . Is . . . PEOPLE!' Labour, Bodies and Capital in the Global Political Economy," *Millennium* 34 (2006): 573–76. Reproduced by permission.

Portions of chapter 5 appeared in an earlier version as Ronnie D. Lipschutz, "Aliens, Alien Nations, and Alienation in American Political Economy and Popular Culture," in *To Seek Out New Worlds*, ed. Jutta Weldes, 79–98 (London: Palgrave, 2003). Reproduced by permission of Palgrave Macmillan.

A somewhat different version of chapter 6 appears as Ronnie D. Lipschutz, "Flies in Our Eyes: Man, the Economy and War," *Millennium* 38 (2009): 1–27. Reproduced by permission.

1

Political Economy, Capitalism, and Popular Culture

βλεπομεν γαρ αρτι δι εσοπτρου εν αινιγματι. ("For now we see through a mirror, darkly.")

—1 Corinthians 13:12

THOMAS "NEO" ANDERSON IS AN INHABITANT of late-twentieth-century capitalist America—or so he believes, along with everyone around him. But the looking glass, as it turns out, is distorted and shows only a very dim reflection of the real world. When the mysterious Morpheus offers him the choice of remaining where he is or "waking up" and entering "Wonderland," a world that we know will be full of strange things and wondrous experiences, Neo hesitates only briefly before reaching for the red pill. What follows exceeds all of his dreams, hopes, and expectations, even though the world he enters is nasty and brutish, not to mention extremely dangerous for human beings. To students of neoclassical economics, Neo's choice must seem strange. After all, in "The Matrix,"[1] he is well paid, well fed, and comfortable—what's not to like? As a "rational actor"—or *homo economicus*, "economic man"—Neo ought to act in his own best interests, preferring comfort, plentitude, and happiness, and he should choose his pill accordingly.[2] Yet Neo is not happy, and so he makes the irrational choice, selecting an uncertain and risky future in preference to the safe and predictable one. The neoclassical economist is flummoxed.[3]

A student of *critical political economy* might, by contrast, see Neo's decision in a different light. Rationality is not everything, one is not always "free to choose," and even if the "truth is out there," it may be necessary to get behind the mirror in order to see clearly. The Matrix is capitalism, and Neo, like those in the audience watching the reflection of the silver screen, is trapped with little possibility of escape. As British prime minister Margaret Thatcher famously said when confronted with opposition to her new economic policies during the 1970s, "There is no alternative" (TINA).[4] But Neo's world is, as things turn out, considerably simpler than ours, and there is an "alternative." Machines keep humanity alive, captive, and trapped within the capitalist Matrix, yet humans can fight, and perhaps defeat, them.[5] In our real world, machines are not that smart, we have choices (don't we?), and the iron cage is of our own making.[6] What prevents us from breaking out into real freedom? The neoclassical economist would say, "This is what people prefer"; the critical political economist would respond, "No, this is what power prefers." Who is correct?

Among other things, this book is about such choices as well as the problem of making them. Using film and fiction as a medium of analysis and a means of illumination, I illustrate concepts, propositions, and practices from both neoclassical economics and political economy—the first defined as accounting for the operation of capitalism and markets, the second explaining how and why capitalism and markets are structured in particular ways that reflect various types of social power. In capitalist society, to which these two analytical frameworks are applied, movies and novels produced for mass audiences—a.k.a., "popular culture"—fill a dual role. On the one hand, they are the products of capitalism, for the most part designed and marketed as commodities to be sold to consumers in large volume. Hence, to be successful in the market, such works must meet certain criteria in terms of costs and revenues, on the one hand, and they must appeal to viewers and readers living in a particular time and place, on the other (e.g., offering gratuitous violence directed toward certain demographic groups, especially young men, possibly as a concomitant to their future participation in war or the competitive market). At the same time, film and fiction also serve to reproduce social being and associated beliefs, contexts, and practices, since these products draw on and mirror those societies and times for which they are produced. As Robert Sullivan, a professor of literature, has explained it, "A Marxian analysis would attempt to look at [a literary] . . . work as a highly mediated 'reflection' of the social conditions (which are in turn subject to the particular economic structure) of its particular epoch."[7] Such an analytical spirit is central to this book.

In this respect, popular culture also reproduces the tenets, principles, and practices that support existing social arrangements—Karl Marx called it our "social being"; Antonio Gramsci, "hegemony"—and it legitimates the very contexts and practices that are showcased. Thus, for example, torture comes to be seen as a routine and necessary means of extracting intelligence from terrorists, a belief advocated on television by both Dick Cheney and Jack Bauer (of "24"). Indeed, we might even say that a work of popular culture succeeds to the extent that it mirrors society and its members' beliefs and practices and in so doing draws on naturalized understandings about social being and, in turn, naturalizes those understandings. The paradox, then, is that even works meant to critique specific aspects and the organization of capitalist society and economy must tap into such beliefs and practices if they are to resonate with audiences and achieve some modicum of commercial success.[8] "The Matrix," consequently, is less an attack on capitalism, per se, than a diatribe against the seemingly invisible power relations and agents that structure the political economy of capitalist society.[9]

The distinction between neoclassical economics and political economy is not hard-and-fast; as a rule, they cast light on somewhat different aspects of the joint processes of social production and reproduction.[10] Neoclassical economics is a discipline and discourse that purports to explain how and why capitalism and "free" markets fulfill individual desires for goods, satisfaction, and freedom, doing so more effectively and efficiently than alternatives.[11] As an analytical-ideological system, neoclassical economics rests on the propositions that (1) people naturally "truck and barter" with each other for the things they want but cannot make themselves or do not possess, (2) money represents a form of stored "value" that makes exchange more efficient than simple barter, and (3) exchange takes place most efficiently in unregulated markets where it is mediated by prices that are a function of the supply of and demand for scarce goods (anything without a price is either priceless or worthless). Moreover, (4) people have preferences, and it is rational for them to calculate the lowest-cost way to fulfill those preferences, and (5) any effort to manage or control production, exchange, or markets is "politics," which interferes with the efficient operation of the system. All else is commentary.

Neoclassical economics cannot, however, tell us *why* capitalist markets are organized as they are, *who* might have a hand in that process of organization, and *how* those arrangements benefit some and not others. Such points and questions are generally naturalized,[12] and to ask about them is to enter the realm of politics (which in neoclassical economic discourse tends to be a pejorative term). This is where critical political economy comes in: it recognizes that there are no markets without politics. Indeed, markets are thoroughly political institutions that require authoritative interventions in the form of rules and regulations in order to function. That means that they are neither natural nor politically neutral.[13] Political economy—at least in its Marxian and critical forms—is concerned not so much with exchange, supply, demand, and price as with how markets and the general economy are structured and configured, why they have those particular forms, and what sources of power shaped them as they are.[14] The critical political economist assumes that social institutions and the relations and practices within them, such as buying and selling, must be organized and operate with the consensus of participants who believe they are acting in their own best interests. Since individuals' interests often conflict with each other, and since individuals often seek to gain advantage over and influence others in order to achieve those interests, those able to shape the rules defining interaction and exchange in social institutions may be able to do so to their own benefit and at others' cost. In particular, in rich societies, corporations and elites can use their economic and "social" capital to induce or pressure executives, legislatures, agencies, and others to pass particular laws and to behave in particular ways that redound to their advantage and to do so in ways that appear to serve the general welfare and interest (thus the so-called Golden Rule: "He or she who has the gold makes the rules").[15]

But the organization of a political economy is not always the obvious result of the deliberate and visible exercise of political and social power by certain parties. As suggested above, the very beliefs, practices, and rules of society may be structured in ways that are accepted broadly as "natural" and inviolable, even while offering preferential advantages and benefits to some individuals and groups. These "mentalities" constitute what Antonio Gramsci called "hegemony," that is, the rhetorical and legal dominance in society of certain social elites and the acceptance of these mentalities as "common sense" by the rest of society.[16] To return to the example that opens this chapter, in a capitalist society, everyone in the United States regards "freedom" as the highest value and a primary goal in life since this allows a person to make those choices he or she most desires and to maximize both economic and social returns and happiness. Inside the Matrix, Neo is free to consume whatever and to live however he wants—so long as he does not interfere with the freedom of others or the security of society; yet he is trapped in that system whose continued operation depends on its broad acceptance by all of its prisoner-inhabitants.[17] Outside the Matrix, Neo is free of the constraints imposed by capitalist society, yet his life is at constant risk, he experiences deprivation, and he can hardly wander about at will. Where is he truly "free"?

Method and Madness

Neoclassical economics and critical political economy are complex and complicated topics—perhaps that is why most people evince only limited interest in them, beyond how much money they can spend before going broke. Most texts in economics and political economy focus on the workings of capitalism as explained through neoclassical equilibrium models of supply, demand and price, trade and comparative advantage, and other related concepts. While such texts offer definitions and equations and incorporate empirical examples and much data, they tend to deal in abstractions, lack much in the way of visual impact, and bear little relationship to "real" social being or how it is experienced by a reader. In this book, by contrast, I use films and novels, most of them produced or published in the United States over the past sixty years, with two goals in mind. First, I describe, analyze, and deconstruct both concepts and practices in economics and political economy: supply, demand, prices, money, inflation, trade, comparative advantage, resources, technology, labor, capital, profit, accumulation, households, class, gender, regulation, and so forth. Second, I show how these concepts and practices are operative in, and integral to, the production and reproduction of the contemporary social order and the hegemony on which it is based. I hope to push the reader/ viewer to consider not only the mechanics of the capitalist economy but also the social contexts and implications of the ways in which production and reproduction are organized, as well as his or her place in that organization (the "matrix" of capitalism if you will).

This text should not be read as a book of film or literary criticism; nor is it a review of a particular cultural genre (e.g., science fiction, even though I draw a great deal on science fiction). I do not refer here to literary or film theories; nor do I write about style and technique—unless they are germane to the discussion. Rather, I focus on the capitalist society with which most of us are familiar and whose symbols, goods, and practices literally saturate our everyday lives as well as the cultural goods we consume. Moreover, in this focus, I rather explicitly limit my selection of works to those produced in and about "the West" (Europe, North America, Australia) or about people from "the West" in what are, to them, foreign lands. It is not that such films and novels explicitly address or focus on capitalism or even economic matters— although some do, and some that do are neither focused on nor produced in "the West." Rather, it is that people are most comfortable with that which is most familiar, and most familiar to most people is the everyday capitalist society in which they live. Consequently, I point to both visible and background elements that illustrate particular concepts and practices and try to examine and highlight some of the contradictions embedded in, and reflected by, such elements.

As an example, consider Coca-Cola. When we (in the global North) encounter a bottle of Coca-Cola, we recognize it as a specific, sugar- and caffeine-laden commodity drink to be consumed at particular times and under particular conditions (e.g., in hot weather, at a party). It is a highly profitable product marketed by a transnational corporation with a presence almost everywhere in the world, and it is a symbol (or signifier) not only of the Coca-Cola Corporation but also of a particular "way of (capitalist) life." When a Coke bottle appears in a film, we recognize it as a probable case of product placement. Even if it is not, we notice and associate. If the presence of a Coke bottle results in people breaking into song, some of us might also detect a reference to an old television commercial.[18] More generally, we make various connections as a result of long-term exposure to the drink as liquid and as signifier.

For instance, in the 1961 film "One, Two, Three," Jimmy Cagney plays C. R. MacNamara,[19] a Coca-Cola executive who tries to sell the stuff to Communist East Germany. We recognize that the company, fifty years ago, tried to use its economic power to penetrate even socialist countries with the not-so-subliminal message that Coke could turn even Commies into capitalists. Contrast such a notion, however, with the reaction of Xi, the !Kung bushman of the Kalahari Desert in "The Gods Must Be Crazy" (1980). He finds a Coke bottle thrown from a passing plane and brings it back to his kin group. They find the bottle very useful, but eventually they fall into arguing over it—not knowing that the world is literally full of such discarded bottles. Xi decides the bottle is an evil thing that must be thrown off the edge of the world, and he journeys to the city to do so. Although we throw away vast numbers of soda bottles every day—for all practical purposes as though they have disappeared off the "ends of the earth"—we rarely impute morality to the bottle itself.[20]

It is also important and informative, as noted above, to pay close attention to the context and background of a work of popular culture: who wrote it and when, how the plot, characters, narrative, ontology, and so on reflect certain contemporaneous signifiers and elements, and how various philosophical propositions are embedded in it. To return to "The Matrix": by now it is a cliché to point out that when a group of Neo's friends comes around to buy his computer hack, the disk is hidden in a hollowed-out copy of Jean Baudrillard's *Simulacra and Simulation* (1994)—although Baudrillard himself claimed that the filmmakers did not understand his work.[21] Or that, as suggested above, Neo must choose between the relative safety of a society governed by mechanical Leviathans within the Matrix and the dangerous and Hobbesian state of nature without, in the "real" world. Such propositions are not always or often so prominently displayed; more commonly they are offered as unseen ontological foundations to the structure of the narrative, in the behavior of the characters therein and, sometimes, as didactic lessons.

At this point, you might ask, does this not read too much into the intentions and even conscious awareness of the authors, screenwriters, and directors? Are you not seeing things that are not there? Does this not distort the meaning of the text or film? One often hears of a film's writer or creator disavowing some interpretation of a hidden or subliminal message or lesson, but such claims are too clever by half. Just as we produce and reproduce society through our everyday activities, without much in the way of conscious or deliberate intent, so do the creators of cultural goods.[22] To make a film or book intelligible to a broad public, a work of popular culture must draw on familiar tropes that allow the viewer or reader to contextualize and comprehend the work. As I have argued elsewhere, this is one reason why foreign films are of limited popularity in the United States.[23] They tend to be framed in terms of culturally distinct assumptions and behaviors and to draw on national varieties of "common sense" that are unintelligible or alien to American viewers. For some, of course, it is precisely that difference that makes such films attractive—think about the pleasure of hearing spoken French even if you hardly understand it or seeing a film set in Paris even if you have never been there.[24] For others, the differences are almost incomprehensible, and they do not want to be bothered.

The Political Economy of Popular Culture

If you search online databases, film sites, and booksellers, you will quickly discover that studies of film and fiction tend to fall into several distinct categories. Some are purely descriptive with, perhaps, some discussion about technical or biographical matters.[25] Others apply various forms of critical analysis to plot, film technique and composition, and genre.[26] Still others address the economics of the industry and how the products are financed.[27] This book takes none of those approaches. Instead, I approach movies and novels as cultural products that, in their composition, can tell us a great deal about the economy and society in which they have been produced. Some works, as we shall see, address the economy quite directly: something in the plot has to do with money or making things or exchange. "Millions" (2004) is an example of such a film. These are pretty easy to understand, although the background assumptions behind the particular plot devices or plot line may not be quite so evident or clear. Others are not so direct: work, production, and exchange are central to the plot, for example, but larger forces are at work. We see this in "Dirty Pretty Things" (2002), in which London's underground economy in labor and organs plays a central role. Finally, in some films and books the economy is almost invisible, yet they are structured in very specific ways determined by relations of production and reproduction. "The Dark Knight" (2008), a highly gendered film, is an example.

This means, then, that we need to expand our understanding of both economy and political economy in order to see them fully in works of popular culture. It is important to recognize and acknowledge that both permeate even those relations and aspects of life we often regard as purely political or social or private. This is not to say economic relations or material stuff—what Marxists call "substructure"—determine everything or that everything we think, believe, and practice is "superstructure" or "false consciousness." It is, however, to argue that we are social beings whose forms of life are shaped, on the one hand, by physical needs and material desires and, on the other hand, by the beliefs, norms, and values into which we have been socialized. The latter play a significant, if not wholly determining, role in shaping the former (substructure), even as the reverse is also the case. To give a mundane (and personal) example, as a scholar and teacher, I believe that books are an ideal way to communicate arguments and knowledge to society. In the same vein, books (sometimes) offer income or status (or both), and they are essential to my prospects for promotion and future income, for which I still have great hopes. I know full well that neither goal, both of which have intellectual and material components, will necessarily be fulfilled through my beliefs and practices, but in writing books I am disciplined, orderly, and a credit to my society.[28]

At the same time, this "double hermeneutic" of theory and practice is not entirely of my own making.[29] When I decided to seek academic employment twenty years ago, I already had a job elsewhere. I also received several other job offers and a choice of what to do in the future. Although I ended up at an institution (University of California, Santa Cruz) well known for its radical proclivities, I did not enter a realm of total freedom: I could decide what classes to teach, but I could not decide not to teach. I could choose my area of research, but I could not choose not to do research. I could select among forms of publication and places to publish, but I could not choose not to publish. (Or, rather, choosing not to do these things meant I would not be employed for very long.) Because my family lacked the income and an adequate down payment, we found ourselves living in faculty housing, first as renters, later as owners, which meant we were subject to the university's rules and in daily contact with other university employees, even when not "at work." My profession and my "production" have strongly molded and determined the very shape of my social being, even when I have not been among other academics. And the political economy of the university—how funds are distributed, by and to whom, and for what ends—has also strongly shaped my work, even when I have been nowhere near the campus. Do my material conditions then determine my consciousness, or is it the other way around?

The quick-and-dirty answer would seem to be yes, but a little reflection suggests a slower and more complex response is in order. After all, although the university (in the generic sense) is a material institution, with land, buildings, students, faculty, staff, budgets, and all the rest, it is also an idea—or, better yet, a discourse.[30] That is, our society has very specific social objectives for higher education, some of which involve material enrichment, others of which have to do with social and scientific enrichment and the search for "truths," and all of which have to do with reproducing society through the production of students, faculty, and research. The regulations that govern life and work within the university are, therefore, directed toward these objectives—not that they are always or ever clear or undisputed—and these rules both enable and constrain those who teach, learn, and work within the institution. As all academics are only too painfully aware, the rules can be changed—usually by administrators, sometimes with faculty and staff input, rarely in consultation with students—in ways that can profoundly affect production in, and reproduction of, the institution. When budgets are cut, economics are at work; when budgets are cut for some and not for others, political economy is at work.

Popular culture is not a social institution in the same way a university is. Rather, it pictures and reflects institutionalized beliefs, practices, and outcomes. Yet, many of the same features that apply to the university apply to popular culture since communication must always involve more than one person. It is possible, of course, to write a novel and hide it in a desk drawer, never again to see the light of day (films, as visual goods, rise or fall on the basis of audience reception, although some go directly to video while others are put on a high shelf in one storeroom or another to live on only as rumor or myth). But the same forms of social consciousness, of rules, constraints, and possibilities, influence the shape and content of the work. To return to Robert Sullivan's discussion of social criticism,

> Good Marxist [social] criticism addresses not only the content of a given text, but also its form. For example, one might argue that Pope's poetry "reflects" (betrays, illustrates, refracts) in its content the stable union of "a bourgeois class in alliance with a bourgeoisified aristocracy," and that its form, the circumscribed, balanced heroic couplet, underlines the equilibrium of such a social structure. To take an extreme contrary example, Eliot's *The Waste Land*: here the content relates to the spiritual bankruptcy and ennui brought about by the failures of Imperialist capitalism, the end result of which was the catastrophe of the First World War. The form of the poem is also historically determined as a consequence of its content: the fragmented vision of the poem demands new forms to give it expression. The important thing to remember is that neither

Pope nor Eliot were consciously trying to mirror the economically determined social structure of their era, but each, a Marxist would argue, are trapped within the ideological confines of their time.[31]

I do not want to overemphasize pure materialism as determining of the shape and content of a film or novel—"ruling ideas" play a major role as well, but inasmuch as "ideology" and common sense are generated through social power and reflective of power relations within a society, we can fairly say that any work of popular (or even high) culture will provide insights into both economics and political economy.

What Is in the Rest of This Book?

In the chapters that follow, I proceed using a more or less logical method. I begin with fundamental concepts in neoclassical economics with reference to particular aspects of critical political economy and then proceed to more structural and contested arguments. Thus, chapter 1 takes on money, while chapter 6 focuses on regulation. This book does not cover everything relevant to the economy, just as one cannot find everything relevant in film and fiction—for example, collateralized debt obligations, or CDOs, a central "actant"[32] in the financial crisis that began in 2007 and really took off in 2008 and 2009, have yet to appear in movies or novels (although numerous online videos seek to explain them). Nor have I dedicated much space to the corporation. And I address some matters that might not seem to fall within the purview of either economy or political economy—in chapter 7, for example, I argue that Heath Ledger's Joker in "The Dark Knight" is a synecdoche for unregulated capitalism and the anarchy it can bring. Brief synopses of the chapters follow.

Chapter 2: Money and Desire

Everyone, it would seem, wants money; yet, if we take debates over the current financial crisis as our cue, very few people fully understand what it is or how it works.[33] Money is usually regarded as, first, a medium of exchange; second, a store of value; and, third, an indicator of the relative prices and scarcity of goods in the market. Sociologically, money is a naturalized device—perhaps it would be fair to call it an element of an economic discourse—that allows exchange of goods to grow beyond simple barter. In this role, money also facilitates long-distance trade, investment, and speculation. But money always seems to be scarce—coming into money, whether legally or not, is always a topic of interest (see, e.g., the novels of Jane Austen)—which is why so much of popular culture is concerned with its acquisition and expenditure.

Wealth and the lifestyles of the rich and famous are also popular topics. For a favored few, accumulation of stuff proceeds beyond the stockpiling of goods and acquisition of real property to profit and personal and social wealth. But economic growth in capitalism is hardly a pure process of matching supply and demand, for desire can extend far beyond that which might seem acceptable. And exchange is not always peaceful, as we shall see in chapter 8. This chapter examines the relationship of money to desire, how the latter is transformed into things that can be bought and sold, and why some people become rich while others do not.

Films and books discussed in this chapter: "Three Kings" (1999); "Millions" (2004); "Wall Street" (1987); *Bonfire of the Vanities* (novel, 1987; film, 1990); "The Big Lebowski" (1998); "Dirty Pretty Things" (2002).

Chapter 3: Bodies and Possessions

Capitalism is, in historical terms, a unique form of social organization[34] in that it seems to mold all aspects of human life into its forms and practices and to place "value" on everything—including human life. Indeed, the term *value* has a dual meaning, applying to the cost of an item as well as to those norms and principles held to be socially important. From the neoclassical economist's perspective, anything of value must have a price (so long as it is not "priceless"), and everything with a price has value. From the perspective of critical political economy, the uniqueness of capitalism arises from a different view: it is grounded in economic and social groups—class, race, gender—and especially those with capital who hold the right and capacity to buy others' labor power and to turn their labor into a source of profit. For the neoclassical economist, the cost of labor and the price of a thing in the market bear no relation to each other, while from a Marxian and critical perspective, there must be a connection, although this is not generally reflected in the price of things. From both perspectives, there is a certain irony in the fact that, today, people are so plentiful that they have no intrinsic economic value unless they are wealthy or have some kind of skill or personal quality that can be commodified, appropriated, and sold in the market. Moreover, in the "old days" people bought and consumed mostly things produced in factories and on farms and sold their labor in order to buy things at the general store. Today, more and more, with people's desire for things ever more easily satiated, they also engage in "body work," producing and consuming the body through dressing, adorning, piercing, tattooing, and modifying it in other ways. The surplus value of the labor that people put into the constant creation and revision of their bodies and identities offers endless opportunities for extraction, reproduction, and accumulation by capital.

Films and books discussed in this chapter: "Soylent Green" (1973); "Invasion of the Bodysnatchers" (1956); "The Return of Martin Guerre" ("Le retour de Martin Guerre," 1982; historical book *The Return of Martin Guerre*, Natalie Zemon Davis, 1983; American film remake, "Sommersby," 1993); "The 6th Day" (2000); "The Net" (1995); "Thelma and Louise" (1991); *Fight Club* (novel, 1995; film, 1999); "Sex and the City" (2008); *Pride and Prejudice* (novel, 1813; many film versions); *The Handmaid's Tale* (novel, 1985; film, 1990), "The Gods Must Be Crazy" (1980).

Chapter 4: Development and Motion

Movement is central to the functioning of capitalism, whether it is the movement of goods in a market or bodies around the world. Capitalism works so well because it is premised on specialization in production and the exchange of the resulting goods. Such specialization might lie in local concentrations of precious gems or cheap labor, in terms of Adam Smith's parable of the pin factory or as a modern parable of "microserfs" writing bits of computer code for a new Microsoft operating system. Through the division of labor and comparative advantage, people can trade with others what they make best (or have the most of) for things they want that others create and are willing to exchange. The result is greater wealth for all—or so the story goes. Experience suggests that markets do not always work to the advantage of everyone, especially where natural resources such as oil are concerned. Sometimes stuff is scarce, and prices rise rapidly to astronomical heights, but if there is too much of something—oil, labor, widgets—suppliers can find themselves at the mercy of buyers who will pay as little as possible. Power is not absent from markets, trade, or development, and those with various forms of power are able to gain the better deal, often as not.

Films and books discussed in this chapter: "Syriana" (2005); "Mad Max" series (1979, 1981, 1985); "They Live!" (1988); "To Serve Man," episode of "The Twilight Zone" (1962); *The Martian Chronicles* (1950); "Blood Diamond" (2006); *The Constant Gardener* (novel, 2001; film, 2005).

Chapter 5: Technology and Alienation

Given that cultural consumption has become an important mode of production and reproduction in late modern capitalism, separation from the "product" of work in both cognitive and physical terms, as theorized by Marx and others, is a widespread effect in contemporary societies. Thus, the trope of "aliens among us" so frequently illustrated in film and fiction usually reflects some form of alienation from labor, society, or both. Aliens are "out of place," and those who are alienated certainly feel dislocated. New forms of technology are often central to the emergence of alienation, whether in cyberspace or "meatspace." This has been a conceit central to cyberpunk, but the proliferation of virtual reality worlds and games on the Internet serves to commodify alienation as players become immersed in, and addicted to, political economies for which they must pay in order to experience escape. One day, perhaps, we and our machines will become one.

Films and books discussed in this chapter: "The Matrix" (1999); *Fight Club* (novel, 1995; film, 1999); "Falling Down" (1993); *Snow Crash* (1992); *Glasshouse* (2006); "Blade Runner" (novel, *Do Androids Dream of Electric Sheep?* 1968; film, 1982).

Chapter 6: States and Regulations

Most of the "economy" we confront in everyday life, in the media, and in the academy can be called "distributive" economics: supply, demand, price, preferences, scarcity, surplus, and so on. In this context, power is seen as a critical resource; hence, the more powerful get to decide on the distribution of goods and other things. Yet, another aspect of the economy goes largely ignored: who decides on the rules that structure the economy? We might say, moreover, that "he [or she] who makes the rules, rules the world."[35] To say, for example, that you cannot charge more than $5 or less than $3 for a pack of cigarettes is to discipline behavior in the market. To rule that "intellectual property rights" limit you to only "fair use" of books and articles is to discipline your mind. There are many such rules, and most are so deeply embedded in our consciousnesses and practices that we are hardly aware of them. Using three works of fiction and nonfiction, this chapter compares and contrasts the neoclassical/realist interpretation of the origins of the economy with a critical analysis derived from social theory in order to show just how regulated and disciplined we really are.

Films and books discussed in this chapter: Lord of the Flies (novel, 1954; film, 1963); *Leviathan* (1651); *Man, the State, and War* (dissertation, 1954, book, 1959).

Chapter 7: Economy and Gender

Not only are the economy and the political economy gendered, but their operation depends on the maintenance of two mythically distinct spheres of production and reproduction: family and state. The family is a feminized trope; the state, a masculinized one. The political economy that mediates and encompasses the two also defines and disciplines the binary. That these two spheres are, in truth, of a piece can be seen in almost all films and novels discussed in this book. In some, gendering is clearly visible and central to plot and character, with cross-dressing and other "nonconventional" behaviors. In others, gender is present as a constraining condition that dictates how characters are to act in "normal" society. But gender is also found in films that barely hint at it at all. Westerns, for example, focus almost exclusively on masculine action and heroics and demean nonmasculine behaviors as signs of weakness. The audience pays attention to this only if the central character breaks with this trope (more often than not, the "not-masculine" character will behave in a masculine fashion; recall Calamity Jane or Annie Oakley, and see "Thelma and Louise," discussed in chapter 3). As we shall see, however, even films with "manly men" are deeply gendered.

Films and books discussed in this chapter: "High Noon" (1952); *Nineteen Eighty-Four—A Novel* (1949); *The Handmaid's Tale* (novel, 1985; film, 1990); "The Dark Knight" (2008).

Chapter 8: Capitalism and Disruption

The hallmark of today's capitalist global political economy is endless transformation. Constantly changing systems of production complicate social relations of reproduction, dispersing people among jobs and professions and to the ends of the earth. Although the common story is that such change is beneficial to all, not everyone emerges unscathed by the "churn" of capitalism, and not everyone is willing to accept the results peacefully. Paradoxically, perhaps, the market itself, although usually presented as a realm of peace and stability, is premised upon certain structural forms of disruption and violence. In placing a premium on the "new" and "profitable," the market pronounces a death sentence for the "old" and "unprofitable." Eventually, things may work out; in the interim, however, that death sentence is also pronounced for all of those people left behind with few or no options for the future. They bear no responsibility for what has happened to their livelihoods, yet they bear much of the costs. Neoclassical economists argue that what becomes of these people is a political matter and not of concern to economics—aggregate social benefit matters most. Critical political economists counter that, on the contrary, such matters are always political and must be addressed, if only because justice and fairness demand it. In the long run, as John Maynard Keynes said, "We are all dead." In the short run, however, we have to live.[36]

Films discussed in this chapter: "Falling Down" (1993); "The Full Monty" (1997); "The Decline of the American Empire" (1986); "The Barbarian Invasions" (2003); "Live Free or Die Hard" (2007); "24" (2001–2009); "Syriana" (2005); "The Marathon Man" (1976); "WarGames" (1983).

Chapter 9: Through the Mirror, Darkly

As cultural products, films and novels mirror the societies that create them. At the same time, however, popular culture also shapes and disciplines societies. Audiences learn about rules and rule, see the consequences of bad behavior, and act accordingly. Sometimes they mimic what they see and read and not always in a positive or beneficial way. The rules, regulations, and practices of global political economy are thus both explicit and implicit in the products of popular culture and serve not only as economic goods but also as mechanisms of social reproduction. For the most part, we only see the reflection of these mechanisms and rarely, if ever, look through the screen at the life behind it. This means not that what we see is somehow "false" but, rather, that we take much as given and never interrogate it. Or, to quote Paul in 1 Corinthians 13:

> For we know only in part, and we prophesy only in part; but when the complete comes, the partial will come to an end. When I was a child, I spoke like a child, I thought like a child, I reasoned like a child; when I became an adult, I put an end to childish ways. For now we see in a mirror, dimly, but then we will see face to face. Now I know only in part; then I will know fully, even as I have been fully known.

2

Money and Desire

W HAT WOULD YOU DO IF A BAG OF MONEY came falling through the roof of your house? Would you wonder from where it came? Would you try to find its owner? Or would you think, finders keepers, losers weepers, then count it out and have a good time? Much of popular culture is obsessed with money: imagining it, finding it, making it, printing it, burying it, digging it up, stealing it, giving it away, and, of course, spending it. And money seems quite simple: I give you this piece of colored paper, and you give me that thing/ food/service (a "good" in the parlance of neoclassical economics; as a rule, "bads" are generally not exchanged for money[1]). Money connotes freedom: if you've got it, you can do whatever you please, so long as what you do is legal. (And even that is not always necessary. As the saying goes, "Those who have the gold make the rules"—and those who make the rules can decide what is legal.) Money represents power: you can use it to get people to do what they might never agree to do otherwise (see the film "Indecent Proposal," 1993). Money represents status: spending on expensive things brings recognition; conspicuous consumption garners attention.

But what, exactly, is money?[2] This question seems especially germane today, when trillions of dollars have evaporated in collapsing real estate and stock markets; when money seems to exist more and more as electronic bits and bytes, newly created out of nothing, on the one hand, and as plastic rectangles, on the other; and when the well-endowed individual can go for days without ever laying hands on "real" money, whether paper or coin. I do not wish to engage here in a lengthy disquisition about money's origins, functions, or symbolic representations.[3] Rather, I want to examine what film and fiction tell us about money and markets and, in particular, how the former serves to grease the wheels of the latter, especially through the creation of property and the cultivation of preferences and desires.

Money, markets, and property are age-old human institutions,[4] but naming them raises the question of value: what makes things valuable (a question we examine below)? We generally believe that money has intrinsic value, especially if it is made of gold or silver, but this is something of a misconception since money cannot be eaten and has no literal "use value"—except, perhaps, as adornment. Money is only as valuable as that for which it can be exchanged. Those who accept money in return for a good or service assume that they, in turn, can use that money to acquire other desired goods or services for sale, use, or investment. As anyone who has tried to get rid of "soft" currency knows, this assumption is not always valid.[5] Indeed, under conditions of hyperinflation, as occurred in Germany's Weimar Republic during the early 1920s and is taking place today in Zimbabwe, the "exchange value," or purchasing power, of money can decline by the hour. People come to think it is better to hold on to food and things that will retain their use value than to accept a rapidly inflating and depreciating currency. They may have to haul around huge bundles of paper bills in order to make the most minor purchases—photographs from 1923 show German children playing with building blocks made of Weimar's nearly worthless marks and people burning them to keep warm.[6]

The reverse is possible too: things can also go from being valueless to invaluable (or even priceless), especially if they become scarce, useful, or stylish.[7] But things need to be scarce to be valuable. Indeed, scarcity is a condition in which demand is thought to exceed supply by some amount, and it is required for something to have value so that it can have a price and be available and attractive for exchange.[8] Sometimes goods are withheld deliberately from the market in order to create "artificial scarcity" so as to support high prices (see the discussion of intellectual property rights later in this chapter and in chapter 5).

The cost and supply of diamonds offer one example of such artificial scarcity. For much of the past century, an international diamond cartel established in 1888 by Cecil Rhodes and the De Beers Company, the Central Selling Organization, contracted to buy the production of most of the world's diamond mines, allowing only enough stones into the world market to keep the price of diamonds higher than they would otherwise be (see below and chapter 4 for more on diamonds).[9] By contrast, despite the Organization of Petroleum Exporting Countries' best efforts, the global supply of oil has had a tendency to rise and fall relative to demand, leading to periods of very high prices (almost $150 per barrel in July 2008) followed by periods of very low prices (approaching $30 per barrel in early 2009). This happens even though the total amount of known oil in the world has tended to rise over time and is currently quite large.[10] And in "The Gods Must Be Crazy," Coke bottles are scarce among the Sho of the Kalahari Desert, who have no access to a world awash in them.

These days, money's value is based not on metal content but largely on faith, as well as supply and demand in currency markets. As we shall see, until the early 1970s, the value of money was generally linked to the value of a precious metal—either gold or silver—for which it could, presumably, be exchanged. The price of goods and services, in turn, had something to do with this intrinsic value. For reasons linked to a growing world glut of dollars in the late 1960s and the accompanying inflation, this link was broken in the early 1970s.[11] Subsequently, the world's currencies were valued only in relation to each other—and especially to the U.S. dollar, the global "reserve currency"[12]—and to some set of changing expectations about how that money might be used and its relative worth in the future. Gold and silver continue to have value, and their prices rise and fall in inverse relation to the speculative prices of various monies in currency markets (that is, when the value of the dollar drops, the price of gold rises). But, for the most part, today's money is "fiat currency"—so-called in the sense that its value is "declared by fiat" through markets or by a government's pronouncement—and has no relationship to anything material except what it can buy and, perhaps, the growth prospects of the economy in which it is issued. While it is possible to make vast profits on currency speculation—it is said that George Soros earned more than $1 billion in 1992 by betting against the British pound[13]—someone, or some number of speculators, is always an equal loser. And if you choose to hedge against a decline in the value of your money by stockpiling precious metals, you might gain on the upside but you could also lose on the downside. Not all that is gold glitters.

In this chapter, I outline "the basics" of capitalist economics—those elements intimately familiar to each of us, that seem "natural" but that we never stop to question or ponder. (After all, is it not something like magic that in exchange for a few pieces of colored paper, the barista in your favorite coffee shop will hand over to you a caramel macchiato frappalattecino, half-caf, nonfat milk? Why?) I illustrate several of the basic propositions discussed above, especially the relationship between supply, demand, price, and money as depicted in two films about people's dreams of vast wealth, "Three Kings" and "Millions." I then turn to the process of accumulation, based on profit and speculation. Here, I draw on two works from the 1980s, the film "Wall Street" and the novel *Bonfire of the Vanities*. In the third part of this chapter, I examine the commodification and value of things that formerly had no obvious value in markets, as presented in "The Big Lebowski" and "Dirty Pretty Things," a topic which we shall consider further in chapter 3.

You Have Three Wishes . . . But, Please, Come Up with Something I Haven't Heard Before

The story of Aladdin and the Djinn and similar tales are all structured, more or less, in the same way. The finder of a magic vessel is offered three wishes by its occupant and almost always asks for "fabulous wealth" or "all the money in the world." Not infrequently, such desires end in tears or worse. While Aladdin manages to do fairly well by his genie, the myth of King Midas warns us that having all the world's gold is not always all it is cracked up to be (but tell that to Bill Gates!).[14] Often, the rapid and painless acquisition of large sums of money is linked to a particular moral stance or lesson, especially if such wealth has not been acquired in a just or Protestant fashion. Yet, as the many films about lost cities, buried pirate hoards, and gold mines illustrate, treasure hunters are always hoping to strike it rich, whether from the ground, the lottery, a casino, a sunken ship, or a bank. Then, in what is a popular bourgeois dream, they will be able to live on Easy Street.[15] After all, the rich do not need to fantasize about wealth—they have it—while the poor may dream of it, but more out of necessity than mere desire since they are likely never to achieve it. It is the middle class that never has quite enough money to meet its needs and is always looking for more (see, for example, the film "Fun with Dick and Jane," 1977, 2005). Still, as many movies and novels propose, ill-gotten gains almost always lead to ill outcomes. (Under the old Motion Picture Production Code, movies could not show criminals being rewarded for their thefts[16]; stay tuned for "The Trials and Tribulations of Bernard Madoff: Ponzi Artist").

"Three Kings" suggests such a moral code, although the plot imposes rather painful experiences on its protagonists before they realize this. The film follows the desert adventures of four American soldiers at the tail end of the "first" Gulf war in 1992.[17] Led by Special Forces major Archie Gates, the group follows a treasure map, extracted from the buttocks of a recalcitrant Iraqi officer, which purports to show the location of a bunker containing a hoard of Kuwaiti gold snatched by Saddam Hussein. Eventually, after a number of adventures, Gates and his confederates find the gold, but the fogs of war and peace conspire to complicate their mission. One of them dies, and as they attempt to flee with the bullion, the rest of the group comes close to being killed several times. Along the way, however, Gates and the others do manage to distribute some of gold to the needy and downtrodden, and they use the rest as bribes to facilitate the flight of Iraqi refugees. In this sense, then, the kings are redeemed despite their many moral lapses.

The attraction of gold is, of course, that it makes its possessors fabulously rich. But Gates and his buddies discover there is considerable difference between getting, keeping, and enjoying their haul. Nor is it easy to keep such wealth secret, since, for one thing, people talk—indeed, that is how Gates first finds the map and how the kings eventually lose their loot. For another, bribes must be paid to keep people quiet, especially when lives and money are at risk. Along the way, there are always deserving people who could use a few hundred thousand bucks. And, finally, gold is not so easy to move around—a common weight for a gold bar is four hundred troy ounces, or 27.5 pounds (at today's prices—about $900 per ounce—worth $360,000); you cannot just fill duffle bags and hike off into the desert. Alas! For the three kings, the gold turns out to be almost worthless. A single bar can be used to barter for food, water, or life; one hundred bars are dead weight. This is an instance in which the "value" of stuff depends entirely on where it is and what others are willing to exchange for it (a $300,000 bottle of designer water, anyone?). Moreover, even though gold might be "scarce" in the wider world outside the Iraqi desert, in "Three Kings," there is too much for it to be of much immediate value to anyone.

Yet, who has not dreamed about "pennies from heaven"? That is the gist of the story told in "Millions," as two young boys acquire fabulous wealth without the headaches of weight, transport, or (just) desert. The money they find is not, however, free, clear, or morally clean, and the plot is based on an imaginary event (one unlikely to take place in the foreseeable future): U.K. currency conversion from pounds sterling to euros. A few days before the deadline for exchanging old money for new at British banks, robbers hold up a train carrying tons of soon-to-be worthless paper notes on their way to incineration. The thieves aim to make a quick profit by exchanging the pounds for euros before the deadline. They throw bags of currency from the train, planning to retrieve them later in the day. One of the bags falls on Damien, a seven-year-old Catholic boy who believes in saints and miracles and is praying in his rail-side retreat for succor for the poor. Damien knows about the impending currency change but thinks the money is a gift from God. He decides to distribute as much as possible to the poor before it becomes worthless. Damien, however, makes the mistake of showing the money to his brother, Anthony, who is much less pious and would rather have a good time. No good deed goes unpunished: the robbers, discovering that Damien and Anthony have one of the missing bags of money, ransack the children's home and destroy their Christmas gifts. Ultimately, realizing that the money is nothing but trouble, as well as a cause of sin, Damien returns to the railway tracks and burns the bag and its contents. There, he has a vision of his late mother, who reassures him that she is fine, and he will be too.

In "Millions," money has value, and lots of money has lots of value—at least until it loses its magical properties and is transformed by fiat into worthless paper. In this respect, then, faith in the soundness and value of money is a collectively held delusion or a form of magical thinking, because if no one believes, no one will be willing to accept money as "legal tender." Damien and Anthony, moreover, have very different ideas about that value. Anthony, a quintessential consumer in the making, wants pleasure, luxury goods—the boys try to buy a car but fail—and real estate. Pleasure provides short-term satisfaction but no long-term material or moral benefits; real estate holds its value for a long time, but gratification is delayed (pleasure and pain are further discussed in chapter 8). Moreover, because the money will lose its exchange value in a few days, Anthony has no time to reflect carefully on how to spend it. Damien, by contrast, knows precisely how to maximize social value and is determined to help the poor, who never suffer from scarcity of poverty. While appreciated, his kindness to others also attracts unwelcome attention since young boys rarely have thousands of pounds to spread around. Thus, even if money is legal tender and scarce, too much leads to insurmountable problems. And although money allows us to buy goods and services, it is not really the money we desire—we want what the goods and services can provide us (more on this shortly).

What do these two films tell us about the political economy of money? First, too much money can be as great a problem as too little. In economic terms, an "excess" in the supply of money tends to drive up the cost of goods and services to the consumer, as people are willing to pay higher prices for the things they need and want (thus, in a hyperinflationary economy, money becomes worthless and bread, priceless). Even low levels of inflation may lead workers to demand higher wages, which will give them more money with which to bid on goods and services, whose prices will rise in response. And the cycle continues. Such a phenomenon, called a "wage-price" spiral, is of particular concern to lenders and investors who hold the debts and interest-paying securities of those who have borrowed on credit. On the one hand, in a highly inflationary economy, the value of fixed-interest debts will decline, as the debtor is paid in money of constantly decreasing value—this is why adjustable rate mortgages have become so widespread; payments rise and fall on the basis of money's future value, as determined by interest rates. On the other hand, investors seek some level of return on the money they have committed to a property, project, or bond, and if the inflation rate is high and the return is lower than that rate, their investment will lose value over time. In other words, inflation is favorable to debtors and not so good for creditors.

This summary of money supply and demand and its effects does not, however, tell us why the value of money varies. Here we have to go behind the scenes, so to speak, to ask who or what controls the money supply. That, in turn, brings us back to gold and silver. Centuries ago, when coins and bullion were virtually the only monetary instruments available for purposes of exchange in markets, and gold and silver flowed into and out of countries in response to levels of foreign trade, a real shortage of money could develop.[18] Moreover, coins were often "debased," as people and kings nicked or shaved them for small pieces of (usually) silver or as monetary authorities minted underweight coins, reducing their metallic content below face value. Under such circumstances, to restore both faith in money and its circulation, governments might either have to introduce large numbers of newly minted coins into the economy or issue paper promissory notes that might, at some later date, be redeemed for metal. Not until people were fully convinced that paper money could be exchanged for goods with use value did they become ready to accept paper in lieu of metal—and even today, some still regard fiat paper money with a jaundiced eye and swear by gold.[19]

Once that psychological barrier was overcome—helped, no doubt, by absolute shortages of coinage—the state, which generally held or authorized monopolies on the production of currency, was able to control its flow into and out of the market.[20] Thus, if prices or the economy were in decline, money could be injected into circulation, which would stimulate spending and stabilize prices and the economy. Conversely, if prices were rising, money could be removed from circulation, which would make less available for spending and lead to deflation. But making this an instrument of fine control is difficult—after all, people are not going to go around giving money away, are they? That would raise suspicions about its value.[21] Governments can, of course, mount massive industrial and development projects, such as building dams, roads, and railroads, and pay construction firms and workers, all of which inject money into circulation. This was one of the bases for Keynesian economics,[22] which began to fall out of favor in the 1970s (although the multi-trillion-dollar fiscal stimulus of the Obama administration and the Federal Reserve indicates that Keynesianism is on its way back in).[23]

Alternatively, an economy's money supply can be managed through manipulation of the interest rate, which both represents the "cost" of lending or borrowing money and serves as a means of assessing its value today as compared to some time in the future (this comparison is called the "discount rate," which is the value of a future sum discounted to today's currency or the interest rate that must be paid on money today to make it worth saving rather than spending). Although the interest and discount rates are conceptually the same, we are concerned here with the former, paid by monetary authorities on loans to the state. That authority—usually a central bank, such as the U.S. Federal Reserve or the European Central Bank—establishes the cost of money for the formal economy[24] based on its assessment of whether more or less money should be flowing into the economy. This cost becomes the basis for the interest rate charged to borrowers (the rate paid out to depositors in banks is always lower). Raising the interest rate increases the cost of borrowing money—in effect, decreasing the supply, because fewer people can or will borrow money and let it loose into the economy, while more will invest in longer-term instruments for saving. Lowering the interest rate does the opposite. High interest rates tend to attract deposits and investors, and in today's world of fluid capital, they will also drive up the value of a currency as foreigners buy the appropriate currency or paper denominated in it. Low interest rates tend to do the opposite.

What, then, determines whether a country's central bank raises or lowers interest rates? This decision depends on whether monetary authorities claim to be more interested in a high level of employment or a low level of inflation and stable prices (or both, even though they can be difficult to achieve simultaneously). In the former case, cheaper money should encourage greater investment in the productive economy, more money flowing into the economy, and more spending on consumer goods. Someone has to manufacture the goods, so employment ought to rise in response to demand (although, these days, this is as likely to take place in a different country and have little effect in the consuming country). In the latter case, there is too much money sloshing around—perhaps from the salaries of all those workers, or maybe someone has discovered buried treasure—so more expensive money will lead investors and consumers to spend less and to be more careful with what they have. This, at least, is the conventional argument.[25]

In fact, central banks often premise their decision to increase or decrease the money supply through interest-rate manipulation on political goals and pressures, notwithstanding all claims to independence and insulation from "politics." It is difficult to take such claims of autonomy at face value. Following the bursting of the American "dot-com" bubble in 2000, for example, the chairman of the Federal Reserve, Alan Greenspan, supervised a series of reductions in the federal discount rate to historically low levels (until 2008). "Easy money" underwrote an economic revival that relied heavily on a subsequent real estate boom—now a bust—which extracted capital from houses and injected it into the economy. While much home equity was spent on imported goods, especially from China, the injection of this money into the American economy also supported high levels of consumption and economic growth until 2007. For a variety of reasons, that project did not create an inflationary cycle—in part because it was not strongly linked to job creation and wage increases. With the popping of the "subprime-mortgage" bubble and the accompanying recession, central banks and governments around the world have reduced interest rates to levels even below those of 2000 and injected trillions of dollars and other currencies into all sorts of financial institutions in order to avoid the political consequences of another Great Depression. As of this writing, we do not know whether they will succeed.[26] Money does not cure all ills.

Mo' Better?

In a capitalist economy, the desires—or "preferences," in neoclassical terms—of those with funds to spend, or "liquidity," are supposed to determine what goods and services markets will supply, a notion captured in the old saw that "demand creates supply."[27] Although it is true that everyone has certain basic needs—food, water, shelter, clothing—the source of desire for things beyond these is obscure. In today's world, for example, one "needs" many things to get along—phones, cars, shoes, apples out of season, computers—even though they are not essential to individual survival or, for that matter, a fulfilling life. More to the point, no one is born knowing that he or she needs and desires phones, cars, shoes, apples out of season, computers, or the myriad of other things for sale; that kind of information and "knowledge" must be communicated and learned. I address consumer education later in this chapter; here, I focus on how one gets enough money to fulfill one's desires, given the cost of stuff. There are two different ways to understand this problem.

The first is the idea from neoclassical economics that the monetary value of goods and services equals precisely what people are willing to pay for them. Assuming that the creation or provision of goods and services involves certain unavoidable costs—materials, labor, equipment, shipping, and so forth—the retail price includes those as well as a premium, or "profit," for bringing said stuff to market. That profit equals the amount people are willing to pay for said good or service above the cost of its provision (if this seems tautological, it is). Those who cannot generate profits or who run short of liquid funds to support a money-losing enterprise will find it difficult to stay in business. So, getting people to accept that the profit premium is worth paying is extremely important to the successful businessperson. Advertising is one way to create both desire and such acceptance.

A second approach to understanding this matter involves the Marxist "labor theory of value," a concept maintained by Adam Smith and others but held in very low regard by today's neoclassical economists. In this instance, the retail price of a good reflects not only the costs of materials, equipment, and shipping but also the value of the labor put into it over the wage cost. Under the labor theory of value, the work time it takes to make two different items sets their relative costs. Say that a hamburger takes ten minutes to cook and a bowl thirty minutes to throw; this implies an exchange rate of one bowl for three burgers. Clearly, some incommensurate considerations are coming into play here. The bowl has long-term use value and probably requires skills more advanced than hamburger flipping. Moreover, even if money is exchanged, there is little economic incentive for someone to go into the business of either bowl making or hamburger flipping. Straight exchange of things is called barter and makes no room for profit. The "surplus value of labor" suggests, however, that these things are actually more valuable to consumers who cannot or will not make them but will pay a premium to obtain them. That is, while a consumer could make bowls and burgers, she has better things to do.

Thus, after the basic costs are factored in, the capitalist appropriates as profit, or the "surplus value of labor," the difference between the wages paid to the worker and the retail price of the product.[28] Clearly there is a problem with this approach. The value of work is not the same as value in the market, even though they are denominated in the same monetary units.[29] Moreover, this understanding of value is not the same as that utilized in neoclassical explanations, especially since different workers bring different skills and expertise to what they do and make, and they receive different wages as a result. Only if everyone were to receive an identical wage might it be possible to determine the magnitude of such surplus value, but that would not take into account differences in quality, utility, and demand for goods.[30]

The image of workers in meaningless, low-paying jobs is a trope of film and fiction, whether it involves making cars, clothing, or lunches, as is the struggle to make ends meet from one payday to the next (see, e.g., "Modern Times," "Clerks," and "9 to 5," among many films). Still, how does the capitalist—the owner of a business or the "means of production"—determine how much to pay her employees? How are wages established for different skills and services? Various occupations have more or less fixed pay rates, although these vary depending on geographic location, the time of year, and the size of the "reserve army of labor," if there is one. This is where the labor theory of value begins to run into serious problems. As suggested above, it is unable to provide a clear basis for the absolute value of a worker's time and labor. Given the existence of labor markets, then, the prevailing wage comes to be set, more or less, by the number of workers with specific skills seeking to fill a certain number of available positions in occupations requiring those specific skills. To be sure, the ultimate price for a good or service must factor in the cost of a worker's time and labor, and a business owner must always seek to keep the cost of labor below the market price of whatever is being produced or offered.[31] But because the amount consumers are willing to pay for specific goods or services, which can also depend on competition among enterprises offering similar wares, also determines price, sustaining a profit is not always easy. Indeed, it is entirely possible for an enterprise to operate at top output, sell most of its goods, and still lose money (the example of U.S. airlines and auto companies over the past decade demonstrates this quite clearly), especially since attempts to raise prices in order to cover costs may well drive away customers and hasten bankruptcy and closure.[32]

But such basic principles of economics are not really of concern here since they can be seen easily in everyday life. Of greater interest is how the wealthy acquire their money and capital, how they make more of it without doing any obvious work, and what they can then do with it. The traditional capitalist—he of nineteenth-century top hat—was assumed to plow a considerable fraction of his profits back into his factories, enlarging them, making them more efficient, and getting more out of his workers, thereby expanding his company's reach and driving competitors out of business (or buying them up at bargain-basement prices, as John D. Rockefeller did in the oil industry). Any surplus beyond such investments might be given to public institutions: Andrew Carnegie endowed public libraries and others have established private foundations. Much, however, would be invested in securities, such as stocks, bonds, and other forms of financial "paper." Such investments were usually linked to underlying material assets and flows of money—industry, mines, plantations, state tax revenues—providing regular dividends in return, at a respectable, but not enormous, rate of perhaps 3 to 7 percent. The idea was not so much to generate profits on the paper as to provide a reliable income stream over an extended period—this is where we get the trope of the widow living on returns from her "blue-chip" stocks.[33] If there is a catch here, it is that, should profit rates fall due to recession, declining demand for goods, or enterprise obsolescence, both the dividends and the value of the paper fall too, in concert with the assessed decline in the value of the underlying asset.[34] A truly serious collapse in the economy, as has occurred in stock markets between 2008 and 2009, can wipe out stock values, corporations, and investors on a massive scale.[35]

Such traditional attitudes toward longer-term investment changed in the 1970s, when high rates of inflation in many rich countries ate away at the value of investors' assets and dividends, and they sought investments with higher returns. Speculation—high risk ventures that involve making money on money—became more popular and, indeed, the stuff of news and legend.[36] Takeovers, mergers, breakups, futures, and hedges all offered new ways to make money "work"[37]—and to work it overtime, as it were. Initially, these activities involved "really existing companies" that made things or provided services; subsequently, speculation focused on the rise and fall in value of the paper itself—selling "long" or "short," buying "futures," and making hedges (there is nothing new about hedging one's bets, although there are always new ways of doing it). Although speculation of this sort is really a form of gambling,[38] it is difficult to portray in film and fiction; that is why Las Vegas appears so much more frequently in popular culture than does Wall Street.[39]

"Wall Street" is a film about speculation on companies; Tom Wolfe's novel *The Bonfire of the Vanities* is about speculation on money itself. Both are morality plays, although the latter is also something of a satire on hypocrisy. Like all of Oliver Stone's films, "Wall Street" is didactic; it attacks what he regards as a tragic, even fatal, American flaw: the insatiable desire for money, lots of it. In the United States of the go-go 1980s—a decade that now pales in comparison to the period between 1990 and 2007—as the country was exiting one of the worst recessions since the Great Depression, money was freedom, and what is more American than freedom? "Wall Street" centers around three individuals and a small airline corporation, Bluestar. Carl Fox is Bluestar's maintenance chief and has been with the company for decades; his son, Bud, is keen to make a killing on Wall Street and thereby become famous. He has therefore spurned the opportunity to work with his father. Instead, he is a stockbroker at small firm, working in the "boiler room"[40] making cold calls to potential investors, hoping to "bag the elephant" that will make him rich. Gordon Gekko is "the elephant," a Wall Street speculator whose infamous creed is "Greed is good," and who buys stock in "undervalued" companies. Bud admires Gekko and wants him to buy Bluestar.

Undervalued companies often become targets for takeover, merger, or breakup for two reasons. First, profits and share value are low because management, it is claimed, is more interested in its own welfare than that of the shareholders (something seen recently on Wall Street). So long as those who run the company get their salaries, bonuses, and perks, they have no real incentive to improve corporate performance. Second, as a result of low share value, the company and its properties may be worth more in pieces than they are whole, as expressed in the company's total share capitalization. That is, if its various pieces are "spun off" as separate companies, and shares in the new enterprises are sold in initial public offerings, investors will pay more to get in early in hopes of garnering high future returns. This will increase the aggregate market value of the pieces and make the speculator, who always retains a large fraction of the share offering, extremely rich. Gekko buys stock in undervalued companies, then tries to generate shareholder dissatisfaction and support for replacing management, promising that investors will realize much higher returns once he steps in and reduces operating costs. Moreover, Gekko buys out dissidents who continue to support management by offering them more for their shares than the share price in the stock market. This gets rid of those who might stand in his way. Ultimately, after gaining control of a company, Gekko breaks it up and sells the pieces. He then walks away, having realized a massive profit.

Gekko's ability to do this, however, depends on "insider information" from someone in the company who knows its weaknesses and management's plans. U.S. federal law limits the use of such insider information by corporate management and employees if they stand to profit unfairly as a result. If inside traders are caught, the penalty can include fines, prison time, and banishment from the financial sector (although it is rare for the severest punishments to be imposed). Consequently, Gekko works the phone all day, seeking information from his many inside contacts on Wall Street, some of whom might be willing to provide tips in return for a cut of the action. If the information is laundered through a "cutout"—someone not directly employed by or involved with the target company—it is much more difficult to prove that the law has been violated. Indeed, if the party who first supplies illicit information is caught in the act, he or she must be willing to testify to this effect in order to avoid the maximum penalties and punishment.

In the case of Bluestar, Bud provides the inside information to Gekko, who buys the company at a low price. Bud benefits greatly. But violating a promise he has made to Bud, Gekko decides to break up the company, sell the pieces, and put its employees out on the street. In reprisal, Bud cooks up a complex scheme that saves Bluestar but at considerable cost to Gekko. Bud does not emerge unscathed either, for he is arrested for his insider activities. Turning state's witness, he entraps Gekko, who will go to trial and prison.[41]

We may presume that Stone's moral is that greed is indeed not good; here, how greed operates is of particular concern to our understanding of both economics and political economy. Historically, greed has been seen as an emotion innate to all human beings, one that can be a force for good or evil. Too much greed is bad (as in the case of King Midas); yet greed is necessary to make markets work (see chapter 4 for more on this point). The things we desire are scarce, and we always want more. Thus, we will work extra hard to acquire what we want, deferring gratification until we can afford those things—and, in the process, generate more wealth for society.[42] Some people want things so badly that they are willing to cheat, steal, and even murder to get them—although too much corruption of this sort risks bringing down the entire system. At the same time, there is a limit to how many things we can consume and use immediately, which is why money is so useful. It is portable, has exchange value, and can be used to acquire more stuff today or in the future. It follows, therefore, that more money is good, and one can never have too much of it.

This is also why lotteries and gambling are so popular, especially among those least able to afford such activities. Because the poor and middle classes do not have surplus funds with which to gamble, they can only hope for Fortuna's windfall. By contrast, people with lots of money can risk large quantities on highly speculative investments; if they lose, they will still have lots of money left. Even though Bill Gates has lost tens of billions in the current bear market, he still has tens of billions left. Still, greed does not always go unpunished; consider the many investors who gave their money to Bernard Madoff. He promised returns greater than 20 percent and fulfilled the promise for a time, but his $50 billion Ponzi scheme eventually went bust. Some of his clients put everything they had into his schemes and were left with literally nothing.[43] Robber barons though they were, even Andrew Carnegie and John D. Rockefeller might look askance at such behavior.

Crumbs

Accumulating lots of money generally means finding ways to persuade others that you can supply what they want and convincing them that what you propose to supply is of great value, be it labor, stuff, or information. It's even better if you can convince potential customers that what you are supplying will increase in value if they buy and hold onto it (you can charge them an annual service fee, whether it grows or not). Do not think, however, about actually having to produce and sell real goods; to accomplish this sleight of hand, you do not actually even need to own what you are trying to sell. Indeed, it is possible to become extremely rich simply through arbitrage, that is, by facilitating exchanges between those who are selling and those who are buying and profiting from the "transaction cost" involved in such an exchange (much as a salesperson gets a commission for making a sale). Since buyers and sellers often do not know how to find each other, especially when shares, bonds, and other securities are involved, a middleman who can connect them is very useful, and he can charge for this service.

That, in a nutshell, is Sherman McCoy's job. McCoy, the protagonist of *The Bonfire of the Vanities*,[44] is a young, very rich bond trader. He owns a fourteen-room apartment on New York's Upper East Side as well as a vacation home in the Hamptons (the eastern, very ritzy end of Long Island). He sends his daughter to a very prestigious private school, bankrolls his wife's prodigious spending habits, and even supports Maria, his beautiful mistress. He is a "Master of the Universe." Unfortunately, Maria's driving practices leave something to be desired; they cause the "bonfire" and lead to Sherman's downfall.

One night, returning from the airport where Maria has picked up Sherman, they take a wrong turn off the highway and go to ground in a rather desolate part of the Bronx. There, Maria hits and badly injures a young black man who might or might not be one of a group trying to rob the couple. Badly frightened, Sherman and Maria flee the scene. As a result, Sherman becomes the target of the borough's ambitious district attorney, who believes he will improve his reelection chances by bringing a white man to trial. Needless to say, in the consequent media frenzy and brouhaha, Sherman loses everything—his family, apartment, car, mistress, job, and millions—learning, perhaps, a certain degree of humility. It is not altogether clear whether Tom Wolfe is beating the reader over the head with a moral or satirizing Wall Street of the 1980s and its dissolute progeny (it is probably the latter).

Of interest here is less the plot than Sherman's occupation as a bond trader. Bonds are no more than fancy IOUs, issued by a public agency or private corporation, as promissory notes to be repaid in full at a certain date in the future, with regular interest payments on their face value until the maturity date.[45] The difference between your taking out a loan or mortgage and the state of New York's issuing bonds is that the latter receives a guaranteed flow of tax revenue with which it can pay interest and principal on the bonds. You, by contrast, pose a much greater risk since you might lose your job and stop paying off your mortgage and credit card debt (sound familiar?). As a rule, therefore, the interest rates paid on bonds are much lower than on mortgages—unless one is dealing in "junk bonds," which are issued by corporations seeking to raise capital without selling shares or borrowing funds. Depending on the rating given them (on a scale of AAA to D, junk is in the range of Baa to D), junk bonds are considered very high risk and, therefore, pay higher interest rates (usually six to nine percentage points above Treasury bills).[46]

Sherman himself does not actually own, buy, or sell bonds; rather, his firm facilitates bond offerings and negotiates trades between buyers and sellers, for which he earns a commission. Using his company's money and credit, he seeks out opportunities to buy bonds from sellers and then searches for investors willing to purchase them. In the interim, his company owns the bonds, but the trick is to hold them as briefly as possible so as not to incur any substantial risk of loss or having to pay the cost of having money tied up in the bonds. Sherman's commission and income are based, therefore, not on his firm's overall profit—although that does show up in his year-end bonus, which can be many times his income—but on the total value of the trade. The commission rate is very small; yet on trades involving hundreds of millions of dollars, even a very small fraction of a percent adds up pretty quickly.

When his daughter, Campbell, asks Sherman how he makes his money, however, he is hard put to explain; even a very smart six-year-old is going to have trouble with indentures and securities. But his wife, Judy, has a much more prosaic and thoughtful way of putting it, comparing Sherman's commission on sales of financial paper to the stuff left behind by baked goods: "Just imagine that a bond is a slice of cake, and you didn't bake the cake, but every time you hand somebody a slice of the cake a tiny little bit comes off, like a little crumb, and you can keep that. . . . You have to imagine little crumbs, but a lot of little crumbs. If you pass around enough slices of cake, then pretty soon you have enough crumbs to make a gigantic cake."[47] Sherman is very greedy for those crumbs, since he must accumulate enough of them to make many slices and support his family's lavish lifestyle. But as Wolfe intimates in no uncertain terms, Sherman is more a scavenger than a creator of wealth, which is also true of Gordon Gekko. Their success derives from their manipulating the greed of others and not getting caught, as well as their own hunger for more and more crumbs. Both get stomachaches and their comeuppance, although, as a general rule, Wall Street bankers and traders get to keep most of their crumbs—so long as the market does not take away their jobs or turn bonds into worthless paper and the government does not freeze their bank accounts.[48]

Why Are There No Love Songs about Broken Kidneys?

Sometimes, what might at first seem worthless turns out to have considerable value—especially if someone wants it badly enough. Why that person might want it is another story, of course. British scholar Michael Thompson once wrote a book called *Rubbish Theory*, which explained why banal knickknacks discarded as junk sometimes became expensive antiques sought by collectors willing to pay thousands of dollars for them (think here of ten-cent comic books from the 1940s or watch "Antiques Roadshow" on PBS).[49] Of course, not everything desirable falls into the category of "formerly garbage," just as not all garbage becomes collectible. The trick here is not so much scarcity, although that is important; also significant is desire. In other words, people have to want an item badly, prefer to spend their money on that object rather than something else, and impute a high enough value to it to spend the premium it commands in the knickknack—excuse me, antique—market. But how do people know they want something? How is desire created? I will return to the second question in the last section of this chapter. Here, I want to look more closely at the relationship of "value" to "rubbish."

Consider, for example the tale of The Dude's oriental rug in "The Big Lebowski." The Dude is that film's protagonist, and although his given name is Jeffrey Lebowski, he is not the eponymous "Big" Lebowski of the film's title. The Dude is a laid-back guy with no obvious source of income, although he does seem to have nice things as well as a car he values highly. One day, The Dude finds himself caught up in a complex and opaque intrigue, as two thugs invade his Venice, California, apartment and threaten him for nonpayment of debts by his nonexistent wife. To emphasize the seriousness of their threats, the two urinate on his oriental rug. The rug itself is of no great value, if it is worth anything at all, but as The Dude says repeatedly and with conviction, it "really tied the room together." Upon discovering that the thugs actually intended to threaten the real "Big Lebowski" rather than him, The Dude decides to seek compensation for his ruined rug. The other Jeffrey Lebowski, who is supposedly very wealthy, refuses to pay for damages, dismissing The Dude as street trash. So, in retaliation, The Dude steals one of the Big Lebowski's really valuable oriental rugs—which are really the property of the Big Lebowski's artist daughter, Maude—and takes it home.

As this is a Coen brothers film, things get more and more tangled and absurd, with kidnappings, million-dollar ransoms, unsolicited sex, various forms of violence, and at least one burning car. The point is that, to everyone except The Dude, his rug is pretty much worthless. He, however, regards it so highly that he is even willing to purloin an (imaginary) ransom he has been tasked to deliver in order to gain just desert.[50] In the end, The Dude loses not only the rug he has taken but also his car and one of his best friends to a heart attack. Moreover, the troubles that befall him turn out to be a good deal more costly than simply buying a new rug. Value and desirability, we might suggest, are in the eye of the beholder, but if others are not convinced of them, even a highly valued thing can be pretty much worthless.

Not all desires are so prosaic or easily fulfilled, and not all value is quite so subjective. Sometimes people desire things that are not only scarce but also exceedingly difficult to obtain. One focus of the film "Dirty Pretty Things" is such an item: a kidney. The film is largely about London's cruel and seedy immigrant underworld, where the "undocumented" try to make a living by offering various forms of sought-after goods and services, many of them more than borderline illegal. Senay, a Turkish immigrant, works as a maid in a hotel, sharing a room with Okwe, a Nigerian cabdriver by day and a hotel desk clerk by night. Although he was a medical doctor in Nigeria, Okwe cannot obtain a license to practice in the United Kingdom. Nonetheless, his medical expertise is in great demand among fellow illegal immigrants, who suffer from a wide variety of illnesses and ailments. Desperate to leave the United Kingdom,

Senay arranges with her hotel manager to provide a passport in exchange for one of her kidneys. Okwe, fearing for Senay's well-being, offers to perform the operation in order to ensure her safety and health. In the event, they drug the hotel manager, extract one of his kidneys, and sell it to the customer. Having obtained their passports prior to performing the procedure, Okwe returns to Nigeria while Senay departs for New York.

Several aspects of desire, supply, and demand are at work in this film. First, of course, there is capital's (capitalists', actually) desire for cheap workers willing to do those jobs nobody else wants to perform. The hotel where Okwe works cannot afford to pay statutory wages; as in the United States, illegal immigrants fill the need at a lower cost. Second, there are the sexual services Senay's employers demand of her in return for both work and official papers. Third, there is the immigrants' desire to acquire those papers that will make them "legal" and enhance their life chances, even if the documents are fake and have no legal "value." Finally, there is the desire for good health, as soon as possible, by whatever means necessary.

Kidneys are in short supply all over the world—most of them are in daily use, and few are willing to risk life with only one kidney. In the United States and Europe, for the most part, such organs are not available through the "free" market. In the former, organs for transplant are generally taken from brain-dead accident victims, and a queue of people awaits them. Elsewhere, however, money talks: the patient far back in line can fly to India, Pakistan, or the Philippines, where the poor are willing to sell a spare kidney to rich foreigners. Organ brokers may pay the donor a few thousand dollars—in the Philippines, there is apparently a surplus of such organs, which decreases their value—while foreign patients can spend as much as $85,000 apiece for installation of their new kidneys.[51]

The shortage of organs for transplant has led some Americans to propose the creation of a "free market" in body parts. The argument goes something like this: the current approach to organ allocation in the United States amounts to a system of government rationing, one that suppresses the full potential supply of organs required to match the demand of patients in need. While the most equitable approach is to make everyone line up for his or her chance to survive, this fails to discriminate among those who are in critical immediate need of an organ and those who might survive for some time on their present malfunctioning organs. Moreover, the absence of a market for organs denies a fair return to the families of brain-dead patients, who probably could use the money, and discourages those who might be enticed by money from agreeing to organ donations. Those closer to death would presumably be willing to pay a premium in order to live, while others would make less expensive arrangements and risk the wait. A market-based approach ignores ability to pay, of course, and a black market in less-than-healthy organs taken from cadavers and corpses could possibly develop, as happened in one instance in Los Angeles.[52] The cases of India and the Philippines are suggestive as well: one can never be wholly sure from where or whom a kidney has come and whether one is getting a great deal or a pig in a poke.[53]

I Want That One! No, That One! No, I Want That One!

In our commercial culture, desire and scarcity are deeply intertwined. Making goods and services appear attractive, necessary, and positional—restricted in order to enhance the social status of owners—cultivates desire.[54] There is little cachet in possession of the commonplace; things appear more attractive when they are expensive and rare and, of course, highly desired. Diamonds are a prime example, as seen in an advertisement issued by the De Beers "Family of Companies" in the midst of the 2008 bear market. The ad cautions greater thought and care in consumption with the caption "Fewer, Better Things":

> Our lives are full of things. Disposable distractions, stuff you buy but do not cherish, own yet never love. Thrown away in weeks rather than passed down for generations.
> Perhaps things will be different now. Wiser choices made with greater care. After all, if the fewer things you own always excite you, would you really miss the many that never could?

Predictably, we are then told, "A diamond is forever."[55] But even cars are sold in this fashion. A Toyota Camry, for example, is common and pedestrian and offers little status. By contrast, the (Toyota) Lexus is presented as both more luxurious and less common, conferring cachet and prestige on its owner. While the Lexus does have leather seats and other fancy accoutrements, the body is essentially built on the frame and engine train of the Camry. In other words, what matters is appearance, the cultivation of desire, and the illusions held by the car's owner. Toyota could produce more Lexi and make more money, but then the Lexus would be no scarcer than the Camrus and could hardly be sold for twice the price.[56] Of course, some things really are rare: there is only one Koh-i-Noor Diamond, and even at its cutdown weight of 105 carats—the original stone weighed 186 carats—its value is hardly calculable. But such rare items present problems of their own. There is nothing to which they can be compared, and their high imputed value may also make them targets for theft ("The Thomas Crown Affair," "Ocean's 12"). This means that their owners may experience only limited enjoyment from possession because the items must be kept either behind glass or in a vault (Queen Elizabeth II rarely gets to wear the crown jewels).

The price of a good or service therefore says something about its relative scarcity but not very much about its quality: one can spend enormous sums on a car or computer and still end up with a lemon. Defects might be specific to the item or general to the product line, but even prestige and cachet cannot ensure that something will work as it should. The difference between a home pedicure and one costing $100 at a high-class spa may not be that great—certainly not big enough to justify the price differential.[57] In this instance, that difference has little to do with supply or quality and much to do with the cachet associated with a spa and its tony character. Most scarcity is of this quality: artificially created by the producer or provider in order to sustain a high equilibrium price (recall the Central Selling Organization described earlier, or check out the price of name-brand and generic pharmaceuticals for an example closer to home). Indeed, as Nobel Prize–winning economist Kenneth Arrow has argued with respect to intellectual property, "If information is not property, the incentives to create it will be lacking. Patents and copyrights are social innovations designed to create artificial scarcities where none exist naturally. . . . These scarcities are intended to create the needed incentives for acquiring information."[58]

All of this is meant to point out that supply, demand, and price, as well as markets themselves, are neither given nor natural. Some authority must structure and organize markets, even if it is involved only in designating the space in which trucking and bartering can occur. For accumulation to take place, demand for a good or service must be created and managed; it does not automatically appear. Although demand is often framed so as to appear linked to a necessity—think gasoline or water—much of that may have to do with commercially stimulated "lifestyles"—think large vehicles or designer bottles of water. Often, suppliers must find ways to create demand for what they provide, or no one will know what it is they "need." Finally, price may have little to do with the use or function of a good. If a good or service does not sell, it might be priced too high or even too low; bottles of wine may not move when offered at $40 in a fancy restaurant yet fly from the cellar at $200 apiece. All of this suggests that the principles and practices of neoclassical economics are not quite as straightforward or transparent as they are often presented. There is more to the mirror than meets the eye.

3

Bodies and Possessions

A S SUGGESTED IN CHAPTER 1, CONTEMPORARY capitalism is a unique form of social organization in human history, for it turns things essential to survival
into things for sale in markets, and it creates desire for other things that have
no survival value.[1] In this and subsequent chapters, we explore in detail the
meaning of this statement. Here it is enough to note that, once upon a time,
people produced what they ate and reproduced their societies because they
could eat what food they produced. Whether hunters, gatherers, or farmers,
they labored with their own hands to ensure the social reproduction of their
children, kin and kith.[2] Yet, even then, in any given place, the fruits of the
earth had limits, a result of the relative scarcity of nature and her resources
in the form of land, seed, and water. When any one of these was lacking, as a
result of drought, disease, or destruction, survival could not be assured, and
if kin groups (sometimes called "tribes") grew too large for those resources
that were available, new ones split off and went in search of sustenance elsewhere.

Still, even if the hungry and starving resorted to the eating of human
flesh—probably more of a myth than a very common practice[3]—they knew,
at least, from whence their food came. Today, our food is generally produced
and sold under conditions not of our own making or knowing. We have to
take it on faith that we will not be poisoned—a faith greatly weakened in recent years by outbreaks of salmonella and other diseases from contaminated
peanut butter, spinach, and who knows what else. And who has not been confronted with a dish of unidentifiable provenance or a package whose contents
seem to consist of entirely inedible substances (is melanine really a foodstuff)?

How can anyone know what it is that she eats or what it once was? Indeed, how do we know it is not ourselves we consume?[4]

That is the central conceit of "Soylent Green," based on Harry Harrison's 1966 novel *Make Room! Make Room!* At the end of the film, Detective Robert Thorn blurts out, "Soylent Green . . . is . . . people!" Do the thirty-five million residents of a grossly overpopulated New York know that they consume their dead in order to "produce" their own bodies? Although Harrison and his fans disliked the film's focus on food, as opposed to overpopulation, "Soylent Green" offers a neo-Marxist dystopian police procedural in film noir style. It illustrates the process of capital accumulation through legalized crime, exploitation of individuals' labor, and extraction of bodily resources (here more than kidneys). It is odd, then, that Thorn was played by Charlton Heston, never known for radical proclivities or politics. Over the years since its release, "Soylent Green" has become a cult film for its imagining of the future. Of interest to us are its insights into twenty-first-century capitalism and the commodification and consumption of the body, figuratively into goods if not literally into food.

This is not, however, a chapter about food, except in a tangential way. Rather, it is about the labor (or work) required to turn bodies into a commodity frontier, an object and means of capitalist accumulation through markets, and thereby to foster body fetishism (parallel to the Marxist notion of "commodity fetishism").[5] Even as capital has sought to create and colonize other commodity frontiers—ecotourism, intellectual property, kitty clones, outer space—it has not ignored the body as a "final commodity frontier." To be sure, adornment of the body is an ancient practice, and the fashion industry dedicated to the transformation of bodies into status objects has a long history.[6] Yet the body today is more than ever a focus of simultaneous production and consumption, of being made by capitalism even as people work overtime on their bodies to make capitalism. Indeed, it can be said that the labor we put into producing and consuming ourselves, and others, is a form of "property" in ourselves. As a result, we are only too ready to sell our bodies as a space to be worked in or on, in order to create distinctive images and identities.[7]

More to the point, people consume not only that material stuff they have acquired with wages earned by physical and intellectual labor but also the very body itself. Increasingly, capitalism finds ways to package physical and intellectual features of the body—genes, body parts, adornments and art, preferences, ideas—and to sell these products of the body back to those who "produced" them in the first place.[8] We produce ourselves to consume ourselves—and vice versa. To the extent that the consumption of goods shapes consumers' subjectivities—how they regard and comport themselves—that act is also closely related to class, status, and hierarchy. "Keeping up with the Joneses" is about more than competition with the neighbors.

In this chapter, we examine how people produce capitalism, and capitalism produces people, through bodies and labor. In addition to "Soylent Green," I explore this topic through several other films—the original "Invasion of the Body Snatchers," "The Return of Martin Guerre," "Thelma and Louise," "The Matrix," "The Net," "The 6th Day," "Fight Club," and "Sex and the City"—and two novels—Jane Austen's *Pride and Prejudice* (1813) and Margaret Atwood's *The Handmaid's Tale* (1986). I begin with some more basics about capitalism, then turn to the topic of "body work," that is, the consumptive labor required to produce a self with social "value" in the eyes of others. In the last section of the chapter, I examine "body fetishism," the literal consumption of bodies in order to reproduce "bare life,"[9] on the one hand, and "identity," on the other. (I will return to the theme of body and bodily production in chapter 5).

More Basics

A fundamental principle of contemporary capitalism, as suggested in chapter 2, is that "everything has a price." There, we saw that, as a result, things not desired or things available in excess are not "scarce" and have no value. Thus, no one is willing to pay for air because there is so much of it and it is so difficult to "enclose" that, to date, it has not been worth commodifying.[10] Ironically, as discussed in chapter 2, things that once had market value and later become worthless "trash" may find a second life as valuable antiques.[11] Today, banks and investors around the world face insolvency because the market cannot "find a price" for their vast holdings of collateralized debt obligations (CDOs) made up of slices of U.S. household mortgages. If no one wants to buy a CDO, does it have any value? Banks certainly hope so, although no one appears willing to guess how much.[12]

In other words, a key element in making capitalism work is "scarcity." Usually, we regard scarcity as undesirable because it suggests that there is not enough to go around, and we tend to imagine that people will fight for such things (see chapters 4 and 8).[13] Yet, as Kenneth Arrow notes, if things are not scarce, they will not be valued in the market.[14] Hence, although commodification involves the literal production of thousands or millions of identical items, there must never be too many on offer because that will render them worthless or, at least, worth less than the cost of making them. This dilemma becomes especially evident when the productive capacities of capitalism outrun the absorptive capabilities of consumers, a condition known as "surplus capacity." If everyone in our society owns a washer, dryer, and refrigerator, each of which lasts fifteen to twenty years, there is little incentive to build new appliance factories (and when people in other countries cannot afford them, there is not much reason to produce them for export). When there are more cars than consumers to buy them, they tend to pile up.[15] Indeed, the existence of surpluses may result in price cutting, dumping, massive job loss, and even corporate bankruptcy (as in the case of Chrysler and General Motors). Then workers pile up too, or become "redundant," as the British like to say.[16] To avoid such conundra, capitalists engage in an endless search for new "commodity frontiers," for the "next big thing" that can be sold for a high price, at least until competitors enter the same market.[17] But all of this is in an ordinary day's work for capitalism.

From a critical political-economy perspective, capitalism is unique because it is grounded in a class with the right and ability to appropriate the surplus value of others' labor. Most people lack the money (capital) or desire to own and operate their own businesses since doing so requires know-how, equipment, a potential customer base, the willingness and ability to operate under initial conditions of loss, and a great deal of faith. People lacking these do, however, "own" the capacity to work for a wage.[18] Indeed, every individual is assumed to possess a set of skills that some capitalist, somewhere, is willing to "buy" in return for wage payments—so long as those skills are not in surplus and are, therefore, "scarce."[19] But as suggested in chapter 2, there are two views about the value of such skill sets. The neoclassical view is that the appropriate wage for skills is whatever the going (or "equilibrium") price is in the labor market. If too many people with the same capabilities compete for a limited number of jobs (e.g., dishwashers), the price of that labor will be low. If too few are available for jobs requiring highly specialized skills (e.g., neurosurgeons), that labor cost will be very high. Some conservative economists rail against even minimum-wage laws, arguing that they "violate" natural market equilibria and destroy jobs, while others point out that even a minimum wage is rarely sufficient for much more than "bare life." And many other factors often influence the availability and price of labor.

As discussed in chapter 2, a Marxian approach relates the value of labor to the exchange value of the final product of the worker's efforts, regarding the difference as the "surplus value of labor." Thus, one could argue that the exchange value of clean plates in a restaurant is quite low—certainly, no one comes to a restaurant expecting to pay extra for a clean plate, even though few people would eat in a place that served food on dirty dishes—so wages for dishwashers are low (collectivization of the restaurant could address this problem, while unions can ensure that such wages are not too low). By contrast, if a neurosurgeon manages to save a patient from death as a result of her labor, the "exchange value" of the patient's life, however measured, could be very high—especially depending on her wealth and occupation (this is one reason why the poor get such execrable health care; the capitalist labor market views them as having little value).[20] From both perspectives there is a certain irony in that because people are so plentiful in today's world, they have no intrinsic economic value unless they are wealthy or have some kind of skill or personal quality that can be commodified, appropriated, and sold in the market—preferably at high value.[21] All those "excess" people—the "reserve army of labor" in Marx's terms, the "unemployed" in the neoclassical view—keep labor costs low or, at least, lower than they would be were labor truly scarce.

At the same time, in wealthier societies production becomes instrumental to the reproduction of capitalism in at least two senses. First, you gotta work to eat—no work, no food, no life, no babies for the next generation. Second, in its shaping of the human body, capitalism also fosters productive work on the self, as people's bodies, organs, and genes are appropriated, transformed, and consumed in a variety of forms. In the "old days," people bought and consumed things mostly produced in factories and on farms. Today, as our desire for material goods is ever more easily sated, we produce and consume ourselves through the constant creation, renovation, and reconstruction of bodies and identities. Not accidentally, this also offers endless opportunities for extraction and accumulation of that value by those offering services, adornments, and alterations. In this respect, the individual's subjectivity, or sense of self, is both the object and subject of commodification and body fetishism. Whereas bodies are converted into consumables in "Soylent Green" and manufactured in "Blade Runner," the ultimate fetish—to be whatever one might wish to be, for a price—involves the literal reshaping and reconstitution of physical and mental bodies, as depicted in *Snow Crash* and *Glasshouse* (I return to the latter film and the two books in chapter 5). First, however, let's look at a more straightforward application of this principle.

Bodies and Their Properties

At the end of the day, we are all consumers. Given our requirements for water, food, and shelter, biology governs our most basic needs. None of these needs has ever been filled without the expenditure of effort and energy. Even hunter-gatherers must work to acquire the necessities for survival.[22] But what happens when such needs have been satisfied? Anthropologists and geographers have argued that once human effort made it possible to stockpile food surpluses, social hierarchies also developed, as those able to control these supplies were also in a position to distribute them to others (recall the story of Joseph in the Old Testament).[23] Controlling food became a means of controlling and managing people. We might also presume that a considerable quantity of such stored food was often sold to lower classes at high prices (something not unheard of in recent times). This would have facilitated the recirculation of limited quantities of coinage through local economies while enhancing the wealth and power of the ruling elite. Much has changed over the intervening millennia, but much remains the same. While the road from such ancient societies to contemporary capitalist ones was neither short nor straight, the basic principle remains the same: use the relative scarcity of food to control those in subordinate positions. Today, such control is also available in other ways.

In contemporary capitalism, it is not enough to meet people's basic needs, for those are satisfied at relatively low profit levels, and it is neither ethical nor practical to deny food to the hungry and water to the thirsty (although vast sums of money can be generated by processing foods and bottling water and claiming special nutritional qualities for both). People must be turned into consumers, and this means not only catering to but also creating and shaping their individual preferences. Of course, it is entirely feasible to sell millions of more or less identical copies of an item without excessive pandering to created tastes. Henry Ford sold nineteen million Model Ts, all of which came in basic black. Eventually, however, people wanted colors and other features—they wanted their cars to be different from other people's. At the time, during the 1920s and 1930s, General Motors offered colors, and Ford found it more and more difficult to compete. The company fell on hard times and never again managed to dominate the American automobile market.[24]

Key here is the individual consumer, with very specific preferences and desires, who can be charged premium prices for goods and services that precisely fulfill those predilections and yearnings.[25] The older system of mass production, called "Fordism," relied on selling large numbers of largely identical items to a mass of undifferentiated buyers. Today, Fordism has been replaced by "neo-Fordism": mostly superficial variations on a basic form are touted as "differences" with which the owner can identify.[26] Think here about a computer that has many extras and expensive bells and whistles but is ultimately no more than a basic $500 machine, like many others. Still, your computer (or car or clothing) can be different and distinct. For that privilege, however, you will probably pay a good deal more than $500, while the manufacturer will make a good deal more profit than would otherwise be the case. That is the very point: to take as much money out of your pocket as you are willing (and prefer) to spend.

As another example, consider pickup trucks. A few years ago, during the height of the automobile boom in the United States, pickup truck commercials were ubiquitous on prime-time and late-night television, when the audience consisted primarily of adults. Although I have no truck with pickups, these ads clearly targeted a male demographic in the twenty-five-to-sixty age range. Ads repeatedly showed vehicles engaged in "manly" activities, such as driving through mud and water, up and down desert mountains, and through brush and jungles, as well as pulling other trucks, carrying hay, herding cattle, and so forth. Note how such advertising works on the viewer/consumer's identity and subjectivity. First, men only! Women need not apply. If they do appear at all it is as decoration (note that in American English "pickup" has a double meaning). It follows, then, that if you are not attracted by trucks, you are insufficiently masculine (women might represent unfair competition for male desire). Second, you can improve your self-image and even shape a new identity if you drive a big pickup, doing the things men do—and there's always stuff to be moved, is there not?[27] Finally, pickups are generally less expensive and more durable than cars, so you can abuse them without fear of losing your investment or being punished (notice the gendered implications of this last point).

What would happen to capitalism if individual tastes were not cultivated in this fashion? What if people were not socialized to be self-interested and acquisitive and did not want more all the time? What would be the economic consequences? Although the original story and several versions of "Invasion of the Body Snatchers" do not address these questions directly, we can infer some of the economic implications of conscious collectivism and collective consciousness from that horror story. Here, I draw on the 1956 film version, in which giant pods grow new versions of people as they sleep—presumably warning us that failing to pay attention to what is going on around us can be fatal. As the residents of the California town of Santa Mira—in Spanish, *mira* means "look"—sleep and are absorbed into the collective mind and body, only Dr. Miles Binnell and his old flame, Becky Driscoll, recognize what is going on. They struggle to stay awake in order to avoid absorption into the vegetable masses. In one scene, Miles confronts one of the pod people, who tells him, "Love, desire, ambition, faith—without them, life's so simple, believe me." Miles and Becky, passionately in love after a long separation following high school, want nothing of a world without desire but cannot escape. As they hide in a cave, preparing to flee via the highway to Los Angeles, Becky falls asleep. When Miles returns from investigating the source of a beguiling melody wafting across the hills—it comes from a radio in a migrant farm worker's truck (is there a message here?)—it is too late. Becky is no longer her old self, even though her appearance has not changed.

Film critics have argued for decades over whether the 1956 version critiques communism, McCarthyism, or both.[28] Kevin McCarthy, who plays Binnell, claimed the film had no political intent and reported that the book's author, Jack Finney, said the same. No matter. Without emotions, desire, and love, what is there to life? Or, as Miles responds in the conversation recounted above, once you become a pod person (a member of the collective), "you have no feelings, only the instinct to survive." For vegetables, survival does not require much more than the basics, enumerated earlier. But this is too simple: survival of the collective is being addressed here, and the collective is single-minded in its will to survive *as a collective.* There is no room for anything else. Nonetheless, what is the collective but the state or, in Jean-Jacques Rousseau's terms, "the General Will"?[29] In the collective state—be it communist or fascist—there is no room for extras; everything must be dedicated to strength and survival. The individual, with her emotions, desires, and preferences—and tendencies to shop and acquire—cannot—must not—be allowed to live, for that way lies fragmentation and atomization. Is it fair to say, then, that what Miles Binnell fears most is not the peace that might come with the absence of emotions? Rather, it is the belief that his "freedom to choose" will be taken away, even if that freedom is constrained by what capitalism makes available and is limited only to capitalism.

Indeed, even capitalism is not truly "free" since, as we saw above, capital seeks to manipulate and control desire for the purposes of capital accumulation, a.k.a., "profit." Working hand in hand, the state and capital routinely construct what might be called the "body of the citizen-consumer," which/ who possesses certain property and properties that enable and encourage consumption as one of society's most highly valued objectives.[30] The conventional "political" citizen, as in ancient Greece, fulfills certain criteria established by the state and is endowed with a set of civic rights. Those rights are based on birthplace, parents' nationality, and perhaps ethnicity, religion, and language, among others. In theory, at least, membership in a national polity offers both benefits and obligations.[31] Some may involve actual cash transfers, including unemployment benefits and taxes, while others offer the right to work or require a commitment to serve in the military. In democratic societies, at least, individual wealth and social status are supposed to have nothing to do with citizenship and its rights and obligations. These are notionally identical for both the prince and the pauper.

If that democracy is also a capitalist society—as virtually all are today (but not necessarily the reverse)—the reality is quite different for, as the old saw has it, "Money is power."[32] Particularly in recent decades, the properties of the citizen-body have been transformed in both concept and practice, and an individual's wealth has become more and more important in providing access to both goods and privileges. Before we examine the body of the new "citizen-consumer" more closely, it behooves us to think historically about how this particular body came to pass and how it is reflected in popular culture. More to the point, the consumer has become the "owner" of her body, a notion we take for granted and hardly ever question.[33] Generally speaking, we regard property as stuff to which the owner has some kind of exclusive access; indeed, "mine!" is one of the first words children learn.[34] But as we shall see, this notion of exclusive property is relatively new and not even correct. And there is a further twist: do we own our selves and our identities? What happens if we cannot prove we are who we claim to be? Why would that matter for economics and political economy? While the plot device of the double (or doppelganger) is an old one, it and the fear of being "snatched" are also staples of contemporary political culture.

Once upon a time there was no such thing as private property. To be sure, people possessed things and had exclusive use of them, but the social and legal concepts that we understand as "private" did not exist. Under feudalism, the dominant form of social organization in Western Europe from around AD 400 to perhaps AD 1200 (and much later in other parts of Europe and the world), the sovereign owned everything. He—and in rare cases she—distributed land to members of the aristocracy, who then "owned" it and could pass it on to heirs—but only at the pleasure of the sovereign. The people who lived on the land were for the most part regarded as part of the land and, therefore, were also the property of the landlords and the sovereign. The very idea that an individual might not belong to a social superior emerged only after centuries of struggle and war.[35]

The residue of the feudal property system lasted well into the nineteenth century—and appears in various forms even today—most visibly in the institution of slavery. Still, even with abolition of slavery, "free" English women could not escape the rules of feudalism. Until quite recently—and, it can be argued, even today—women in marriage had no independent legal or economic existence. As the property of their husbands, they were bound to do his bidding, no matter what.[36] The reverse was never the case, as the novels of Jane Austen and their many film versions show. To take just one example, the entire plot of *Pride and Prejudice* revolves about the efforts of the Bennet family, with five daughters, to ensure that none is left to age in poverty.[37] Under the English laws of primogeniture in effect at the time, only the eldest surviving son could inherit his father's estate (and title, if such existed).[38] If there were no son, the property went not to the oldest surviving daughter but to the nearest male relative of the paterfamilias—a brother, cousin, or nephew. Moreover, although the widow retained some residual rights to her husband's property, his survivors could be turned out of their home by a new (related) owner. This is the dilemma confronting the Bennets in *Pride and Prejudice*. Once Mr. Bennet dies, all of his property and money will go to his cousin, Mr. Collins. Elizabeth, the heroine (and stand-in for Austen), rejects Mr. Collins's marriage proposal, which threatens the family's future. Ultimately, after much spurning and misunderstanding, she falls in love with the very wealthy Mr. Darcy, thereby ensuring that no one will be cast into the streets after Mr. Bennet departs this earthly vale. That similar, if not identical, conflicts and dilemmas exist today is amply illustrated by fights over the division of property and wealth following the death of affluent family members, especially if they have been married more than once and had children by different spouses.

Although the institution of marriage has been liberalized extensively since Austen's time, it has not been long since any property a woman brought into a state-sanctioned union legally became her husband's property.[39] Moreover, the male in a marriage held considerable power over the female in any number of respects, thereby making her his to command. One version of such a property system underpins *The Handmaid's Tale*, which tells the story of a single woman in Gilead, a New England society that at some undefined future time (but almost certainly the 1990s or thereafter) has reverted to a highly patriarchal and extreme form of Protestant fundamentalism. The eponymous "handmaid"—she is never named except to be called "Offred" (from "Of Fred," meaning that she is the possession of her master, Fred)—is a feminist, whom the authorities have caught, imprisoned, reeducated, and "repurposed" to the task of bearing children for infertile couples in "proper society." In effect, Offred's body becomes the property and tool of her owners, the Commander (Fred) and his wife (Serena Joy). Offred performs various menial household tasks, such as doing the shopping, but her primary function is to participate with the couple in a monthly ménage à trois, called "the Ceremony," during which she is meant to be impregnated with the Commander's sperm. Inasmuch as Fred, like Serena Joy, is (probably) infertile, and a handmaid's failure to bear a child condemns her to exile in the Badlands, Offred finds it prudent to start a not-so-secret affair, arranged by Serena Joy, with the Commander's driver, Nick. He is most assuredly not infertile. When the baby is born, he or she will become the child and property of the Commander and will be raised as the couple's own, to carry on the family line. Offred will be returned to the Reeducation Center, along with other handmaids, to be sent out again to other infertile couples as the need arises.[40]

Atwood wrote *The Handmaid's Tale* during the 1980s, a period when the influence of the neoconservative movement and right-wing Christianity was ascendant and Ronald Reagan was in the White House.[41] As a Canadian, she was free to imagine one outcome of then-current trends and backlashes in the United States and to put them in novel form without having to fear the opprobrium of fellow citizens. As a feminist, Atwood clearly feared that women's many political and social gains over the preceding two decades could be easily erased were the state to decide to do so (and, presumably, she saw this to be the Reagan administration's intention). And as a novelist, she drew on George Orwell's *Nineteen Eighty-Four* in order to say something about American society and its dystopic tendencies.[42]

For our purposes, the key point in the novel, which Atwood never directly addresses, is the state's power to create and destroy property rights and, in so doing, to change fundamentally the legal status and social standing of specific groups and individuals. In the novel, the Gileadian state captures wayward and "loose" women who can bear babies but refuse to recognize the power and legitimacy of the new regime. Their property in the self—their rights and freedoms as well as their access to money, which facilitate mobility and escape—is simply canceled by fiat. Women become the property of their husbands, if they have one, or of the state, which at its own discretion can dispatch them wherever it sees fit and even kill them if it so chooses.[43] Of course, Atwood also draws on the American institution of slavery to frame Gilead's misogynistic system and even suggests in the "Historical Notes" section that Gilead, like the antebellum South, is doomed.

Atwood's vision might seem extreme, but even in today's supposedly enlightened society, women are still commonly treated as property. Margaret Davies and Ngaire Naffine note that in "the very structure of heterosexual marriage . . . the man . . . retains property in the self while the woman is cast as his object,"[44] a point starkly illustrated in "Thelma and Louise." In that film, the eponymous protagonists encounter a string of men, each of whom believes that he has the right to possess them and attempts rape, theft, or kidnapping. As a consequence, the two women kill, injure, or imprison each man. By the end of the film, Thelma and Louise are fugitives from the (male-dominated) law that will almost certainly lock them up for the rest of their lives. In prison, they will become the property of the male state, to be abused in perpetuity or even executed. Rather than give in to such a fate, Thelma and Louise drive their Thunderbird over the edge of the Grand Canyon. In this instance, at least, male claims to property rights in women have been foiled, but only at the cost of the two women's destruction of their own bodies.

It might seem absurd to propose that Thelma and Louise are victims of capitalism as opposed to male hormones, hubris, and stupidity (on this, see also chapters 6 and 7). One could argue that the abuse of women by men is as old as human history—think of the cartoon trope of Stone Age man dragging Stone Age woman by the hair—and long predates even the first glimmers of capitalism. Yet, it is largely due to the legal status of married and unmarried women that the two come to their untimely, if deliberately chosen, end. Thelma has legally been the captive of her spouse by dint of the property-protecting marriage contract, while Louise is a "free woman on the prowl," assumed available for enclosure by any passing man who by taking her, even without consent, imposes on her an implied contract. As "prisoners of love (and capital)" there is only one way to escape—although even the death of the weaker party does not render contracts wholly void since both heirs and the state can assert property rights over whatever she might have left behind.

What about the rest of us? Might not we and our identities also be considered "prisoners" of capitalism, entwined in an iron web, subject as we are to the property-protecting contracts of its various institutions and corporations?[45] Note carefully that any credit agreement signed by a customer/debtor is contingent on provision of documentation proving (1) that the individual asking for credit is who she claims to be, and (2) that her "creditworthiness" and credibility meet the creditor's exacting standards. By contrast, the creditor is never required to demonstrate his liquidity, the legality of the funds he loans to the debtor, the veracity of the contract, or the credibility of the lender. For that matter, he is not even required to reveal how he might be spending funds loaned to him by the state—depositors and investors in various recent bank failures, bailouts, and Ponzi schemes discovered this much to their great sorrow. Should the debtor fail to make timely payments, the creditor is legally entitled to assert property rights in the income, accounts, and possessions of the former (the debtor has few, if any, such rights) and can even see her to prison. But imprisonment extends far beyond the instrumentalities of credit and debt. It is also deeply embedded in our very identities through lifetime socialization in the language, limits, and practices of capitalism.

Consider again the case of Thomas "Neo" Anderson in "The Matrix." Recall his first encounter with Morpheus, who asks whether Neo does not feel "that there's something wrong with the world." In speaking about the Matrix, Morpheus observes that it "is everywhere, it is all around us. Even now, in this very room. You can see it when you look out your window, or when you turn on your television. You can feel it when you go to work, or when go to church or when you pay your taxes. It is the world that has been pulled over your eyes to blind you from the truth." We need not, for the moment, bother ourselves with what the "truth" might be—it is enough to observe that there is not much difference between the Matrix and capitalism. The latter is everywhere, and we have so internalized and naturalized it that we can hardly imagine a different world (remember TINA, "There is no alternative"?). Prior to his meeting with Morpheus, everything—every thing—that Neo has imagined he is or does or owns consists of no more than electrical impulses crossing the synapses in his hibernating brain. The reality outside—if there really is one (for insight into this metaphysical problem, consult Daniel Galouye's 1964 *Simulacron-3*, later filmed as "Welt am Draht" ["World on Wires"] in 1973 and "The Thirteenth Floor" in 1999)—is, as far as the audience can tell, starkly different from that inside. Inside the Matrix, not only does Neo have a well-established identity, but he is also well known to the surveilling overseers who closely track his imaginary-virtual activities.[46] Outside, he is Neo (and the much-awaited Messiah), but that's it. Indeed, his only function and purpose in the world is inside the Matrix, where he is the One sent to free what's left of humankind. In fact, when the Matrix is destroyed in the final film of the trilogy, the billions of sleeping humans who dream of comfortable lives while fueling it with their electricity all die. Only those few thousand living outside actually become "free." (This notion of freedom also appears in "Fight Club.") I shall return to "The Matrix" in a later chapter; suffice it here to point out that we are all like Neo, "born into bondage, born inside a prison that you cannot smell, taste, or touch." Whether it is enough that some of us, mostly in the planet's wealthy North, are "free to choose" among a myriad of goods and services is more of a philosophical (and ontological), than an economic or political, matter.[47]

Who Are You? Are You Really Here? Why?

For many centuries, as the foregoing discussion suggests, there was little distinction between person and property. That is, the person was constituted through certain status characteristics that were very much like property ("propriety") and closely associated with land. Subsequently, the legal persona came to be identified with the documented individual.[48] In the absence of appropriate, authorized and authorizing documents, as we saw in "Dirty Pretty Things," not only does the state not recognize one as a legal person endowed with civil, social, and economic rights, but it is almost impossible to own anything other than very personal items. A myriad of plays, novels, and films, ranging from the works of William Shakespeare to "The 6th Day" starring poor Arnold Schwarzenegger, have depicted the practical and other difficulties associated with "not being yourself." In the latter, Schwarzenegger plays Adam Gibson, who arrives home one day from work only to discover that he is already there, celebrating his birthday. The Adam in the house is a clone, but how can the Adam outside the house prove who is real and who is not? Identification documents can be forged; how much more difficult is it to prove "legal" existence when you and your copy are identical in every detail, and your copy possesses all the documents? This being a Schwarzenegger flick, plenty of mayhem and murder takes place before things get straightened out. Unusually, the cloned Adam is not destroyed. With the help of the "real" Adam, the cloned one skips town for South America while the real one regains his rightful place as male head of household.

"The Return of Martin Guerre" illustrates even more clearly such confusion over identity and its economic implications. Martin Guerre was a French peasant who left his wife, Bertrande, and son in 1548 and vanished. In 1556, a man claiming to be Guerre appeared in the village. Bertrande, believing him (or, according to some accounts, seeking a husband), accepted the "returned" Martin as her spouse. They lived together for three years, had two children, and even claimed the inheritance from Martin's father when he died. But Martin's uncle, married to Bertrande's widowed mother, was never fully convinced that this was the "real" Martin Guerre, and he brought an accusation that the returned Martin was an impostor. The case was going against the uncle and his wife when, quite dramatically, the real Martin Guerre reappeared. The impostor was found guilty and hanged.

One might ask, so what? Why does it matter if one person convincingly impersonates another, especially when the original has disappeared? (Today, we would call this "identity theft"; see the discussion below of "The Net" and chapter 5). The problem has largely to do with property. In most societies, especially under capitalism—and even sixteenth-century France was moving toward capitalism—inheritance forms an important part of the social order and political economy. If all property were confiscated from the newly dead, great estates and fortunes could not be passed on to heirs, condemning families to penury and causing the collapse of the social hierarchy. That the false Martin Guerre inherited the property of the real Martin's father did not matter very much in the grand scheme of things, but it did threaten the legitimacy of the family structure on which Catholic France was based. After all, if anyone could claim the identity of another, be that person dead or missing, how would paternity be ensured (especially inasmuch as determining maternity is rarely a problem)? And if the wealthy and powerful could not prove their legitimate right to rule, would not chaos ensue as the poor sought to steal from, and even replace, the rich and powerful?[49]

Indeed, it is not too inaccurate to argue that identity is a form of property, especially if it provides access to goods and money. Although no one is born with an identity—it has to be learned and created—today one leaves an "electronic spoor" almost everywhere one goes, whether in reality or cyberspace. People demand to see a photo ID or other government-issued identity document, and more and more, this is likely to be accompanied by various forms of biometric identification.[50] It is far from easy to get "off the grid," and it is increasingly difficult to move around and stay under the electronic radar. Identity theft can impose insuperable contractual obligations on those who have been "duplicated," but it is also regarded as theft of property—though no longer a capital crime, as in Martin Guerre's day, it is still a serious felony. And we can see why so much effort is made to prevent such theft: If debtors could escape creditors by stealing another person's identity, the entire basis of credit and profit would be undermined and with it the stability of the capitalist order.

In 1939, Woody Guthrie wrote and performed a famous ballad called "Pretty Boy Floyd." Among other things, the song is widely recalled for its penultimate stanza:

> Yes, as through this world I've wandered
> I've seen lots of funny men;
> Some will rob you with a six-gun,
> And some with a fountain pen.[51]

Today, property is stolen less often with a pen and more often through electronic legerdemain (as vividly evidenced by various financial scams during 2008). The point of identity theft is not to eliminate someone's online doppelganger—that would also destroy the very point of the theft, which is to "prove" the thief's cyberidentity to software programs asking, "Halt! Who goes there?" The point is to spoof electronic identification-verifying systems and algorithms into thinking the thief is the victim. But what happens when your electronic identity is completely deleted from the cyberworld? Do you then cease to exist?[52]

The relationship between the material and electronic body[53] is another element of "The Matrix": if you are "killed" in cyberspace, your "real" body also dies, and vice versa. More prosaically, Angela Bennett in "The Net" is "deleted."[54] The plot does not bear a detailed recounting but revolves around a secret program designed to allow access to top-secret computer systems as an element of something like a total information awareness program.[55] A group of computer hackers with evil designs seeks to acquire the program, and they pursue Angela to get it. The bad guys erase her electronic identity from the global communications network, substituting a new one with a criminal history. As a result, she becomes a fugitive from police and security agencies. Only if she can find someone who can testify to her "real" identity will Angela be able to retrieve her old life—although it is not at all evident why she or someone who "really" knows her should be believed (think about how expired IDs are rejected, even though you remain the same physical person). Angela's basic problem is that, as a full-time computer nerd, she has few real-life friends and is hard put to find someone who knows her in person. Her only recourse is to reveal the plot herself and notify the FBI of what is happening, without anyone's help. Of course, at the end of the film Angela recovers her identity and returns to her old life, now determined to make some friends outside of the Net.

To reiterate the point made above, because proof of identity is so critical to the many economic, civil, and social transactions we engage in every day—not only to verify that we are who our credentials claim we are but also to provide testimony to our individual creditworthiness, existence, and just deserts—our identities have the properties of property. When you go to the ATM and punch in your personal identification number (PIN), you are not withdrawing money from a physical pile of cash you have stored in the bank—unlike taking money out of a piggy bank or from under a mattress. Rather, that PIN is one of many electronic representations, or signifiers, of you that, combined with information embedded in the ATM card's magnetic strip and database information about the size of your bank account, result in an exchange of electronic bits and bytes for paper money. By itself your PIN has no intrinsic value if not associated with the data on the card that signify you and the "existence" of your property in the bank—which "exists" only in virtual form. Think about the matter this way. If you go into a bank, show your identification, and say, "Give me money," the teller may regard you strangely but will probably comply. If you skip showing your ID, he or she is likely to hit the alarm button.

Body Work and Working on the Body

Creating identities, pursuing preferences, and fulfilling desires is hard work. At a very early age, we begin to learn who we are and why we are here, as well as all the gendered social, civil, and economic roles that we are permitted to claim. And appearances matter. Girl babies are clothed in pink, and boy babies in blue, even though at the ripe old age of three weeks, what does it matter? As we get older and learn about sumptuary (dress) standards and expectations, such distinctions seem to become more and more important, especially if status is involved. The rich and powerful have always taken great pains with their appearances, although one would be hard put to argue that this constitutes "labor" in any real sense of the word (at the same time the very rich and powerful often have servants whom they pay to help them dress, a task that can take hours).[56] To be sure, appearance can be an important ancillary of accumulation insofar as it helps to clarify relative status and to legitimate those with whom the wealthy might wish to associate (hence the reason for medieval sumptuary laws as well as the contemporary demand for suits and ties).[57] But while the furrier makes a handsome profit on the mink stole he sells to the socialite, clothing is only one among many signifiers of status and income available through capitalist markets. As the ranks of the well-off have grown, moreover, such cues have become more and more difficult to maintain and upgrade[58]—especially given the broad availability of counterfeit goods. In recent decades, as a result, identity has also come to displace social class as a status marker linked to material signifiers.[59] Indeed, to the extent that anyone and everyone can acquire a distinctive identity, it might be regarded as a "great leveler," a kind of mental and material post-Fordism.

This suggests that "body work" is a simultaneous process of both consumption and production: the production of an identity requires consumption of specific goods, while consumption of those goods generates surplus value that can be extracted by capitalists for profit.[60] Capitalism based on body work seeks to add value to material goods through "body fetishism." In mainstream social science, identity is conventionally linked to ascriptive characteristics associated with certain definitions of culture, such as language, foods, religion, myths, beliefs, and collective social practices, and identity groups hew to different sets of such characteristics.[61] Historically, such distinctions were regarded as the basis for concepts like tribe, ethnicity, and nation.[62] While such characteristics can be socially constructed and commodified—witness the proliferation of ethnic restaurants in any U.S. city or the integration of "culture" into fashion—they are not infinitely malleable. Moreover, membership in a cultural group does not require body work, that is, labor put into endowing one's own body with a specific and distinct identity.[63] By contrast, from the perspective of capitalism, identity is a plastic attribute rooted in fear and desire, and it is almost endlessly malleable. Not only can one purchase those accoutrements necessary to acquiring a new bodily identity, one must also work continuously to ensure that one's identity is visible for all to see and that it does not become too "common," thereby losing its status distinctions.

Consider, for example, bicyclists.[64] The University of California, Santa Cruz, campus, where I have taught for almost twenty years, comprises two thousand acres at the foot of the Santa Cruz Mountains on the central coast of California and is especially attractive to mountain and competitive bikers. Although most student bicyclists are more interested in function than form, truly committed competitors own very expensive machines and wear costly and often brightly colored Spandex outfits, awash with boldly displayed corporate logos. Some bicyclists are also quite militant in defense of their "right to ride" and hostile to those who rely on fossil fuels or feet to get around. There is no dearth of accumulation possibilities available from catering to such bicyclists, and specialty stores, magazines, books, and websites keep them well informed about what is required to stay at the cutting edge of the sport and its fashions.[65] While one is "free" to be a bicyclist, one is not "free" to be just any kind of bicyclist-consumer. It takes work, mental as well as physical, to be and remain a mountain or competitive biker, to be accepted and recognized by others, and to maintain that identity. The return to an individual's investment in biking is, moreover, a form of human capital whose expenditure further helps to establish one as a member of that identity group and which one can call upon in the event of an accident or other problems.

This is a caricature, of course, but only to some degree, and it is akin to any one of thousands of similarly commodified identities, many of which are even more costly to maintain. On the one hand, an individual invests considerable labor (and capital) in acquiring an identity that sets her off from others. On the other hand, that identity has meaning only if others also work hard to acquire and display it—and understand its meaning. (In this instance, those who march to the beat of a different drummer do not constitute a market.) Such identity groups make very attractive the exploitation of bodies as sources of profit and accumulation, which in turn fosters innovations in equipment, adornment, and appearance that the committed must acquire in order to maintain and keep current their identities.

"Sex and the City," the film sequel to the HBO series, is about body work and fetishism, the relentless consumption of things for the purpose of maintaining a distinctive identity and status. This film's story line also does not bear repeating—and it never gets very complicated anyway—although it seems to suggest that LOVE® is worth more than money, which the audience can hardly take as a serious moral given how much stuff, especially clothing, is consumed over the course of 145 minutes. Ostensibly, Carrie Bradshaw and her buddies are in search of LOVE® (and SEX), but it is curious how LOVE®always seems to equate to STUFF, most of which is outrageously expensive (even as a successful writer, it seems improbable that Carrie could earn as much as she so wantonly spends). In every scene, Carrie and her friends are wearing different new, very stylish outfits; wearing the same clothes for too long or too often signals that one is falling down "on the job." Shopping is the film's major activity, outranking even LOVE® (and SEX). Nor is there any dearth of product placements, each conveying the importance of consuming, or being seen only with or in, the "right" commodities—as evidenced when Carrie's personal assistant, Louise, rents high-end handbags (this is not something made up for the film; it really happens).[66]

Body fetishism peaks when one of Carrie's buddies, Samantha, who owns a talent agency in Los Angeles with her live-in movie-star lover as the sole client, flies to New York. Samantha has come for an auction to acquire an estate ring that she covets. Bidding starts at $10,000 and rapidly escalates as Samantha competes with an anonymous person communicating by telephone (can you see where this is going? I did.). She finally quits at $50,000. Of course, a few days later her lover—the bidder on the phone—presents her with the very same ring. Thereafter, the ring is Samantha's feature signature. After all, not many women so casually sport such expensive (and garish) jewelry, do they? In this instance, she becomes an identity group of one.[67]

Another instance of body work appears in "Fight Club," in which the never-named narrator (Jack) becomes so alienated from his job and possessions that he dissociates and splits into two, his alter being Tyler Durden. I will return to Jack's problems in later chapters. Here I only note Jack's conversation with himself (i.e., Tyler) after his condo is destroyed, with all of his carefully acquired possessions blown out into the street below: "You buy furniture. You tell yourself: this is the last sofa I'll ever need. No matter what else happens, I've got the sofa issue handled. Then, the right set of dishes. The right dinette. . . . I mean, you did lose a lot of nice, neat little shit. The trendy paper lamps, the Euro-trash shelving unit, am I right? And, now it's gone. . . . But maybe, just maybe, you've been delivered."[68] Note here that body work and fetishism have nothing whatsoever to do with subsistence or even the physical body and everything to do with identity. Indeed, such activities are generally possible only for those with incomes far above subsistence levels (one tends not to find such behavior among the world's five billion poor, although they receive plenty of instruction on how to engage in it). While it might be necessary for those with sufficient incomes to purchase a new computer every two years, a new car every three, and a new fridge every ten, saturation levels are quickly reached. Thus, advertisements for even status goods tend to play up identity angles: masculinity for trucks, speed for computers, sex for perfumes, LOVE® for diamonds. You are what you consume. And what you consume, so to speak, is yourself. This brings us to "Soylent Green."

Hello! My Name Is Sol, and I'll Be Your Dinner This Evening

Both "Soylent Green" and *Make Room! Make Room!* take place in New York City in 2022. The city is an urban nightmare. Creature comforts, employment, and anything beyond basic necessities are practically nonexistent. Virtually all housing is communal, and for many home consists of no more than a riser in a building stairwell. A perpetual heat and smoggy, yellow-green haze envelop the city, giving the film an opaqueness mirrored by its sometimes confusing plot. The inhabitants dress in drab, uniform-like clothing and spend their time wandering aimlessly about the streets in search of something to eat. The governors of this hellhole are mostly responsible for ensuring that food and water are available to the city's residents so that riots do not break out.[69] The basic foodstuffs are crackers—Soylents Red, Yellow, and Green—produced and distributed by the eponymous Soylent Corporation. This company is a monopoly that controls access to the oceans, from which it extracts plankton, as well as all agricultural lands outside of the city where, presumably, soybeans are grown. Both raw materials are transformed into Soylents Red and Yellow. More recently, the corporation has begun to market Soylent Green, a high-protein cracker of unclear origin that is in great demand but in limited supply. As it is sold only on designated days, vendors often run out rather quickly, leading to bread riots. The police then bring in "the scoops," garbage trucks with front loaders, which pick up the rioters and dump them into the truck bed for disposition.

Not everyone in New York is so badly off. A small and shrinking middle class lives in real apartments, has jobs and beds, and sometimes even acquires food other than Soylent crackers. Detective Robert Thorn belongs to this group. He has salaried work—although not a uniform or suit—which entitles him to the small apartment he shares with his "police book," Sol Roth (played by Edward G. Robinson, appearing in his last film role). Roth searches out the information and intelligence Thorn needs to solve his cases.[70] Occasionally, while investigating a case, Thorn pilfers things and foods—a tomato, a carrot, a tattered bit of beef—no longer available on the street, which make his and Sol's lives a little less unpleasant. For the most part, however, bourgeois life in 2022 is pretty nasty.

Finally, there is a very small group of extremely wealthy men, most of whom seem to be members of the Soylent Corporation's board of directors. They live in large, opulent, and comfortable apartments with clean water, soft beds, air conditioning, and beautiful women. The last are called "furniture," and while their function is never spelled out explicitly, it is fairly evident. These men can buy food, liquor, and other luxuries without limit. And they are privy to very secret information about the corporation's food sources, to wit, that the oceans and the plankton are dying. Indeed, a threat by one of their number to publicize this information and to reveal the source of Soylent Green leads to his murder.

Thorn is assigned the case although it is evident from the outset that certain parties do not want him to apprehend the killer. When he begins to get too close to the truth, Thorn is ordered to stop his investigation. When he refuses, the corporation orders a bodyguard to kill him. With Roth's help, Thorn discovers that the oceans are dying, although he is certain that this cannot be the reason for the mysterious murder. Sol Roth provides the answer. He is old, tired, and ill (as was Robinson when he made the film) and decides to "go home."

In the language of 2022, that means euthanasia at one of the state's special centers for old people. Thorn tries to stop Roth but is too late. For some reason—perhaps he is loath to let Sol go—Thorn decides to follow Roth's body to its final resting place. He hops aboard one of the garbage trucks that transport the dead and arrives at a giant factory that manufactures . . . Soylent Green! The upshot is that Thorn cannot be allowed to reveal what he has discovered. Returning to the city, he staggers into a Catholic church where he seeks confession and absolution. By now clearly insane, Thorn is carried away by police as he cries out, "Soylent Green . . . is . . . *people!*"

Waste not, want not, even if it is people on the plate.[71] The late economist Julian Simon famously called humans "the ultimate resource," but he was also known for arguing that humanity could "never run out of resources."[72] What Simon had in mind was quite different from "Soylent Green" but not so removed from his claims as one might think. The concepts of "human capital" and "human resources" reflect the notion that people and their relationships are like money, and where there is money, there are opportunities for profit. To be sure, human bodies have been a "technology of production" for millennia as slaves and sex objects, but in those instances direct ownership of the "worker" mediates between labor and capital. The very stuff of the body itself, however, has never been fully commodified (although blood banks are almost a century old, the growing trade in organs is changing this, and molecular biology works with DNA, which is life's "building block").

The production system depicted in "Soylent Green" closes the cycle. In the world of 2022, what is in greater supply and surplus than human bodies? When the oceans are dying, and the farms cannot produce enough, what better source of protein than the newly dead? And how better to feed the teeming billions than by "growing" crops of humans for systematic harvesting, processing, and conversion into edibles from which a few can profit enormously (foreshadowing, perhaps, the cultivation of babies as replacement "batteries" in "The Matrix")? After all, is capitalist prosperity not dependent on the continual discovery of new market niches and ways to fill them? That the Soylent Corporation is a state-sanctioned monopoly hardly matters in this case, for where else can the hungry turn for food?

The economic system that underpins survival in "Soylent Green" presents us with an interesting twist on the Marxist theory of the surplus value of labor and offers some insights into certain forms of commodity fetishism too. In his vision of the communist future, Marx argued, there would be no surplus value of labor or profit, for there would be no production of goods beyond that necessary to provide for everyone's essential needs. Each individual would be supplied through public distribution, working in the morning, engaging in cultural activities in the afternoon. That was the utopian dream; to the extent that it was realized, really-existing socialism did not quite achieve this blissful vision.[73]

In "Soylent Green" we see something rather different, and whether it is meant to be a fully debased form of capitalism or an ironic parody of state socialism is not altogether clear. Here, the labor of New York's residents is not incorporated in the production of goods and services for which they receive wages that they can spend on those goods and services (in contrast to Henry Ford's workers). Instead, their energy and skills go directly into the work of "growing" the body, as it were—in a setting of perpetual scarcity, survival is hard work. Although food is acquired through private exchange in the market, the vast majority of the population lives on state-supplied welfare payments, and their monies go to purchasing the Soylent crackers on which they depend for survival. When they are ready to die, the elderly go to an institution where they are efficiently euthanized, shipped to the factory, and turned into high-protein Soylent Green crackers, which the population on welfare eagerly buys and consumes. Even so, there is not enough Soylent Green to supply public demand, which allows the Soylent Corporation to sell the crackers for a high profit that allows its board members to live quite well.

In other words, the surplus value accumulated by the owners and directors of the corporation through the production and sale of Soylent Green is the difference between the cost of the work it takes to keep a person alive and the cost of turning his or her body into crackers. So long as the supply of bodies does not decrease—which it cannot do under conditions of high population growth—the cycle can be maintained. There are, evidently, several problems with this economy, not the least of which is that it violates the laws of thermodynamics, but no matter. My point is that labor is expended on the body, which then supplies the free raw material for the food that the body "worker" must purchase to survive, which provides the body . . . and so on.

The obvious punch line here is that "capitalism devours all" and, left to its own devices, will lead only to the "stark utopia" decried by Karl Polanyi in *The Great Transformation* (2001).[74] It is only logical in an overpopulated world where everything else is dead or dying that the ultimate resource, as well as the ultimate profit center, becomes the body itself, its very material substance (and how apropos of such a self-centered society as ours).[75] But even in our world, which does not (yet) much resemble that of "Soylent Green," this is not so far from truth. The body may very well be the "final commodity frontier" and a source of windfall profits, even if we are not quite yet at the point at which we must literally feed on human bodies to survive.

4

Development and Motion

A NOTHER MAJOR HALLMARK OF CAPITALISM IS MOTION: the movement of bodies, money, resources, and things from place to place, across space, and around the world. Such motion and mobility are related to both scarcity and desire. Aristotle theorized that the movement of things through space relied on a prime mover, who or which provided the thing being moved with a purpose, a teleology, an end, even a desire.[1] In the case of capitalism, we speak of relative scarcity and the desire for things where they are scarce—which their market price reflects. Things must therefore move from where they are plentiful and their price is low to where they are scarce and their price is high. Because such mobility is tied up with spatial differences in supply and demand (and the cost of labor and inputs), we call such movement in the economy *trade*, a term that in its banality conceals a great deal about the force and work needed to get things moving. Generally speaking, a "trade" involves exchanging one good for another or for a sum of money. But why it is necessary to trade and how the conditions facilitating trade come about are not, perhaps, quite so obvious.

Neoclassical economics and critical political economy explain trade differently. The former constructs arguments around comparative advantage and division of labor, which are both premised on the relative costs of production and mobility. Critical perspectives are more apt to see trade in terms of uneven development, through which those with wealth and power shape markets and the capitalist economy in their favor. Here, mobility is linked to primitive capital accumulation and extraction of surplus value through unequal power relations. This is not to say that one account is correct and the other not—although those deeply invested in each explanation often make such claims—but, rather, that different parts of the elephant are being examined and explained.[2]

This chapter looks at how and why things move in, and because of, capitalism. I begin with the production and movement of "natural resources," using a recent film about oil, "Syriana" (2005), as well as some older movies from the "Mad Max" series, all of which help to illustrate a number of concepts and propositions regarding trade and its associated features. In the second section, I examine the logics of uneven development and exploitation, turning to a 1962 "Twilight Zone" episode, "To Serve Man," as well as Ray Bradbury's *The Martian Chronicles* (1950) and the film "They Live!" (1988; short story by Ray Nelson, "Eight O'clock in the Morning," 1963). Finally, I explain the concepts of comparative advantage, the global division of labor, and uneven development through "Blood Diamond" (2006) and John le Carré's *The Constant Gardener* (book, 2001; film, 2005). I will also return to these topics in later chapters in this book.

How Low Can You Go?

By the time Adam Smith published *The Wealth of Nations* in 1776, the basic principles of international trade were already well developed although not well understood. It was left to Smith, observing society around him, to frame the basic psychological incentives for such trade. He argued that people naturally "trucked and bartered" in order to acquire things they did not already possess and could not make for themselves.[3] That is what markets are for, although they do not emerge spontaneously but, rather, are organized and regulated settings in which exchange (arms-length trade) can take place, whether in goods, services, or money. Smith also articulated the principle of "division of labor" in his famous example of the pin factory. The allocation of specific repetitive tasks to individual workers in an assembly line was more efficient and less costly to the capitalist than allowing each worker to make complete, individual items.[4] Not until some decades later, however, did David Ricardo frame the principle of relative comparative advantage.[5] This came to be one of the foundational elements of "free trade," the notion that exchange should be premised only on the costs of production and should exclude all other impediments in the form of taxes or tariffs artificially imposed for "political" purposes.[6]

All of these notions and associated practices rest on the desire to "buy cheap and sell dear," to minimize the cost of production and maximize profit and accumulation, as we saw earlier. To be sure, in a complex society people have different skill sets, and the costs of activities associated with the production of goods and services vary considerably depending on those skills as well as the availability of resources, capital, and technology. Thus, in poor societies with limited investment funds and lacking access to expensive mining technology, it may cost less and be easier to use low-wage human labor to dig up diamonds or coal (both forms of carbon) in deep mines. In rich societies, it is often less costly per unit of material produced to rely on giant shovels and dump trucks and to strip the tops off mountains to get at coal and other minerals. But—and here is one irony—it might also be less costly for rich societies to import coal and diamonds from poor societies, perhaps in exchange for computers and flat-screen televisions, than to mine their own coal or diamonds. Thus, the "global division of labor" assigns certain tasks to some societies and other tasks to other societies, depending on their cost and their price in the market. Although this division is usually ascribed to the "efficient" operation of capitalist markets that allocate resources in the most "cost-effective" ways, the result is just as much a consequence of differentials in power and wealth between rich and poor as it is the former's incentive to maximize profit and accumulation.

As the term suggests, relative comparative advantage involves the comparative, rather than the absolute, difference in the costs of producing things and providing services among different places. To extend the example above, even if the rich society can produce its own coal more cheaply than it can buy it from a poor country, importing coal might still make sense if the rich country can export more expensive goods to the poor one. For example, coal might cost $100 per ton in the rich country and $110 per ton freight on board in the poor country. At the same time, the rich country can manufacture computers for the equivalent of $500 per ton and sell them to the poor country for the equivalent of $1,000 per ton. The upshot of such a comparative advantage is that it makes more economic sense to trade computers for coal, even if the absolute cost of the imported item is higher than the absolute cost of a non-imported one. The markup is greater, and there is more profit in making and exporting computers than in mining, selling, and buying coal domestically.[7]

The same notion applies to labor, as we see in goods and services as diverse as windshield wipers, computer code, household servants, and call centers. Even though both high- and low-skilled workers are available in a rich country, they can also be quite costly to employ compared to workers in other countries (e.g., software engineers earn $100,000 per year in Silicon Valley compared to $50,000 or less in Bangalore, India). As a result, consumers have to pay more for domestically produced goods and services and for "legal" servants so that businesses and service workers can cover their costs and subsistence. But highly skilled workers are also available in poorer countries (e.g., China and India), and the goods they produce can be shipped to the rich countries at relatively low cost, where consumers can buy them for less.[8] Similarly, as we saw in "Dirty Pretty Things," low-wage workers can be imported into rich countries, where they will work for less than "legal" ones. Of course, one result is that both skilled and lower-wage workers in the rich country might no longer have jobs or the income with which to buy the cheaper imported goods. To the extent that consumption is integral to continued economic growth, as is the case in most industrialized countries, the resulting decline in consumption can lead to recession or worse. As the current economic crisis suggests, however, the well-off generally do not rely solely, or at all, on waged income, and they have ways of making it through economic downturns. The rich are unlikely to change their behaviors in the absence of strong political incentives or financial inducements.

One final point: for the most part trade does not take place among countries; rather, it occurs among and within companies. Thus, although official trade statistics might suggest that Glutco has contracted for the import from China of windshield wipers with a wholesale value of $1 million—a transaction that shows up in U.S. government accounts as an exchange of money for manufactures—it might well be that the wipers were made at a Glutco-owned factory in China, shipped by a Glutco-owned transport company, and distributed by a Glutco-owned wholesaler to Glutco Auto Supply Stores. In such a case, we are looking not at international trade but, rather, at intracorporate transactions involving transfer prices charged by one subsidiary to another (usually so as to reduce taxes in any particular jurisdiction). We do not know for certain (1) if the wipers are actually worth more or less than the price reported in the various transfer documents, (2) what kind of profit or loss each Glutco subsidiary might realize on its portion of the transaction, (3) how much profit might be repatriated back to headquarters, or (4) what might be the actual cross-border monetary value of the transaction. Not only is such information considered proprietary to the corporation, but no one outside the company keeps books on such trade. Hence, when you hear about "ballooning" trade deficits and "unfair" trade practices, be sure to check your wallet.

Oil Eyes and Gas Gauges

In many ways, oil is the archetypal item in global trade. The world consumes about thirty billion barrels of the stuff every year and because so much oil is found in countries that do not use that much, up to half of world production must be moved from where it is produced to where it is consumed, from one country to another. Moreover, oil is much cheaper to extract from some places than others. For example, getting a barrel of oil out of the ground in Saudi Arabia costs a couple of dollars. Doing the same thing in the North Sea might run as high as $20 per barrel or more, while oil extracted from Alberta tar sands costs about $35 to $40 per barrel. For a variety of political reasons, it could make more sense for a country to import less oil, produce more at home, and invest in renewable and sustainable substitutes. From a neoclassical perspective, however, it is easier and makes more economic sense to import lots of oil. Today, oil is so plentiful and so cheap compared to many alternative sources of energy that incentives to find substitutes for it are limited. Indeed, oil is hardly scarce by any standard. Known world petroleum reserves stand somewhere between one and three trillion barrels (compare this to current world consumption, above), and there might well be equivalent quantities tied up in tar sands, oil shale, and other petroleum-bearing sediments and formations around the world. Notwithstanding fears of oil running out, it is relative scarcity among places that really matters.

Relative scarcity, as discussed in earlier chapters, is not purely a function of supply and demand. It also depends on the circumstances of possession, control, and use, as well as consumer desire. Some parts of the world have a great deal of oil, while others have only limited amounts. About two-thirds of the world's known petroleum resources are located in what is called the "Oil Corridor," an ancient ocean bottom stretching from the Arabian Peninsula through Iran and Iraq and up to the Caspian Sea. Russia has a great deal of oil, as does Venezuela, but much of the rest is scattered in other places around the world. From a Western political perspective, as a result, a lot of this oil is in the "wrong" place. Rich industrialized countries consume vast quantities, but with the exception of Canada and the United States, they do not control very much and must import most of what they use. Even the United States, the third-largest oil producer in the world (after Saudi Arabia and Russia), uses so much that it must import 60 percent of its consumption. Relatively speaking, therefore, oil is scarce for rich and industrializing countries, and this fact motivates petroleum politics to a significant degree.[9]

As the lifeblood of modern civilization, oil is desired not only for its functional purposes but also as a means to power. Those who possess or control oil, it is widely believed, hold a substance for which the world will pay any price (at least $147 per barrel, based on the peak price reached on July 11, 2008). Conversely, withholding oil from global markets not only further drives up its price but can also offer oil-producing countries political leverage over those who lack, desperately want, and will pay anything to get this commodity. In other words, oil producers might hold a comparative advantage in terms of not only supply but also political leverage and what it might be used for.[10] "Syriana" presents one view of relative oil scarcity and associated politics; "Mad Max" and "Road Warrior," another. The plot line of the former is too impossibly complicated to summarize here (even film critics have trouble with it). Suffice it to say that the movie brings together several contemporary themes—oil, terrorism, politics, economics, and espionage—all related to the enormous supplies of petroleum found in the Oil Corridor and linked to uncertainties about the reliability of flows to the West.

In "Syriana," the constant and growing global demand for oil—about which everyone knows—and the geopolitical efforts to control it and direct its flow stand as background to the machinations of the plot's many interwoven forces and players. In the film, the politics of a Middle East oil emirate ruled by the al-Subaai family (note that Kuwait is ruled by the al-Sabah family) intersect with the American interest in maintaining good political relations within, and reliable oil flows from, the region. The older of the emir's two sons is a reformer interested in democratization, while the other is willing to continue his father's repressive policies as well as maintain a U.S. military presence, both of which ensure uninterrupted oil production. In the event, the emir chooses the younger son as his successor even while the elder plans a military coup as the first step in his plans for liberalization. The CIA, fearful that democracy might mean the end of American influence and the flow of oil, orchestrates the assassination of the older son and his family so as to avoid a ticklish problem.

The agency is right to be concerned: "free" elections in the Middle East have not always returned U.S.-favored candidates to public office. Indeed, the United States has not been a strong fan of democratization in the Middle East, seeing it as an opportunity for radical Islamists to win elections and take power (as was the case in elections to the Palestinian legislature, a situation more recently avoided in Lebanon). Were that to happen in one of the major oil-producing countries, some believe, its government might well restrict oil production and flows to the West—as happened after the Arab-Israeli war in 1973—and even force the United States to withdraw its military from the region. In a truly "free" global oil market, moreover, the highest bidders would get the oil, and high prices could have severe economic and strategic consequences for the United States and its industrialized allies (were the global oil market "free" in any meaningful sense, moreover, the United States might well consume a great deal less of the stuff).

But relative scarcity is not a permanent problem, for, ironically perhaps, too much oil can be as great a problem as too little. If the price of oil and gasoline rises too high, users will begin to search for ways to reduce their consumption. This might mean less driving, less flying, and fewer services or a shift to more energy-efficient systems and practices. When energy demand declines, the excess of supply leads to a fall in price, as happened after July 2008, when the price of oil dropped precipitously to below $40 per barrel. Because each barrel of oil generates less income, producers may decide to increase their output in order to maintain the revenue flows needed to pay their domestic bills. Ultimately, however, governments are forced to spend less, and their windfall wealth disappears, like water into desert sands. The worsening of economic conditions in oil-producing countries has been known to generate political and social unrest—part of what is sometimes called the "resource curse" (see below)—and there is no reason to think this will not happen again, even to the West's largest oil suppliers in the Middle East (Saudi Arabia being the most important among them).[11]

The enormous wealth associated with large oil revenues has other pernicious effects. One of them is called the "Dutch disease" after the impacts of large inflows of natural gas revenues into the Netherlands during the 1960s. In that instance, a surge of foreign revenue raised the value of the domestic currency, thereby making domestic goods more expensive and imported goods cheaper. As a result, domestic production of food and goods declined, while imports rose. At the extreme, the Dutch disease can decimate entire productive sectors and drive them into the ground, as happened to agriculture in Nigeria. After oil revenues began to flow into that country in the early 1960s, it became cheaper to import food than to produce it domestically.[12] Floods of money also make it easier for public officials and private parties to engage in "rent-seeking" activities as opposed to productive ones. These might include having workers provide various otherwise unavailable services to well-heeled foreigners or a newly rich government (e.g., drivers, bodyguards, access) rather than laboring for much lower wages on farms or in factories. Finally, if the inward flow of capital is not handled carefully, the domestic money supply can grow, leading to uncontrolled inflation. None of this conduces to a stable or peaceful society. In a larger sense, then, the resource curse may lead to social instability and violence, corruption and theft, loss of ethical standards, and mass impoverishment. Nigeria is the poster child for this effect.

What will happen when oil really runs out? This is a growing concern among those who believe the world will soon reach "peak oil," if it hasn't already.[13] Whereas oil is plentiful in "Syriana," it is absolutely scarce in the "Mad Max" series. Both "Mad Max" and "Road Warrior" are set in a ruined, postapocalyptic landscape, one not too far removed from a Hobbesian "state of nature" (see chapter 6). While all three films in the series revolve around fast cars, violent men, and the struggle for gasoline, the former two most explicitly depict the conditions and consequences of scarcity. An energy crisis and nuclear war have led to the collapse of civilization, the breakdown of the national and global fuel supply systems, and the emergence of marauding motorcycle gangs who seek gasoline, food, and women in the few remaining

towns of the Australian outback. In "Mad Max," Max Rockatansky is an officer working for a small police force that seeks to protect the townspeople.
In "Road Warrior," he has left the force after the death of his wife and son at
the hands of one of the gangs. Gasoline is central to the film, as townspeople
struggle with bikers for control of the last remaining oil refinery in Australia.
It comes as no surprise that, with Max's help, the townspeople manage to
escape to the northern coast, carrying with them a supply of fuel and leaving
behind a booby-trapped facility that will never again produce any gasoline.
(One is left to wonder what the refugees will do when their supply of gas runs
out—but that question is never explored.)

It is worth noting here that the scarcity of gasoline is less a matter of supply than the availability of technology (the source of the oil stock to feed
the refiner is never made clear either). The third film in the series, "Beyond
Thunderdome" (1985), opens with Max driving a camel-powered truck. He
needs no gasoline to get around. Were it not for the leftover desire for mobility and the tools to fulfill that desire—cars, trucks, and motorcycles—there
would hardly be any need for gasoline. One could argue that cars and fuel
are necessary concomitants of contemporary life, but it is possible to subsist,
and even to have a fulfilling life, without ever laying eyes on an oil-powered
vehicle.[14] Admittedly, most of those who lack high mobility are very poor and
perhaps not all that happy with their lives. Still, it is not difficult to imagine a
society much less obsessed with mobility and freedom yet able to provide its
members with all they desire and an efficient transportation system too (see
Europe for an actually existing example).[15]

We might recognize, however, that the postpetroleum future envisioned in
the "Mad Max" series is more about people's imagined loss of mobility than
it is about the mobility of oil or capital. One theme that reappears over and
over in film, fiction, and other texts is the conviction that the poor and weak
of the world want nothing more than to take away the possessions of the rich.
A deep and abiding belief in a God-given "right" to energy and automobility
serve to fuel relentless attempts to control the flow and price of oil and to
regard others' efforts along these lines as pernicious and evil. It is a staple of
the academic and policy literature, as well as popular culture, that people will
come to blows over that which is scarce, although one's own intentions in
this regard are always presented as beneficial and benevolent. Similar conceits
appear in any number of science fiction films, including "Independence Day"
(1996), in which aliens attack Earth for its water and other natural resources.
And do not forget that in *War of the Worlds*, H. G. Wells imagined his Martian tripods invading Earth in order to escape their "dying planet." That the
pursuit of such wealth almost always inflicts serious injury on the innocent

is written of as an "unfortunate but necessary" cost of economic prosperity. The wages of sin, indeed!

Are You Ready to Order, or
Do You Want More Time to Chew on Your Choices?

"Soylent Green" is not the only work of popular culture that links moving bodies with degustation and the economy. A *Twilight Zone* episode called "To Serve Man," based on a 1953 short story by Damon Knight, offers a similar narrative, this time about uneven interstellar development, comparative advantage, and free trade. The Kanamits, very intelligent, large-headed aliens, arrive on Earth bringing with them a vast array of advanced technologies that make life more comfortable and prosperous, free of disease and war. In short order, the Kanamits solve all Earth's problems, turning humans into indolent, overweight beasts (not all that different a theme from that found in 2008's "WALL-E"). They then offer Earthlings the opportunity to travel to their home planet, and many eagerly apply. But the political authorities are mystified by the Kanamits' great generosity—it counters everything they know about geopolitics and human behavior—and they are certain there is more to the aliens' benevolence than meets the eye. They manage to steal a Kanamit book with the title "To Serve Man," which, once laboriously deciphered, turns out to be a cookbook.

Why does the theme of smart people exploiting stupid ones appear so often in popular culture? The reason is not difficult to explain. Americans seem perpetually concerned about being shortchanged by con men and wiseguys, especially those with various magical devices and gizmos (e.g., *The Wizard of Oz*, 1900). It has always been thus when technologically advanced peoples encounter less technologically developed societies (but see the discussion of *The Martian Chronicles* below). The Europeans' imperial conquest of much of the world and subsequent exploitation of the labor and resources of the conquered and colonized have made some parts of the world very prosperous and others quite poor. Yet such conquest and colonization is almost always rationalized as part of a "civilizing process,"[16] even if it also involves the deaths of millions, as was the case in the Belgian Congo.[17]

Moreover, that such exploitation might occur without great awareness— and even with tacit cooperation—on the part of "natives" is also a common trope. This is the theme underlying John Carpenter's film "They Live." John Nada (i.e., "nothing"), a homeless worker in Los Angeles, finds a pair of sunglasses. When he puts them on, the glasses reveal the presence of aliens with skull-like faces and a plethora of disciplinary commands, such as "Obey" and "Marry and Reproduce," written on billboards, money, and other common items. Nada and his friends, who also put on the glasses, realize that the aliens are here to transform the world's environment and to steal resources and other things that might have economic value on their home planet. For space travelers, in other words, Earth is a Third World planet good only for plunder and extraction. The humans' response is to launch a rebellion, one that might or might not eventually succeed, but the point is to demonstrate how capitalist practice is also a means of fostering obedience and supporting exploitation (an argument central to "postcolonial" literature).[18] In this instance, moreover, aliens will colonize Earth and strip it of wealth, while humans are reduced to slaves or even exterminated (shades of "The Matrix"!).[19] Recovering from such a social and ecological disaster, inflicted by a superior civilization, would be no easy matter. In this light, it is puzzling that so many of the world's wealthy blame those living in ex-colonial countries for inflicting their impoverished conditions on themselves.[20]

A slightly different story of underdevelopment, exploitation, and destruction appears in Ray Bradbury's *The Martian Chronicles*, a series of stories in which Americans flood the Red Planet and turn it into a large strip mall. The book is striking in its implicit depiction and condemnation of developmentalism and Americans' heedless treatment not only of other peoples but themselves as well. The year is 1999. Bradbury's Earth and Mars are a baroque mixture of past and future. Rockets are as ubiquitous and personal as automobiles, while houses are sentient, fully automated, and able to care for themselves. At the same time, it is still 1950. Oppressed by the white man's laws and prejudices, African Americans flee the South to Mars, where they hope to live in freedom. Houses on Mars are built with wood shipped from Earth, and television does not exist. Although the indigenous Martians are far beyond Earthlings in terms of technology and ethics, the settlers from Earth wipe them out with imported diseases (as happened to Native Americans). In the end, rampant commercial American civilization is exported to Mars and reproduces something like the "Old Capitalist Frontier" with all of its sordid ways and people looking to get rich quick. In 2026, atomic war breaks out on Earth. All of the settlers fly home, fearful of missing the Big One and being stranded on the Red Planet. A very few stay behind as the new "Martians." Did Bradbury see only a burnt-out cinder as the future of American capitalism?

Why have some human societies become rich and others not? This remains a focus of intense debate, primarily outside the community of neoclassical economists, who explain it as "simple economics" (but even within these ranks, there are notable dissenters from the conventional wisdom).[21] As already suggested, one of the keys to capitalism's success is "uneven development." This, too, is a Marxist concept not generally recognized in neoclassical economics, which calls it "underdevelopment" and blames differences between "developed" and "underdeveloped" societies on culture, governance, and weak enforcement of laws, rules, contracts, and property rights.[22] The technical and critical literatures on "development" are vast, and I do not intend to rehash them here. Suffice it to say that development has been held up as a global economic and social ideal since at least 1949, when President Harry S Truman gave his famous speech outlining the Point Four Program.[23] Setting up industrial societies and the United States as examples of the large-scale benefits of steady economic growth, both policy makers and financiers sought out opportunities to invest resources in developing countries, hoping to transform them into democratic, capitalist societies (this as an element of the Cold War conflict with the Soviet Union). Notwithstanding the trillions of dollars that flowed from north to south—and here it is important to note that trillions of dollars also flowed from south to north with the net flow being impossible to determine—social and economic development has been very uneven and largely to the advantage of capitalists, wherever they are.

Some countries, such as Japan, Korea, and China, have realized enormous levels of growth as a result of market-oriented strategies. Many others, as across Africa, have not. It does appear, however, that political intervention in the organization of markets and their political and social relations is a critical element in the process of both enrichment and impoverishment. Where states are riddled with fraud and poorly organized markets, social investments tend to be small or nonexistent and corruption rampant (e.g., Nigeria). Where the rules structuring the political economy are well defined and tend, for the most part, to be enforced, development seems much more likely (e.g., South Korea).[24] While corruption is rife in China, that country's economy and population are so large and there is so much inward investment combined with the reliability of a strong state that even relatively lax organization of the political economy does not seem to impede growth.[25] Yet, even in China, hundreds of millions of people, mostly rural, have realized little or no benefit from the new economic policies of the past three decades.

In many ways, uneven development is the flip side of comparative advantage. Some places possess greater capital and social resources than others in the form of finance, technology, and capabilities (as a consequence of historical developments and colonialism, these are mostly in rich, developed countries, as I discuss below). Capital can be used to extract further capital in the form of raw materials and labor from poorer places unable to put their own resources to "good use"—a process sometimes called primitive capital accumulation (PCA) in that resources are extracted with minimal payment or none at all. (Whether "good use" might also include leaving resources where they are is generally not a consideration.) Due to frequently "unequal terms of trade," finished, manufactured goods tend to be more expensive and to rise in price more rapidly than unfinished ones: it takes a lot of fish to pay for a copy of Windows. As the rich places sell things to the poor ones, the latter gradually fall farther and farther behind, unable to sell anything but raw materials and labor to the rich. Were capitalism to foster "even development," there would be much less comparative advantage and trade among locations. Why buy an imported auto when a comparable one is available locally? (In fact, as noted earlier, there are many reasons to buy foreign, and the bulk of global trade continues to take place among rich countries; Japanese autos sell quite well in the United States and Europe, even though the latter produces perfectly serviceable and high-quality cars.)[26] From the neoclassical point of view, however, such "unevenness" is simply comparative advantage at work. Some countries are strong in terms of specific manufactured goods and advanced services; others, in providing raw materials and cheap labor. There is no systematic or structural impoverishment of the poor by the rich or any intention to cause it. After all, as we asked in chapter 3, would you pay a neurosurgeon's wages to a housecleaner (or vice versa)?

A critical perspective looks at the situation differently. Were poor countries able to produce finished goods that displaced comparable imported ones, they would become less dependent on both stuff and capital from rich countries—even if their own goods were more costly. If poor countries could achieve such autonomy, they might also become more politically and economically radicalized, which, as we saw above, the rich greatly fear. Consequently, not only did old colonial powers deliberately prevent industrialization in their colonies—and even, as in the case of India's textile industry, deliberately destroy it[27]—but they continue today to organize international trade and its governing regulations in ways that often disadvantage poor countries. We should only note in passing that the rise of China has significantly overturned this pattern of rich countries' exporting high-value products to poor ones. At least until the onset of the current economic crisis, the United States was becoming more likely to export raw materials to China while the latter shipped all kinds of manufactured goods in the other direction.

Bloody Diamonds!

One element seems to arise in both development successes and failures: primitive capital accumulation. This is also a Marxist concept, although a version of it appears in liberal economics, in John Locke's arguments to the effect that improving land by working it makes that land one's property. Both Marxist and neoclassical economics assume that beyond the cost of their extraction, resources are "free" and belong to no one (otherwise rents would have to be paid to their owner). Land and resources not being visibly exploited or "developed" through farming, logging, fishing, mining, and so forth, are assumed to be unused or "waste" and to have no legal "owners." It is then a fairly simple juridical matter to declare such resources the "property of the state" and to redistribute them to the rich and powerful (the political consequences may, of course, not be so straightforward). That is, while capital is required to extract resources, be they minerals, timber, or oil, those materials are there for the taking by anyone with the capability to do so. All that is required is for the state to allocate ownership of those resources to some party, either itself (that is, the "people") or its agents or designated private parties. After all, if trees are simply standing there, and no one has legal claim to them—an oft-contested point—who has the right to harvest and sell them and to receive money in return? Applying Locke's arguments, we see that anyone who puts labor into felling timber has made it his or her property, giving him or her the "right" to sell the "improved" or extracted resource to others. That first step—taking something "raw" and undeveloped and turning it into one's own wealth—is primitive capital accumulation (PCA).

In many parts of the world, states have asserted national property rights in land and resources. This includes the vast public lands of the United States (to which many private corporations desire access). Anyone who wishes to explore for resources on such lands must pay the government for a lease. If anything marketable is extracted, such as oil or coal, royalties on production, constituting "rent" to the owner, must also be paid. Private landowners with subsoil surface rights also receive royalties, as in the old television show "The Beverly Hillbillies." But those lacking such mineral rights can literally lose their land to coal strip-mining and other similarly destructive activities and see it piled up into unfertile hills or washed down devastated valleys. In other words, resources are not literally free for the taking, but the market price for raw materials is usually low compared to the final products in which they are incorporated (gasoline is one exception to this rule; the cost of oil comprises a major fraction of the price at the pump, and prices tend to rise and fall in concert with that of oil).

While the concept of PCA is not normally applied to labor, it is not entirely incorrect to think of wages as generally including a considerable "free" component.[28] Recall that the labor theory of value tries to link the value (price) of a finished product to the value of the labor required to make it. "Profit" can, consequently, be understood in two ways. From the neoclassical perspective, it represents the premium over the total costs of inputs—labor, raw materials, rent, technology, and so forth—that demand for the product supports. Profit, in other words, represents what consumers think something is worth, which is why cheaply made goods can sometimes command premium prices. From the perspective of the labor theory of value, however, a major portion of profit is the difference between the lower wage paid to the worker and the full value of that labor. In other words, the capitalist attempts to pay the lowest possible wage to the worker in order to generate the greatest profit, even if that wage is less than what the worker needs to survive.[29]

Unions attempt to put upward pressure on wages through collective withholding of their labor from capital, but they must always remain aware that reducing a company's profit margin to zero may result in no jobs at all. In places where there is a reserve army of labor, it becomes possible to maintain wages at very low levels—this is the "equilibrium price of labor" in neoclassical terms. Indeed, low labor costs become a "comparative advantage," one that China has exploited to great benefit, although some companies are beginning to find its wage rates "too costly" and have relocated to Vietnam (which forbids unions and strikes). At the limit, the difference between low wages and outright slavery begins to disappear, the latter being purely primitive capital accumulation. To put the point more bluntly, the prosperity of the United States was built, partially at least, on the "free labor" of millions of African slaves and their descendants over the two centuries up to 1865 (arguably, it was built further on low wages paid to them following emancipation, as well). The current value of this contribution to the American and world economies must almost certainly be in the tens of trillions of dollars.[30]

There is no need to enter into the further details of this debate, however, since "Blood Diamond" provides an excellent illustration of PCA. Briefly, the film traces the global trajectory of a large and rare pink diamond from the mineral fields of Sierra Leone, during the height of that country's civil war (1991–2002), to the vaults of the Central Selling Organization in London. Solomon Vandy, a fisherman captured by the Revolutionary United Front (RUF), is forced to dig for the gems that pay for RUF weapons. In return he receives minimal subsistence (not even "slave wages," as it were). Vandy finds the pink diamond, but his efforts to keep his discovery secret are futile. As the news spreads, more and more people try to steal the stone. One of them is Danny Archer, a Rhodesian soldier of fortune engaged in the arms trade and linked to a South African mercenary who, in turn, does business with a shady European diamond company. The third major character in the story is Maddy Bowen, an American journalist looking for a good story about "blood diamonds" that she can sell back home.[31]

After a good deal of bloodshed and violence, Archer manages to acquire the diamond, but he is mortally wounded in one of the film's many gunfights.

As he lies dying in the early dawn light, splayed out as on a crucifix, Archer repents and returns the stone to Vandy. He and Bowen spirit the diamond to London, where it is auctioned to a South African diamond merchant for two million pounds. Bowen publishes a widely read exposé of the trade in blood diamonds and becomes famous. The diamond itself is carefully carted off to the closely guarded vaults of the diamond company, like the Ark of the Covenant retrieved by Indiana Jones and buried in a vast U.S. government warehouse of ancient wonders. There, the stone will remain hidden, along with tens of thousands of other stones, so as to keep the retail price of diamonds far above their "real" value.

Although the film is fictional, the civil war in Sierra Leone—as well as similar wars in other West African states—the presence of mercenaries from southern Africa, and the trade in diamonds for arms are drawn from "real events," as the saying goes. During these African wars, competing military forces enslaved men, women, and children to work in the diamond fields, and a large fraction of the stones dug up and sold or traded for weapons from various suppliers of small arms ended up in the international diamond trade.[32] All of this became an international cause célèbre, leading to the creation of movements, organizations, high dudgeon, and, eventually, the Kimberley Process Certification Scheme. The last represents the diamond trade's effort to certify every stone's origin and thereby reduce trade in blood diamonds. According to the scheme's website, "Diamond experts estimate that conflict diamonds now represent a fraction of one percent of the international trade in diamonds, compared to estimates of up to 15% in the 1990s." Whether this is really the case is difficult to say with any certainty.[33]

Even Kimberley-certified diamonds are not wholly clean, however, since the difference between a miner's salary ($20 to $50 per hour maximum) and the retail cost of a one-carat diamond ($2,800 to $10,000 in the summer of 2009) is considerable (even if the diamond cutter's labor costs are factored in).[34] And for much of the industry's history, especially in southern Africa, diamond miners were virtually enslaved. This is an example of PCA both in terms of the resource and labor. Diamonds are virtually "free" for the taking, even though a great deal of labor goes into finding them, and they only acquire value and become capital higher up the production chain through managed scarcity. By exercising near-monopoly control of the flow of diamonds into the world market, the Central Selling Organization was long able to maintain retail prices at artificially high levels (a typical markup between wholesale and retail diamond prices is 300 to 400 percent).[35] Even so, governments make a tidy sum from their role in the diamond trade, for mining companies are often required to sell their production to a state agency that, in turn, certifies each stone as "conflict free."

A considerable fraction of this wealth—and the revenues generated from other natural resources and raw materials such as oil, metals, and timber—tends to vanish before ever reaching the state treasuries or benefiting the inhabitants of the producing countries. In some instances, prominent individuals have acquired legal title to the resource-producing lands. In other cases, they stand somewhere in the revenue flow and are able to divert funds to bank accounts in faraway places. Nigeria offers an archetypal example of this problem. The country sells around two million barrels of oil per day. Oil costs somewhere between $1 and $10 per barrel to produce and sells for $50 to $100 per barrel. The government should see revenues of $25 to $100 billion per year. From this, we might expect Nigeria to be a rich and prosperous country. Not so: per capita incomes today are less than at the country's independence in 1960, and most Nigerians have to get by on $1 or $2 per day. Moreover, it has been estimated that somewhere between $100 and $150 billion or more in Nigerian oil revenues have simply disappeared over the past several decades. Meanwhile, the Nigerian economy is a mess, its oil-producing regions are enmeshed in conflict, and the country cannot even feed itself. And all of this is a consequence of too much oil and too much money.[36]

As noted earlier, this state of affairs has been called the resource curse. Countries that should be wealthy and well-off as a result of ownership and production of more or less "free" resources are, instead, impoverished, underdeveloped, and conflict ridden. Why? Several reasons have been offered. A macroeconomic policy perspective attributes the problem to a lack of monitoring and accountability by and within governments. Funds are poorly handled, there are few, if any, mechanisms for keeping track of the vast sums involved, and there are many opportunities for diverting money. Rather than spending the funds on projects that will provide employment opportunities and increase agricultural and industrial productivity, governments are wont to spend them on subsidies for food, fuel, and housing, social services for the well-off, and grandiose enterprises and infrastructures with little practical value. The resource curse is nothing that a modicum of "good governance," along with a healthy dose of democracy and accountability, cannot fix, according to majority opinion.

Critically speaking, however, the deck is strongly stacked against meaningful development or escape from the curse. The influx of large sums of money, as noted earlier, tends to drive up the value of the local currency, which makes it cheaper to import goods and commodities than to produce them domestically (and these imports often come from rich countries that can produce more cheaply and often subsidize their export trade). As a result, agriculture goes into decline, industries go out of business, and high rates of inflation follow. This means that the cost of food and other basic necessities can climb out of reach (hence, the need for domestic subsidies). Should the state try to eliminate the subsidies, strikes and riots would likely result. Rather than development we see a small group of people getting wealthier, the masses becoming poorer, and little else. This does not mean there is no economy—indeed, the gray and black markets tend to be very active and vibrant—only that the opportunities for significant accumulation are quite limited for those not in the upper class or among political, social, and military elites.

Bad Medicine

The Constant Gardener illustrates another version of primitive capital accumulation, albeit by transnational pharmaceutical corporations, that involves "body work" rather than extraction of raw materials. While the novel and film differ on certain key points, the overall plot elements remain the same. A low-level British diplomat in Kenya, Justin Quayle, finds out that his activist wife, Tessa, has been murdered, apparently because she discovered that a northern pharmaceutical corporation is trying to cover up some very deadly side effects of a drug it is testing. Moreover, the company is illegally running drug trials on Africans. The cover-up not only encompasses Kenya, however, but extends all the way up to the British government, which is more interested in global drug sales and economic growth than the injury and deaths of largely anonymous Africans. In an afterword to the book, author John le Carré wrote, "By comparison with the reality, my story [is] as tame as a holiday postcard."

Both the novel and film have been praised widely by those who believe Big Pharma is the font of evil and vilified by those who see the story as liberal-lefty propaganda. It cannot be denied, however, that drug trials have been conducted in Africa and not always with salubrious results (at least one author charges that AIDS was the result of such a drug trial gone terribly wrong, although his claims have been much disputed).[37] Africa is an especially attractive place to conduct such trials for several reasons. The first is the sheer dearth of medical care, and for those suffering from one disease or another, the opportunity to receive treatment is very attractive. The second is that, in contrast to many drug trials in the global North, Africans are paid very little for their participation—if they receive any remuneration at all. Finally, although such testing is notionally subject to the ethical and procedural restrictions imposed by state regulatory agencies, such as the U.S. Food and Drug Administration (FDA), the fact is that monitoring and review are almost nonexistent in Africa. In all respects, therefore, it is much less costly to conduct drug trials in Africa than in America or Europe.

This, then, is a form of "comparative advantage," "free trade," and PCA. In this instance, bodies for testing are both relatively and absolutely cheaper in the global South than the global North, and regulatory costs are lower.[38] And the low level of testing restrictions makes it relatively easy to conduct drug trials in the global South. Indeed, this is the principle by which manufacturing has been outsourced and sent offshore from North to South over the past twenty years since labor is much cheaper in poor countries than in rich ones (although labor mobility itself is not subject to "free trade"). Yet it does not seem altogether ethical that drugs that will mostly benefit the well-off are being tested on the poor. Is this a comparative advantage or a gross injustice? It depends on whom you ask. From a neoclassical economic perspective, the "low cost" of organizing a drug trial is a decided advantage. Such testing is quite costly in the global North, and companies can bear considerable liability if something goes wrong among those who receive the drug. Even though it might be more difficult to ensure a rigorous trial in poor countries, what with people dropping in and out and not always following protocols closely enough, a "reserve army" of potential participants can always be tapped. The benefits accrued from public relations campaigns describing a company's activities on behalf of the poor and sick are also worth something in northern markets.

From the more critical view, the calculation is not quite so simple. The offer of "free" pharmaceuticals and medical care in return for participation might appear to be a fair exchange, but it places a low value on human life and work. The larger benefits to a company if a test is successful and the FDA accepts the results can far exceed the costs of the trial. Moreover, there is a greater injustice when the finished drugs are sold in African pharmacies at prices that few can afford. Nor do trials or drugs make any significant contribution to local "development." The pharmaceutical company will take the results of the trials to its labs where the drug will be refined and packaged and then sold to well-off consumer-patients who have health insurance or deep pockets. The drugs will not be manufactured in African factories, and none of the eventual profits will be repatriated to either the participants or the countries in which they live. There is not much difference here between the extraction of resources and drug trials. The results of both are "finished" in the global North and reexported to those few who can afford to buy them.[39]

5

Technology and Alienation

TECHNOLOGY IS IMPORTANT TO CAPITALISM; it is the fourth in a quartet of inputs that also includes capital, labor, and resources. But technology is also socially problematic for as a social creation it can also alienate, or distance, the worker from that which she creates and, indeed, from the world around her.[1] Writing in *The Economic and Philosophical Manuscripts of 1844*, Karl Marx referred specifically to "social alienation":

> The worker becomes poorer the more wealth he produces, the more his production increases in power and extent. The worker becomes an ever cheaper commodity the more commodities he produces. The *devaluation* of the human world grows in direct proportion to the increase in value of the world of things. Labour not only produces commodities; it also produces itself and the workers as a *commodity* and it does so in the same proportion in which it produces commodities in general. . . . This fact simply means that the object that labour produces, its product, stands opposed to it as *something alien*, as a power independent of the producer. The product of labour is labour embodied and made material in an object, it is the objectification of labour. The realization of labour is its objectification. In the sphere of political economy, this realization of labour appears as a *loss of reality* for the worker, objectification as loss of and bondage to the object, and appropriation as estrangement, as *alienation*.[2]

In short, the spiritual and ontological linkage between the creator and her creation ·is broken as the subject of the creative act is turned into an object. Since the beginning of the Industrial Revolution, the means of creating goods has been taken out of the hands of the craftsman [sic] and put largely under the control of the capitalist and his technological systems. Consequently, the worker is alienated not only from her creations but from and through the tools with which she works as well as from the eventual exchange of her products, in which money is traded for things in impersonal transactions. One might further argue that by replacing both labor and use value with exchange value, capitalism turns us into "aliens." We are disembedded, as Karl Polanyi might have put it, from the very conditions of our social and material existence.[3] Not to push the point too far, but imagine if, at birth, newborn babies were auctioned off to the highest bidders so as to realize their full exchange value to their biological parents—this would be the complete disembedding of life from social and material existence.[4] But perhaps this is being too harsh on technology.

This chapter reflects on the theme of technology and alienation and, in particular, how the former both distances us from, and increasingly absorbs into itself, the very bodies and society that capitalism has done so much to produce. Not everyone takes such a dystopic view, of course. Nonetheless, beginning with Mary Shelley's *Frankenstein: The Modern Prometheus* (1818) and terminating, at least at this writing, with "Terminator Salvation" (2009), the cyborgian combination of human and machine has become a trope common to both film and fiction.[5] It is rare, however, to find authors or directors who wholeheartedly endorse such a transmogrification; possibly they are dubious about a time when all humanity will be lost to the "soul of the machine," as it were.[6] In this chapter, I begin with a general examination of alienation, which should be regarded as a necessary element of successful capitalism, inasmuch as it is that separation of product from labor that makes our economic system so productive. Still, too much alienation can be extraordinarily destructive, as is evident in "Fight Club."

By contrast, technology is both a tool of alienation and enormously attractive to consumers who seek not only functionality but also the status of the "latest" gadget. "The Matrix" (1999) is perhaps the quintessential expression of the combination of the two—technology and alienation—positing a world in which capitalism manipulated by unseen forces (shades of *The Wizard of Oz*, 1900!) is literally a prison for both mind and body (a theme further explored in "eXistenZ" [1999] and "The Thirteenth Floor" [1999]). Lest we think this a mere fiction, consider "Falling Down" (1993) as a parable of America's Manifest Destiny—"Westward the Course of Empire!"[7]—in which the separation between technology and producer nonetheless leads to their fusion in an alienated and ultimately doomed man/cyborg. Later in the chapter I turn to the realm of "cyberpunk" in Neal Stephenson's *Snow Crash* (1992) and Charles Stross's *Glasshouse* (2006). There, I consider how technology facilitates further commodification and transformation of bodies and minds. Finally, I return to a theme first broached in chapter 3, the literal production of bodies as depicted in "Blade Runner" (1982). In that film, a group of technobiological creations seeks to overcome the alienation inherent in the four-year lifespan imposed on their genes by their human creator (who is curiously impotent and alienated from them).

Each of the works discussed in this chapter posits the alienation of individuals from both society and themselves and the problem for and threat to the body politic they pose. In those alien and alienated body/texts, produced and printed courtesy of the American political economy for the edification of American consumers, the genesis of alienation, aliens, and alien spaces can be found in capitalism and accumulation. Each offers a different means of dealing with the internal and social contradictions resulting from life under capitalism. And each puts its audience in a curious and paradoxical position, problematizing good, evil, and everyday life, even as it distances and alienates viewers who think that what they see on the screen "can't happen here."

Set the Wayback Machine, Sherman!

Technology signals change and progress.[8] It allows us to do things we could not, were we forced to depend solely on our own strength, wiles, and intelligence. Not only did technology allow humans to become hunters and farmers and, more recently, "symbolic analysts" with computers, but it has also been central to war and the state, to industrialization and economic growth, to consumption and comfort.[9] Where would we be without it? Still, who among us really knows what is inside those black boxes, those iPods, computers, and cars, we buy so eagerly and use with such alacrity?[10] How do transistors work? What is electricity? Who put the edge on mass-produced knives? Do we really need to know much about the insides of the things we use in order to use them? Is alienation from our technology really necessary so that we will buy things rather than build them ourselves?

In a sense, we are aliens in our own social existence—very little about it is "natural."[11] It might be helpful at this point to note, therefore, that aliens are found not only in outer space but also in the home and all around us. As both dictionary and discourse remind us, the term has four common meanings. The first is the creature, whether extraterrestrial or of this earth, who confounds "normalcy" and what it means to be "human." The second applies to those individuals who are not native to the country in which they reside, a conception that often connotes a sense of unbridgeable cultural difference as well as contrasting tastes and preferences. The third means "out of place" and also encompasses "alienation," here referring to those who feel that they do not belong to the society of which they are members.[12] Finally, there is the dual conception of the "alienation" of an individual from her stuff, whether the product of her labor or tangible things bought and sold. In all four senses, "aliens" come to be regarded as threatening presences, possessed of a drive or force that, if not stopped, will absorb, consume, or subvert and transform the body politic. Consequently, much of American popular culture invites, and even incites, violence and war against aliens.[13]

But perhaps the alien "problem" is better understood in terms of the internal cohesion of the body politic as visible in the repeated and destabilizing efforts of the alienated to escape from the containment established around them by capitalism's social norms and traditions. Paradoxically, neoclassical economic practice and the capitalist market make escape feasible even as they construct an "iron web" from which there is no escape. As I have argued in earlier chapters (and will again in chapter 8), both state and market have long propagated fear of the world outside the former's geographic borders and the latter's cultural norms as a means of fostering internal discipline and self-regulation. The invocation of "alien" can be understood as one tool to this end, among many. I address the topic of capitalism and violence in chapter 8. Here it is more appropriate to draw connections within the iron web of discipline imposed by both state and markets.

For Hobbesians, as we shall see in greater detail in chapter 6, internal discipline has long been a reason for, and function of, Leviathan, the state. At the same time, the state must ensure that conditions within, necessary for production and reproduction, remain undisturbed by conditions without. Thus, many interpreters of Thomas Hobbes—who was not, strictly speaking, a "Hobbesian" in the common realist understanding—transposed the state of nature among men alienated from one another into relations among states alienated from one another. As a result, they were always subject to and prepared for war. In the absence of the shadow of a violent future, present conditions of relative peace and tranquility within states and among them might lull both men and women into thinking Leviathan excessive or even unnecessary. They might, moreover, believe that markets left to operate "freely" could provide whatever political guidance and discipline were needed—a central principle of libertarianism as well as neoliberalism.[14] In other words, the continued power and authority of the state depends upon the alienation inherent in a state of nature among states, one that must be maintained in order to legitimate the state and the domestic social order that it guards.

Still, claims of danger from the outside have sometimes become difficult to mount and sustain. It is not that states have not persistently armed against each other and threatened crisis and war or that they have not gone to war and killed millions in the process. Rather, it is that the progressive expansion of economic exchange among societies—capitalist "globalization," to which we return in chapter 8—has repeatedly disrupted the cultural, social, and moral borders the state establishes and polices. This, in turn, has served to propagate the belief system that E. H. Carr derided as "idealism," the notion that extensive webs of economic intercourse would serve to mitigate conflict and prevent war.[15] To some degree, Carr was correct; such "idealism" has turned out, again and again, to be unfounded. At some level, however, he completely missed the point. Social containment is undermined by capitalism and the individual self-interest it reifies, with the result that the cohesion of the body politic is weakened and can, under certain circumstances, dissolve into Hobbes's mythic "state of nature" (see chapter 6). To avoid such conditions, state authorities have often found it helpful to engage in the escalation of domestic threats, ranging from relatively mundane anarchists and "lone wolves," such as Nicola Sacco and Bartolomeo Vanzetti and James von Brunn,[16] to real and imagined planetary terrorists, such as al-Qaeda and those depicted in films such as "Independence Day" and the various versions of "War of the Worlds." In this light, it seems plausible to suggest that domestic social instability triggers the fabulous panoply of alien threats and dangers.

Consider 9/11. Most, if not all, of the hijackers who took over planes and flew them into buildings and the ground on September 11, 2001, were educated, middle-class men.[17] Much of their anger seems to have derived from disgust with, and alienation from, their own societies and leaders, and they acted in hope of destabilizing them through alienation from the United States. Moreover, that disgust and alienation was linked to what they saw as moral corruption and dissolution visible in the libertine behaviors of Western capitalist societies.[18] Although external evils are often posited as corrosive of the body politic, the sources of social destabilization are more commonly internal to societies. To acknowledge and act on this truth would, however, destabilize the belief system that legitimates the social systems governed by individual Leviathans—hence, the frequent invocation of alien threats.

It should not escape our attention that alienation and alien threats are almost always associated with advanced technology and the mysteries of its operation. Invaders from off planet always arrive with superior gadgets. By contrast, invaders from on planet may not have superior technologies but use existing ones in unexpected ways (as on 9/11). In some sense it is the black-boxing of things,[19] which obscures what is inside of them and the operators' minds, that generates alien invaders ("Danger! To be opened only by authorized service personnel!"). The fear is pervasive, for example, that hackers' viruses and worms will take command of our computers and turn them into "bots," zombies that propagate throughout cyberspace, just as the aliens (or alien bugs) in "Invasion of the Body Snatchers" or Robert Heinlein's *Puppet Masters* (1951; film, 1994) colonize people's brains, transforming them into bots too.[20] This is linked, in turn, to the nagging notion that our trajectories in life are already determined and that nameless forces we cannot see, hear, or feel control the universe and our fates (be they gods, demons, or Fortuna).[21] At the same time, many find the possibility that there is no omnipotent, transcendent guiding force in charge so disturbing that they have been willing to fight and die to prove otherwise (even as no proof is ever forthcoming as a result of those wars and deaths).

Fighting with the System

Jack, the narrator of "Fight Club," feels this way. A first viewing of the film suggests that Jack is so alienated from his life and work in the capitalist system that only pain and the possibility of death will sensitize and bring him back—which is why he seeks out support groups and twelve-step programs. But vicarious suffering through others is not enough. As a result, he experiences a dissociative psychic break and splits into two very distinct and distinctive personalities. Tyler Durden, Jack's alter, is everything Jack is not: brash, violent, sexy, abusive, destructive. Durden, in full touch with himself and his emotions, is more importantly deeply committed to fighting and destroying the system. Jack, by contrast, is a "tool of capitalism." He works as a risk-assessment specialist or, in the language of neoclassical economics, a "cost-benefit analyst."

Cost-benefit analysis attempts to reduce everything in life (and death) to comparable monetary values in order to decide whether to undertake an action.[22] Jack searches for defects in automobiles after an accident has caused injury or death in order to determine whether it is less expensive for his company to recall all defective cars for repair or to reach out-of-court settlements with those who are killed or injured by the defect. In chapter 3, I briefly addressed the question, what is a human life worth? Here it is enough to recognize that Jack's job leads him to both a psychological and existential crisis, which alienates him from himself. Although those around him recognize that he and Tyler Durden are the same person, Jack does not. The audience, seeing Jack and Tyler as two distinct characters, experiences an epistemological and ontological crisis along with Jack. Is Durden real or a projection of Jack's deeply disturbed mind?

Jack and Tyler have different solutions to their joint dilemma. They create the "Fight Club," which is very much like a men's support group, except that it lionizes hand-to-hand combat, pain, and suffering. As a result, Jack no longer needs to seek and absorb vicarious pain experienced through others' emotions (as aliens sometimes try to do with humans). Now he can feel his own pain, and it is more real than any of the material things he has ever possessed. Ironically, however, videotapes of Jack "fighting" with Tyler show Jack beating himself up, knocking himself out, and splashing his own blood and teeth all over. Jack's pain is self-inflicted, and his alienation continues to grow.

Tyler's "solution" to the dilemma is to destroy the causes of Jack's psychic break. He turns the growing legions of Fight Club participants into a secret army whose ultimate goal is the destruction of credit card companies, the enablers of Jack's alienation and, of course, signifiers of capitalism. But because Jack sees himself as essentially law-abiding and peaceful, he is horrified to discover not only that he and Tyler are the same person but also that in his war on capitalism, the latter has managed to secretly induct almost everyone, including the police, into his army (indicating how widespread alienation from capitalism has become). Ultimately, Jack is unable to halt the destruction of the credit card companies' buildings, even though by shooting himself in the head, he manages to "kill" Tyler and heal the psychic break.

"Fight Club" is both very subversive and very cynical. On the one hand, it follows in the spirit of those bumper stickers that proclaim, "I'd rather be smashing capitalism." On the other hand, it suggests we are all so alienated from our lifeworlds that only the virtual masochism and pain inflicted by capitalism and its stuff keep us from dissociating entirely. Should we be amused or horrified? Or both? The genius of the film is, perhaps, that the audience is never quite sure (and in this the film's critique of capitalism is far superior to that of "The Matrix"). At the end of the film, Jack is "reunited" with his similarly alienated, but not split, "love," Marla Singer, as they stand watching buildings explode, implode, and pancake (very disturbing after the endless reruns of the collapse of the World Trade Center towers—the film was released in 1999, so it foreshadows rather than echoes 9/11). Whether Jack has found peace with his alienation or managed to overcome it through the destruction and havoc he has wreaked is left unanswered.

Jacking into the Market

"The Matrix" offers another version/vision of capitalism and alienation, although here the splitting that results is of a somewhat different nature. The film hardly qualifies as a great work of art or culture, yet it has achieved cult status and generated a plethora of learned journal articles and books.[23] That such a film should be so popular, especially with the academic literati, is somewhat puzzling. For one thing, it is extraordinarily violent, notwithstanding attempts to aestheticize the violence through liberal use of slow motion and intimations of philosophical conundra.[24] At the end of the day, however, all the film's characters are merely emptying assault weapons at each other. Moreover, there is nothing particularly insightful, innovative, or even provocative about the film's basic plot device—that we do not live in or experience "true" reality. Plato wrote about this notion, as have many others. And as the film reminds us with its sly reference to Jean Baudrillard, these days everyone who is anyone writes about simulation and reality (as I do in this book). So what's all the fuss about?

As I have suggested in earlier chapters, the most interesting element of "The Matrix" is its implicit commentary on contemporary capitalism, as it plays with concepts of alienation (and false consciousness) writ large. Moreover, in drawing on a long history of philosophical, religious, and literary thought about the material and spiritual worlds, the film confronts us once again with questions about "the real." If money is a social construction, is it real or imagined? And what about the capitalist system itself? Is the key point "I am therefore I think," or vice versa?

Dualism is the notion that the physical world we perceive and in which we live is not the "true" reality. As an idea, it is as old as (if not older than) organized religion and as recent as certain versions of postmodernism.[25] Historically, parallel-world dualisms found in religion and philosophy tend to bemoan human ignorance, sin, error, and folly and claim that a better, more-perfect world exists elsewhere to which we might aspire and might even go when we die.[26] It is not that we lack wisdom. Rather, our baser appetites dominate our ability to reason and see what is true. Why this is so and who makes it so is more problematic. Does the source of error lie within us, or is someone or something out there pulling our strings? (And why do we so often feel, as Morpheus points out, that there is "something wrong with the world"?)[27]

"The Matrix" is also an inverted allegory about globalization and the alienation from the real world promoted by commodity fetishism, the broadly advertised opportunities consumers are offered to purchase escapes into fantasy worlds (whether real resorts or virtual ones), and a general mystification about how the capitalist system operates. Not only is the everyday "reality" encountered by the participants in the simulacrum of contemporary life depicted in "The Matrix"—although filmed in Vancouver, it might as well be taking place in Los Angeles or any other North American city (a car chase in the third film of the series was filmed in Oakland, California)—fully bourgeoisified, but it is also a replica of the very world of the film's audience. That this world comes to repulse the audience is only one of the many tricks played by the filmmakers.

As in "They Live" (discussed in chapter 4), however, the underlying conceit is that alien forces—from whom people are alienated—control the horizontal, the vertical, and the focus, as well as the content. "The Matrix" clearly draws on such notions, treading well-worn ground in its positing of evil beings manipulating the appearance of reality, controlling the destiny of humanity, and limiting the possibilities of doing and being good. Who are these Others but the mysterious "They," those who conspiratorially manipulate an imaginary market utopia in which billions of humans "live"?[28] Those who, at great personal risk, seek the "truth" and discover that in this virtual world they are alienated from a brutal and sordid reality, which some nevertheless imagine to be "freedom," are, like Neo, marginalized or vaporized (the fate of dissenters in *Nineteen Eighty-Four,* too). Their plugs are pulled and they simply cease to be, like the characters in a video game. We might note that the same holds true in today's "real" market utopia, with the exception that our alienated seek succor in electronic fantasy worlds, many of which are set in rather desolate and grim postapocalyptic landscapes but promise, nonetheless, a certain form of Hobbesian "freedom" to game players as well as profit to game producers.[29]

But another theme here is not, for the most part, prefigured in the literature of dualism. In explaining the origins and organization of the virtual world in which humans "live," Morpheus, the leader of Zion's "freedom fight-ers"—"cyberterrorists" in contemporary national-security jargon—tells Neo that the Matrix is control and that every human being is a prisoner in it. "As long as the Matrix exists," he says, "the human race will never be free." And in what might be another case of false consciousness for both humans and the machines that govern both the virtual and real worlds, he elides the economic roots of the Matrix in twentieth-century capitalism. Nor does Morpheus ever stop to wonder whether the illusion of freedom in a virtual, albeit totalitarian, utopia might be more attractive than the terror of freedom in a devastated and hostile dystopic reality (that experiment is left to Cypher, who discov-ers that having left the Garden, he can never return). "The Matrix" might be understood, paraphrasing Max Weber, as an allegory about the "iron cage" (or "web") of globalized market capitalism and its foundationally totalitarian nature. (The Matrix is also Leviathan, of course, maintaining order and secu-rity, albeit without a social contract, as such. As we all know but are reluctant to acknowledge, the state is essential to the proper operation of markets, but no one has ever asked you to sign any such social contract.)

Who, then, really controls the Matrix? In the "real" world where humans slumber, the governors are artificial intelligences: machines, androids, rep-licants, computers. In the virtual world where people are "awake," the gov-ernors are avatars with human faces. Who can tell the difference and how? Both are human creations—in the potted pre-Matrix history of Morpheus as well as in the film-making "reality" of the Wachowski brothers—as is the materialization of humanity's quest for a peaceful and comfortable Utopian order whose nightmarish quality is visible in the endless rows and columns of pods that Neo sees only after he stops dreaming in his womb and uses his eyes for the first time. Everyone is quietly in place, in order. Babies are cultivated like corn or wheat to produce uniform products for the "world market." People are valued only for the energy they generate, which is little more than the power in a common battery. As Pogo might have said, "We have met the consumer, and he is us!" Alienated from ourselves, we are no more than commodities, fetishes for those who manipulate the market. (Or, to further paraphrase René Descartes, "I consume, therefore I am.")

We begin to see here why the iron web of capitalism might figure so centrally in "The Matrix" and what it has to do with the audience watching in a quiet and orderly fashion. Although not an explicit part of history as told to Neo by Morpheus, we recognize that artificial intelligence was/is a commercial venture conducted primarily for profit and only secondarily to enhance human or machinic capabilities. The search for human perfection in the face of what is commonly accepted as fallible human nature is another well-known mythological and literary trope. As such stories warn us, hubris is often a cause for divine displeasure—not to mention unintended consequences. But this desire for perfection is also basic to the teleology of liberalism. Although perfection can never be achieved, the boosters of free markets claim that they can improve the human condition until the world is a happy place and every human being's wants are met. (How does this differ from Marx's utopia?)

As the economic crisis that began in 2007 seems to suggest, however, our "reality" is not bound for such a utopian telos, no matter how often some expert opines that "prosperity is just around the corner" (or a year or two or three away). Indeed, the type of deregulated markets that, between the 1980s and 2007, seemed to underpin trends toward universal happiness has now been revealed as a good deal more brutish. As Karl Polanyi warned in *The Great Transformation*, "Our thesis is that the idea of a self-adjusting market implied a stark utopia. Such an institution could not exist for any length of time without annihilating the human and natural substance of society; it would have physically destroyed man and transformed his surroundings into a wilderness."[30] "The Matrix" is a story of such a "stark utopia." It is also our story. We are born into the matrix of capitalism, as it were, and escape is impossible. We have come (or have been made) to believe, moreover, that there are no alternatives except those too awful to contemplate, as are visible in places like Africa or the increasingly desolate spaces of periurban America. Our alienation is complete.

Over the Hill and into the Woods

Neo seems a largely passive tool in the real-virtual war of "The Matrix" (although this might just reflect Keanu Reeves's acting style). Beyond following

Morpheus's instructions, Neo is merely pursuing his historical destiny, flying through the air and shooting a lot of guns. Others see fit to take matters in hand, although they are also victims of history, as it were. In "Falling Down," William "Bill" Foster[31]—"D-FENS," according to the license plate on his car—is one such person, alienated by the forces of history and capitalism's constant story of social change (see chapter 8). Foster, whose mother reveals that he "protected us from the Communists," has lost one of the most valuable properties an individual can possess, a well-paying and respected job. An aerospace engineer by training, Foster has been laid off from his position at a defense corporation as a result of federal budget cuts, economic recession, and disappearance of the Cold War enemy (a.k.a., "the Communists"). Little does Foster's mother, or anyone else for that matter, imagine that her son is about to become a new alien threat, a once "normal" white male transformed through alienation into a cyborg bristling with weapons, determined to restore his and the nation's lost past (compare this to the first appearance of the Terminator and his persona, equipment, and mission in the eponymous 1984 film).[32] Alas! You cannot go home again, especially if you've been swept away by the gales of capitalist churn and change.

The film opens on one of those blisteringly hot days so familiar to Angelenos. Trapped on the freeway, his car stopped in immovable traffic, Foster is a prisoner in an iron (and concrete) web, in a place and situation as banal as one can imagine. But he means to find freedom and give meaning to his suffering. While his fellow freeway travelers wait like sheep to continue their journeys, Foster breaks ranks and breaks away. He abandons his car and the iron web. "Hey! Where are you going?" demands an irate driver resentful of Foster's sudden escape. "Home. I'm going home," Foster replies.[33] Scaling the nearby embankment, he goes AWOL over the hill and into the 'hood on the other side. There, he thinks, he will find the "real world" and the route home. Instead, he finds his personal hell.[34]

Foster has become frozen in time by the Cold War and neither understands nor realizes that the 1970s and 1980s are over—a can of Coke now costs 85 cents, and a phone call, 50 cents!—or that globalization has changed the world. He cannot speak the local languages—Korean, Spanish, even English is something of a mystery—he cannot read the writing on the walls (graffiti), and he certainly has no understanding of local customs or practices. Marked as an outsider by his haircut, tie, white shirt, and Samsonite briefcase, Foster is an alien on planet Earth, lost in a "traveler's tale." As Angela Gulick explains,

> One way that utopian authors . . . let readers know important background details about the utopian world is to create something called the "traveler's tale."

In a traveler's tale, the narrator is an "alien" who has dropped in on the utopian society, either through time travel or by crossing a physical barrier. As readers, we learn what the narrator sees, hears, and most importantly, what he/she is told by a utopian citizen. In other words, the narrator is dependent upon a native citizen's knowledge and perspective for any kind of information. So too is the reader. Thus, readers are also "aliens" who have dropped in on a strange, new society and in need of context and history.[35]

Not only has Foster crossed a physical barrier by going over the hill, but he has also time-traveled into a dystopic future. In so doing, he has lost work, identity, status, and property,[36] those individual characteristics that have kept him imprisoned.

Once "liberated," Foster proceeds cross-country in a westward direction, across Los Angeles and toward his "manifest destiny," passing through a series of increasingly hostile and incomprehensible terrains and adventures.[37] As he travels, Foster becomes militarized, militaristic, and machinelike, acquiring a gym bag full of guns, a camouflage outfit, and a very bad attitude. Moreover, he finds no "friendlies" in Los Angeles except, perhaps, the police who are searching for a guy who has become a threat to the social order. He also discovers that he is "economically unviable," in the words of an African American man being hauled away by the cops from the front of the bank where he is protesting. By the time Foster reaches Venice (a.k.a., "home"), where his ex-wife and daughter live, he has been turned into a fully alienated mechanical monster unable to survive in the new dispensation. Just as he is ignorant of the economic and social transformations of the 1980s and 1990s, Foster is also unaware of the changes to his own social being. He is puzzled when people suggest that he has become irrational and violent and shy away from him in fear. As the film comes to a climax, he runs to the end of the Santa Monica pier, intent on killing his wife and daughter before committing suicide. There, Foster threatens Detective Martin Prendergast with a water pistol and is shot in return. Foster falls over the railing and into the ocean, splayed out in a cruciform pose (again!), dying for capitalism's sins.

To Foster, D-FENS is a response to the dangerous and alien world he has encountered, one that stands between him and the past to which he so longs to return. He has lost his identity—defense of the United States, his job and status, his property, his home and family, his very reason for being! By the film's conclusion, Foster may as well be one of the tentacled aliens seen in a hundred other films, on the run from police and military who are on a mission to eliminate the enemy. The "truth" about the new political economy must not be allowed to escape. That truth is that Foster is much more than an "angry white male." American reviewers could not see this, and it took a British film critic to suggest that Foster's alienation was not his alone. She observed, "In the new world order, with no discernible outside enemy for America to define itself against, it's not just D-Fens who is cracking up, but his country. It is the status of the States that's under question here."[38] Foster made us safe from the Communists, and now he is out of a job. His economic viability is shot, and there are no job openings or any need for his skills and knowledge. Nor is there anyone to narrate his traveler's tale. If America's innovative means of destruction brought down the Soviet Union, they also left a trail of human ruin and rubble at home. It is worth noting that all three aliens discussed so far in this chapter—Jack, Neo, D-FENS—are only able to deal with their alienation through violence. What might this tell us about escaping from the iron web in which we are entangled?

What Do Androids Pay for Electric Sheep?

To be sure, novels and films about aliens (foreigners and others) threatening England and the United States date back to the late nineteenth century, with most warning that those Others want what we have and will stop at nothing to get it.[39] Ridley Scott's "Blade Runner" is a different kind of "alien" movie, one in which androids (artificial humans, or "replicants") seek to overcome their alienation from the human race by laying claim to "life, liberty and property." The film is based upon a quite different novel by Philip K. Dick, *Do Androids Dream of Electric Sheep?* (1968)[40] centered on the "manufacture" of human beings in and by postmodern capitalism. For our purposes, we might ask the following questions: Who belongs in a particular political economy and how can its "real" members be identified? Who ensures that "outsiders" (aliens) do not get in, especially when they are indistinguishable from "insiders"? And what are humans worth compared to aliens (whether offshore or off planet)?

"Blade Runner" is best known for its mise en scène, a postmodern film noir set in the Los Angeles of 2019, a megalopolis perpetually shrouded in clouds and smog and drenched by constant rain (quite unlike the sunny city we know from most films and television). The city is an agglomeration of damp, moldering, crumbling, abandoned structures of both twentieth-century and "modern" provenance, laced with crowded, torn-up streets and (like the broad boulevards of the contemporary Los Angeles basin) lined with small (open-air) shops and businesses. Old Pontiacs crawl through the streets as flying cars speed above. In this Third World city, much like the New York of "Soylent Green," the rich are on top and the poor are on the bottom. Enormous wealth exists side by side with grinding poverty. The city is inhabited by a polyglot mixture of Hispanics, Asians, Middle Easterners, and others, in constant movement yet with no evident destination, speaking a creole of

Japanese, German, Spanish, and English. High above the ruined streets, the few remaining Anglos—most have emigrated to off-planet colonies—live in opulent, elaborate, and highly secured buildings, enjoying comfortable apartments and the latest in fancy electronic gadgetry. Yet, as in contemporary America, the rich and poor need each other (someone has to clean up after the stockbrokers and designers have gone home). All that keeps Los Angeles going are the cops, who protect, serve, and maintain the social order in the interest of the rich and powerful. As Rick Deckard's supervisor, Sergeant Bryant, puts it, "If you're not cop, you're little people."

In this space-faring world of 2019, "little people" are plentiful, but it is too expensive and troublesome to ship them to the off-planet colonies to do heavy labor and service jobs—and humans still have some residual rights. Consequently, replicants have been created to do the dirty work. Replicants are "more human than human," according to Emmett Tyrell, the childless founder of the company that makes them. Judging from those that appear in the film—Roy, Pris, Leon, Zhora, and Rachael—replicants are also always white.[41] Indeed, says Tyrell, the only difference between a "real" human being and the latest model of replicant, the Nexus-6, is its four-year life span. Replicants nonetheless pose a threat to the social order because they are not "real" humans. They have been banned from Earth, having banded together in the past to kill their human masters. Any that get to Earth must be hunted down and eliminated. That is the job of Rick Deckard, a "blade runner," who kills them.

It is not so easy to distinguish replicants from reals. The only effective way has been to test a suspect's retinal response to emotional stimuli via an interrogation having to do with the killing of animals. A real human's empathic response to such questions is much stronger than that of a replicant, which does not possess a complete range of emotions.[42] The Nexus-6 have been given memories to eliminate this shortcoming. The idea is to make them more accepting of their short, four-year lives by leading them to believe they have lived long ones. The change also enhances both emotion and empathy, which eliminates the possibility of detecting who is a replicant and who is not. As a result, the blade runner's job has become much more difficult. But the blade runner himself is also different since he can kill only if he lacks empathy for others of his kind (Harrison Ford, who shows little emotion in any role, was perfect as Deckard). Ironically, perhaps, the unempathic Deckard must now test and kill emotion-bearing replicants. Is he also a replicant or only an emotionally damaged human being (a long-standing debate among the film's fans)? By the film's conclusion, all four of the replicants Deckard targets are dead, but only one has died at his hands. Moreover, Deckard has fallen in love with Rachael, a fifth replicant, which ends his usefulness to the police who are now set to hunt him down.

Who is "real" and who is not is of less interest here than the political economy of "Blade Runner," particularly capitalism's manufacture, exploitation, and alienation of human beings through various forms of advanced technology. Replicants force us to ask several questions. First, what makes someone a "real" human? The four who are the object of Deckard's laborious hunt have been manufactured to work for humans, but unlike free humans, they cannot sell their labor. Though superior to people in strength and intelligence, they are, all the same, slaves to and within capitalism. There are at least five distinct "models" of replicant in the film: Leon is a "combat model"; Roy, a nuclear-fuel loader; Zhora, an assassin; Pris, a "basic pleasure model" (Rachael, Deckard's love object, does not have a named "function"). In other words, replicants are commodities—service mechanisms—for sale, and they are not all that different from those who migrate to the United States in search of low-wage work. The specification of "roles" for different "models" is not that different, either, from the "body work" described in chapter 3. To the extent that adornments, accoutrements, and attitudes become the identifying characteristics of particular groups, their members replicate a specific "model"—and those characteristics can be commodified and offered for sale to the public at large.[43]

The film also poses a larger question: what is the value of a human life? And by whom is it valued (or not)?[44] So long as the replicants remain "out of sight and out of mind" and perform the tasks for which they have been created, their individual value is strictly limited to their labor power (whether they receive wages is never made clear, but as "slaves" it seems likely they do not). The Nexus-6 replicants' memories give them subjectivity, reflexivity, a sense of self, and an identity that, together, make them unwilling to work gratis. Indeed, their experiences make them valuable beyond what they do, what they earn, and what they cost. Roy's dying monologue illustrates the relative value of those memories (even if they make no evident sense): "I've seen things you people wouldn't believe. Attack ships on fire off the shoulder of Orion. I watched C-beams glitter in the darkness at Tannhäuser Gate. All those moments will be lost in time like tears in rain. Time to die." Deckard reflects, "I don't know why he saved my life. Maybe in those last moments he loved life more than he ever had before. Not just his life, anybody's life, my life. All he'd wanted were the same answers the rest of us want. Where did I come from? Where am I going? How long have I got? All I could do was sit there and watch him die." In a very real sense, aliens save our lives every day. They do the dirty work, and we reap the benefits. Without them, our societies would not function. Yet, we regard them as "people out of place" with little or no value beyond the labor their physical bodies provide.[45] Deckard, too, is an "alien" alienated from himself because his job is to alienate others from their lives. Once he is no longer useful, he becomes "economically unviable" and expendable. Capitalism makes us; capitalism can kill us. All that matters, it would seem, is what we are worth to capitalism and capital.

Bike with an H-bomb

The technoelectronic revolution of the past fifty years has generated intense speculation about its consequences for the human body. Predictably, capitalism has played a central role in such expectations, especially in terms of creating "cyborgs," the material fusing of human and machine. A parallel strand of futurism involves what might be called "cyberborgs," the transfer of mind into machine as reflected in "cyberpunk" literature.[46] The best-known cyberpunk novelist is, arguably, William Gibson, who coined the term *cyberspace* in *Neuromancer* (1984) and set the standard for an emergent genre in popular culture. Neal Stephenson might well be the best cyberpunk writer of the 1990s, at least in terms of the capitalist societies he imagines arising from new technologies and their applications (although, as I shall suggest below, Charles Stross gives him a run for his money).[47] Stephenson's opus *Snow Crash* depicts a near-anarchical society—set, once again, in early-twenty-first-century Los Angeles—in which the United States has nearly ceased to exist. Instead, hypercapitalism has broken American society up into sovereign bits, into "franchulates" such as CosaNostra Pizza and MetaCops Unlimited, and "burbclaves" such as New South Africa and Mr. Lee's Greater Hong Kong ("not affiliated with the People's Republic of China"). Citizenship is subsumed in brand loyalty and membership in franchulates and burbclaves. The citizen-consumer is king.[48]

Everything is for sale and everything—eating, sleeping, washing, and praying, protection, prison, and roads—has a price. This society has replaced the Constitution with a three-ring binder that offers guidance for all contingencies facing a business. The world of *Snow Crash* is also the ultimate information-based economy, one that exploits the profit potential of the brain and the intellectual products of the individual mind. As in every other cyberpunk story, Stephenson's Los Angeles is bifurcated into a "real world" (reality, or "meatspace") and a "cyberworld" (here called "the Metaverse"). "Jacking into the Metaverse" is akin to transferring one's consciousness into an avatar in a giant memory bank where one can play "Second Life" 24/7. In commercial terms, the cyberworld is much like the real one, although not as impoverished. It is also amenable to all kinds of individual feats and activities impossible in meatspace (by contrast with "The Matrix," death in the Metaverse does not mean death in meatspace).

The novel's two main characters are Hiro Protagonist and YT. Hiro is a Japanese/African American pizza deliverator and computer hacker who wields two katana swords like mighty pens and sells his services to anyone who can pay for them (he is also one of the creators of the Metaverse). YT ("Yours Truly") is a Kourier messenger. She speeds around the city on a souped-up skateboard and, like fluid and mobile capital, moves quickly and freely through fragmented society collecting intelligence and delivering documents. Contrary to our expectations, however, YT is a fourteen-year-old blond female whose mother has no idea what she is doing (none of this is revealed until well into the book).

One of the novel's several antagonists is L. Bob Rife, a telecommunications mogul and owner of the Metaverse who aims to gain control of the world's computer hackers in order to establish a monopoly over the global flow and production of information. Rife has management problems, however, inasmuch as he does not control his software programmers. They go home at night with their thoughts, which are his property. As he argues to a television interviewer,

> If you'll just follow my reasoning for a bit, that when I have a programmer working under me who is working with that information, he is wielding enormous power. Information is going into his brain. And it's staying there. It travels with him when he goes home at night. It gets all tangled up into his *dreams*, for Christ's sake. He talks to his wife about it. And, goddam it, he doesn't have any right to that information. If I was running a car factory, I wouldn't let the workers drive the cars home or borrow tools. But that's what I do at five o'clock each day, all over the world, when my hackers go home from work.[49]

Another bad guy is Raven, a Siberian Aleut, ex-Soviet submariner. The world recognizes Raven as a "sovereign power" because he possesses a personal nuclear deterrent, an H-bomb stolen from the sub. Mounted in the sidecar of his motorcycle, the device will detonate should its hyperlink link to Raven's brain ever be broken. The novel's plot is, perhaps, unnecessarily complex—this is one of Stephenson's weaknesses as a writer—but it is exact and incisive in depicting capitalism taken to extremes, the market run wild, a system in which individuals search relentlessly for any advantage they can turn into cash or credit (not all that dissimilar from the American economy just prior to its recent crash).

To gain control of everyone's minds, whether hacker or not, Rife is determined to loose on the world a biological/cyber virus called "Snow Crash" that will infect people's neurolinguistic networks and turn them into mindless, babbling followers of his religious cult. Hiro discovers the purpose of Snow Crash, who is behind it, and the threat it poses to American capitalism; to wit, if people are not "free to choose," as Milton Friedman put it, they will not buy. The economy will collapse, and collectivism will be restored (indeed, Rife's monolingual vision of the world looks suspiciously like an impoverished version of the Soviet Union, which fell apart as Stephenson was writing the novel). Hiro and

YT ally with other "good capitalists" to stop Rife, Raven, and the rest of the "bad collectivists." (This synopsis does little justice to the world Stephenson conjures, but it is sufficient for my purposes to imagine a world in which everything and everyone is commodified).

In the America of *Snow Crash*, information has been both liberated and privatized. The CIA has merged with the Library of Congress to form the Central Intelligence Corporation (CIC). The CIC maintains a database to which everyone has access (for a fee) and into which anyone can upload information (and receive payment, should a customer appear). Although Hiro should be fabulously wealthy, as coinventor of the Metaverse, he has hardly a penny to his name. Most of his meager income comes from stuff he dumps into the CIC database, although, as the novel begins, most of his intelligence is of no interest to anyone. YT, by contrast, is hardly competent to navigate the Metaverse but delivers information in meatspace, where she is an invaluable repository of knowledge. She flows smoothly with the traffic on society's privatized highways and knows the location of every franchulate and burbclave in the Los Angeles basin. This mobility helps little when she is kidnapped by Raven, but it is critical to defeating L. Bob Rife and his grandiose plot to gain control of everyone's mind.

In earlier chapters, I introduced the concept of "body fetishism." In *Snow Crash*, we see the apotheosis of what might be called "intellectual fetishism," which transforms mental work into material goods. Here we go beyond the materiality of bodies as portrayed in "Soylent Green" all the way to Julian Simon's infinitely "renewable resources" in the form of human beings.[50] Ingenuity and innovation, he argued, are unlimited. A better mousetrap can always be built, a more popular book written, a better set of lyrics and beat to set people dancing. But under capitalism, such innovations are of only limited value if they can be copied and manufactured without restrictions. Hence, we have developed a means of commodifying the fruits of the mind by making them scarce—namely, by employing patents, copyrights, and trademarks. We call the result "intellectual property rights" (IPRs).[51]

Though not new, intellectual fetishism as practiced today is certainly more widespread than in the past. As Peter Drahos and John Braithwaite explain, patents, the first IPRs, were invented in sixteenth-century England to grant monopolies to certain manufacturers and suppliers of goods to the throne.[52] During the nineteenth century, the patent system was extended to new inventions in a further development of John Locke's arguments about labor and property and on the theory that inventors and designers ought to be rewarded for their commitments of time and money. Copyright extended this notion to printed matter, again on the principle that writers and musicians deserve to benefit from the "work" put into their creations (it has recently been extended for periods far beyond the death of the creator, some say in order to protect the Disney Corporation's title to Mickey Mouse).[53] In the past, however, IPRs applied only to material objects, such as machines, devices, books, and sheet music. Moreover, they were of limited scope and duration and unenforceable outside the jurisdictions in which they were granted. What we call "intellectual piracy" was widespread, although hardly the stuff of high politics. Today, as a recent case in China indicates, it is taken as a serious crime.[54]

Still, the very notion of stealing ideas is a peculiar one inasmuch as nothing is ever created ex nihilo or without the varied contributions of many individuals and generations.[55] Indeed, it can be (and has been) argued that knowledge constitutes a global commons to which everyone contributes and from which everyone benefits. The creation of IPRs thus represents a form of enclosure—privatizing that which was formerly open to all—imposing access restrictions on that which ought to be widely available for free.[56] Yet, if human ingenuity and innovation are unlimited, how can the products of the mind be privatized and fetishized, especially if inventors and innovators are drawing on a pool of knowledge available to all? As with enclosure of the English commons, the creation and assertion of property rights is something of a trick and a cheat. But the conceptual basis of IPRs goes further, representing a form of "primitive capital accumulation" and a means of appropriating surplus value from mental "labor," something possible only in a social context in which one's body is also property.

An example of this can be seen in the kinds of databases that contribute to the flood of mail-order catalogues, fund-raising appeals, and electronic spam that so plague us today. Underlying their collection and distribution are assumptions about the targeted consumer's preferences (which are confirmed if the targeted recipient actually purchases something). These preferences are inferred from information regarding reading and buying habits, preferences and tastes, and other characteristics that all require some degree of individual mental and material effort. Such information is compiled in databases that, in turn, are sold as commodities to manufacturers, service providers, nonprofit organizations, and spammers. But who really "owns" your preferences? Buyer or seller?

To be sure, when I buy something from you, the knowledge that I have made a purchase is no longer strictly proprietary—or is it? One might imagine individual predilections to be a private matter, of concern to others only on birthdays, holidays, and other such occasions (certainly this is the case with the purchase of certain socially marginalized goods). Nonetheless, an exchange of money for goods manifests a preference that, if recorded, acquires the character of property and, indeed, amounts to a theft of the intellectual labor needed to acquire that preference. Such information, linked to a name, address, and other such bits and bytes, is now owned by whoever has "labored"[57] to enter it into a database. It can then be sold to others who seek unwary buyers for their wares and services. We beleaguered consumers are hardly conscious of this sleight of hand until besieged by unwanted catalogues in the mailbox, phone calls during the dinner hour, and endless e-mail entreaties about sex organs and secret bank accounts.

Snow Crash seems to approve of individual alienation in contrast to L. Bob Rife's desire to bring everyone together again. Does the creation of mass databases containing personal information foster the former or the latter? On the one hand, each of us becomes simply a collection of electronic bits and bytes, not all that dissimilar from Neo in the Matrix or Angela in the Net. If enough of those characteristics could be collected about each of us and given consciousness, how would that differ from life in the Matrix? On the other hand, even as we are compiled in databases, we are each really no more than another largely identical consumer in meatspace, to be sold another gadget or CD of greatest hits. We are the "batteries" that sustain capitalism so long as we continue to generate the necessary wattage. As we have been lulled into comfortable passivity, is it any wonder that pain and violence appear as the only way to escape the iron web?

Manufactory

But why stop with splitting the body? Why not eliminate altogether the distinction between reality and cyberspace? What if machines could place your consciousness into any material body you wished, saving all the old specs in backed up databases just in case you wanted to be the old you again? That is the central plot device in Charles Stross's *Glasshouse*, which imagines life after the "Singularity,"[58] that time coming in the next twenty to fifty years when the global magnitude, power, and speed of global computer processing's RAM and ROM[59] will exceed humanity's, and artificial intelligence will outpace its "wet" human counterpart. What will happen then? Will electronic consciousnesses emerge?[60] Will humans be able to upload their consciousnesses into electronic universes? Will new forms of "body work" become new sources of capital accumulation? Of the last, we can be fairly certain—there is no reason to think that the profit motive will disappear.

Once again, the novel's plot is rather too complicated to summarize here in full. In any event, we are interested in the technological conceit behind the plot. Indeed, the book is, in many ways, a literary chimera combining conventional ideas about cyberspace with rather fanciful applications of nanotechnology (Neal Stephenson has also written about the latter in *The Diamond Age*).⁶¹ In Stross's twenty-seventh-century universe, humans can "back up" their consciousnesses and body architectures and be de- and reconstructed through nanotechnological methods. Their consciousnesses can also be inserted into any organic or machinic—or combined—form they might desire or imagine, be it human or not.

Contrary to expectations, however, this society is not a capitalist one in any sense we might find familiar. After all, what is the point of production and exchange when anything can be made to order through cyber- and nanotechnology, and scarcity cannot exist? Stross seems to regard identity as essentialist at its core: material experiences are a form of learning but do not alter the individual's basic sense of who she/he/it is. The characters in *Glasshouse* are "free to choose"—at least so long as they are not hacked and make sure to back themselves up frequently (a lesson we have all learned through bitter experience with Windows). The idea of the "self-made" wo/man is an old trope—indeed it hearkens back to John Locke—relying upon the transforming and "improving" powers of capitalism and accumulation to remake the body and the self, in one's eyes and the eyes of others. But it helps to be rich. No one speaks, after all, of the "self-made" bum, service worker, or academic.

Still, the notion that one can make of oneself anything one chooses is powerful, and its implications have not been lost on capitalists. Growing numbers of social programs, educational projects, and self-improvement seminars all propagate the idea that individuals possess "assets" that they can use to increase their "human capital." Such assets include "a range of skills, knowledges, experiences, habits and values . . . often understood as personal resources."⁶² The personalization of capitalism in the body was noted by Michel Foucault and commented on by Colin Gordon, who wrote,

> The idea of one's life as the enterprise of oneself implies that there is a sense in which one remains always continuously employed in (at least) that one enterprise, and that it is a part of the continuous business of living to make adequate provision for the preservation, reproduction and reconstruction of one's own human capital. This is the "care of the self" which government commends as the corrective to collective greed.⁶³

Or, as Foucault put it, "the stake in all neoliberal analyses is the replacement every time of *homo economicus* as partner of exchange with a *homo economicus* as entrepreneur of himself, being for himself his own capital, being for himself his own producer, being for himself the source of [his] earnings."⁶⁴ So, even bums, service workers, and academics can "make" themselves and profit from their labors.

Are There Any Conclusions Here?

At the end of the day, films and novels focused on technology and alienation feed into a pervasive sense of unease and paranoia—most acutely expressed in "The X-Files"—that things are neither as they seem nor as they should be. There is a disturbance in the Force, but the Force itself is the source of the disturbance. Exposure to the dark side of capitalism and reassurance that it can be put to rights can be a powerful draw, but these works are fantasies, and no one really expects salvation (there are Christian films and novels for that purpose, such as *The Chronicles of Narnia* and the *Left Behind* series by Tim LaHaye and Jerry Jenkins). Cultural critics and the guardians of hegemony are likely to attack "straight" films positing in an outright and linear narrative fashion that things are out of whack or subject to conspiratorial control as inaccurate and ideological. "Pay no attention to the man behind the curtain," we are warned in *The Wizard of Oz*. A peek now and then, however, does not hurt.

6

States and Regulations

A LMOST EVERYONE HAS READ *Lord of the Flies*.[1] William Golding's 1954 fable of English public-school boys stranded on an island is familiar to most American and British high school students, although few seem enamored by either the book or its "lessons." The standard classroom interpretation has something to do with an absence of authority, the evil in men's souls, and the descent into bloodshed and war that is inevitable in the state of nature. Almost everyone deplores the brutality, violence, and murders that take place in the novel. And perhaps some recognize the irony in the boys' "rescue" by British sailors, as the island is about to be immolated by fire not long after the rest of the world has been subject to atomic bombs. For the most part, this would seem to be where the storytelling and lessons end.

Except that they do not. *Lord of the Flies* is also about economic and political liberalism and how bodies are subject to regulation and discipline within that particular system. That Golding applied Thomas Hobbes's notion of the state of nature to his South Pacific gedankenexperiment hardly comes as a surprise; that there is more to *Lord of the Flies* than *Leviathan* might. Intentionally or not, Golding interrogated the very foundations of English society and, especially, its class-based political economy, which relied on "epistemic" violence to impose order.[2] Few would call Golding a theorist, yet his novel contains a great deal of social as well as political theory. Even fewer would call Thomas Hobbes an economist, yet *Leviathan* contains a great deal of political economy. In both cases, moreover, we can glean considerable insight not only into the fallacies of conventional international relations and geopolitical theories but also into many of the basic elements of neoclassical economics and critical political economy.

By the same token, few would seek to make a connection between *Lord of the Flies* and Kenneth N. Waltz's *Man, the State, and War.*[3] Published by Columbia University Press in 1959 and based on Waltz's 1954 PhD dissertation,[4] the latter is rarely examined as either a work of economics or political economy, much less myth or fiction. Indeed, Waltz aimed primarily in this book to explain why wars happen. In doing so, however, he fell prey to some of the foundational fallacies that economists in particular hold about capitalist society and its organization and functioning, specifically their canonical and ahistorical claims about *homo economicus*, rationality, and endogenously given preferences.[5] This foreshadowing of what later emerged full-blown as "neorealism" in his *Theory of International Politics* (1979) dealt with the formation, or lack thereof, of an "international society" that could limit or even eliminate war. Although Waltz tended to abjure Hobbes's state of nature, he was nonetheless impressed by the extreme individualism of the state under conditions of international "anarchy."[6] That a number of his arguments can be found in *Lord of the Flies* is, perhaps, less a reflection of Golding's notions concerning the causes of war than Waltz's unreflective application of what we now call "social theory."

In this chapter, I take a somewhat different analytical approach to capitalism, political economy, and popular culture than in earlier ones by establishing a conversation among *Lord of the Flies, Leviathan,* and *Man, the State, and War.* I do this as a means of interrogating neoclassical economics and critical political economy as well as making a first investigation of the foundations and sources of social violence within societies and among them (a topic to which I return in chapter 8). I compare Golding's and Hobbes's stories of "origins" to illustrate how fairly straightforward notions of supply and demand, production and reproduction, and the social division of labor belie the possibility of the presocial state posited by both. Indeed, that both Hobbes and Golding were commenting on English society and its history rather than a mythical anarchy only reinforces this often-ignored point. Waltz, of course, wrote about the conditions outside of societies rather than within them, but we may take the sources of violence that concern him to lie not in the anarchy he posits but in the lessons learned by both statesmen and schoolboys as they are socialized into "proper" behavior toward their fellows and inferiors. To paraphrase a more recent believer in extreme individualism, "TINA!" ("There is no anarchy!").

Why regulation rather than law? Regulation—understood here not only as lawlike commands but also as internalized rules of discipline and civility—is central to this chapter because, absent a well-regulated capitalist society whose members are attentive to their own behavior and appetites, the market is very likely to degenerate into something resembling anarchy.[7] Although it is common to regard the idealized "free market" as requiring only minimal regulation—if it is regulated at all—really existing markets are far from this ideal. Each in his own way, Ludwig von Mises, Friedrich Hayek, and Milton Friedman all deplored states that sought to control economic transactions, the cost of goods, and their form and quality, among other things, for political ends.[8] But even the simplest of markets requires some rules: when and where it is to be held, what can be sold, who can sell, who can buy. Regarding even primitive exchange as a form of "contract" implies rules and regulation. And the most basic rule of the market is, Thou shalt not steal from or kill those with whom thou art dealing.

In this chapter, I segue between the three works rather than moving methodically through each. I begin with a brief synopsis of *Lord of the Flies*, arguing that it can be read as a work of political economy whose logic of violence is rooted in an English social division of labor rather than the absence of authority or regulation. Next, I address the proposition that we can read *Leviathan* as a work of political economy rather than merely political theory, in this case of a seventeenth-century England in social turmoil. In the third part of the chapter, I show how the onset of violence on the boys' island follows from their socialization into the regulatory framework of English class society, based as it is on forms of epistemic violence. I then discuss how Waltz, having drawn on recent political history to make his arguments, nevertheless regards history as irrelevant to understanding the social causes of war. Consequently, not only is his an ahistorical analysis, but it also misses completely the role of socially learned and remembered histories in triggering violence and war, whether inside or outside.[9] Finally, I conclude by arguing that not only is anarchy a myth, as Cynthia Weber has made clear, but it also serves to obscure and mystify the role of social relations and forces as well as their histories in accounting for violence and war, whether on a Pacific island or this island called Earth.

Flies in the Ointment

Lord of the Flies recapitulates the World War II experiences of British children evacuated from London, this time by plane in the face of imminent atomic war.[10] Rather than landing in the countryside, however, this planeload of public school[11] boys crashes on a deserted South Pacific island, with all adults lost.[12] Some boys survive—others go down with the plane and grownups—and our first glimpse of them is an encounter between two at the edge of the jungle. Ralph emerges onto the beach, strips off his clothes, and plunges naked into the water. The other—whom we soon find out wishes not to be called "Piggy"—carefully takes off his shoes and wades into the water, informing Ralph that he cannot swim and that his auntie worries about his "asthmar." This appears truly as Hobbes's imagined state of nature. The boys "spring up like mushrooms"[13] from the forest, shed the trappings of civilization, and are reborn from the ocean into a new world waiting to be made by them.[14] Or is that what this is? Hobbes acknowledged his state of nature to be a fiction but one necessary to account for society's origins and order. Nonetheless, from the opening scene in *Lord of the Flies*, we can deduce that Golding had certainly absorbed the gross features of Hobbes's reasoning even if we cannot tell what more he might have gained from reading *Leviathan.*

Walking along the beach after bathing, Ralph and Piggy find a conch shell. Piggy instructs Ralph on how to coax a sound from the shell—a skill that presocial beings would almost certainly not have known—and his summons brings other boys scrambling out of the jungle and onto the beach. Piggy's knowledge and counsel enable the birthing of this new society of boys (men). Not only does he know how to blow on the shell, but he also recognizes it as a *skeptron*,[15] the symbol of political authority whose momentary possession conveys the right to speak in the public sphere. As finder of the conch, Ralph is to be the boys' leader. Piggy, in turn, is to keep track of boys and rules, who is present, and whose turn it is to speak. At this very moment, however, a worm—or is it a snake?—crawls out of the apple:

> Within the diamond haze of the beach something dark was fumbling along. Ralph saw it first, and watched till the intentness of his gaze drew all eyes that way. Then the creature stepped from mirage onto clear sand, and they saw that the darkness was not all shadow but mostly clothing. The creature was a party of boys, marching approximately in two parallel lines and dressed in strangely eccentric clothing.[16]

By contrast with the boys in Ralph's group, the new arrivals do not emerge from the jungle as lone individuals. They already are a society. The moment they arrive, and perhaps foreshadowing the story's Armageddon-like ending, their "leader" asks, "Where's the man with the trumpet?" Finding no such man, Jack Merridew argues that he should be leader because "I'm chapter chorister and head boy. I can sing C sharp."[17] Social knowledge again. Piggy points out that Ralph is already their leader, but Jack invokes "democracy," seeing here the opportunity to become the sovereign by popular plebiscite (who in a state of nature knows of "democracy"?) and to make "rules" that bind everyone to his diktats. Enamored with this, the boys revel in the idea of "making rules" and punishing violators. In the event, Ralph wins the vote and benevolently rewards Jack with leadership of the "hunters" (his chorus of boys). Thus does the state come into being, albeit hardly in an ahistorical or presocial manner.

Exiles in Paradise?

Later in this chapter, I will return to our story of the castaways and argue that Golding has, unwittingly or not, illustrated the precise problematic that Hobbes sought to address in *Leviathan*: How can individuals be brought to acknowledge and obey a rule-making authority so that they can go about the business of producing, consuming, and being rescued? Golding tries to have his boys begin the world anew, but they fail because, as we shall see, they cannot shed their history or social baggage. Thomas Hobbes, by contrast, looked at the world—or, rather, mid-seventeenth-century England—and sought ways to reestablish social authority after it had been called into question by the religious and political controversies that began in the sixteenth century and culminated in the Civil Wars of the 1640s and the regicide of Charles I in 1649. When he wrote this best known of his works, Hobbes was an exile in Paris, having fled England in fear for his safety as king and Parliament came to blows. In *Leviathan* he sought to make a systematic and scientific argument about the restoration of order and authority in a way that provided for individual liberty and property without permitting excessive license or the defiance or destruction of hierarchy. This was not a new problem for England, even in his time.

Beginning in the early 1500s, with Henry VIII's break from the Roman Catholic Church, England's political hierarchy had come under growing challenge from a variety of emerging social and material contradictions. In creating the Church of England, Henry had no intention of destroying the sovereign's divine rights or, for that matter, significantly altering the new Anglican dispensation's similarities to the old Catholic one. Nevertheless, the rise of Protestantism, capitalism, and science across Europe all brought into question the God-given traditions and practices that the Anglican Church retained from the old one. These included rights to rule, to own property and men, and to participate in political society, all of which remained tightly linked to the new church's doctrine and dogma. In particular, although old social relations were breaking down even before 1500 and new ones had yet to come into being, changes in people's possessions, land titles, and subjectivities challenged the status and standing of nobility, religious authorities, and others in governing roles.

The collapse of social order in seventeenth-century England resulted, in part, from an emerging capitalist political economy. For as long as anyone could remember, English society had been based on a feudal order rooted in land, and land could be redistributed only by will of the sovereign.[18] A market in land was developing even before the advent of English Protestantism, but the beliefs, rules, and practices that legitimated the social order, deeply encoded in the organization and practices of both state and church, were slow to adjust. The result was a growing "contradiction" between the material base of society and its ideological superstructure. Men lacking the "right" to buy large tracts of land were, nonetheless, doing so, while nobles were becoming insolvent and selling parts or all of their estates. Accepted rules determined who stood where in the social and political hierarchy but there were no rules to deal with unauthorized changes in that order or to determine who stood where as a result of those changes.

Struggles to impose a new set of regulations on the preexisting social order culminated in the two English civil wars between 1642 and 1651. Throughout the turmoil before, during, and after the wars, various groups, sects, and movements, including lower-class ones such as the Diggers and Levellers, tried to assert their "natural rights" in contravention of custom.[19] The Royalists resisted the tides of history and capitalism that, for a time, favored Parliament and its supporters. Hobbes, by contrast, was a practical man. He did not see the need to legitimate the sovereign through authorization by God. It was enough, in his view, that propertied men in society agreed on a leader, whom he called "the mortal god."[20] This was the beginning of liberal political theory and practice in which, today, we are all immersed. At that time, such arguments were regarded as atheistic and heretical, and Hobbes later came under parliamentary threat of trial for heresy. The "invitation" issued by England's upper classes to William of Orange to depose James II as King of England in 1688, an event celebrated ever after as the "Glorious Revolution," demonstrated that Hobbes was not far from being right.

Although *Leviathan* is usually regarded as a landmark in political philosophy and Hobbes as the founder of liberal theory, it is equally apposite to read him as a political economist, for the problem he sought to answer—matching the supply of regulation to the demand for reliable order—is a quintessential one in capitalist societies. Traditionally and historically, human societies regulated themselves through religion, which encoded hierarchy, rules, and relations in rituals and laws. Originating from a divine source, these could not be challenged or changed (at least in theory) and were internalized and naturalized through repeated belief and practice. Of course, such regulations could be challenged and changed, which happened not infrequently as a result of crisis brought about by changing social and material conditions and practices. Then, new religious rituals and practices, or even new religions, would emerge to fill the "authority gap." The later invocation of "natural law" represented exactly such a process, albeit one in which God was no longer available. Still, even "natural" laws must be produced before they can be consumed and naturalized. Property owners and power holders are particularly concerned about naturalizing rule, right, and possession, and so they seek a source and supply of order to meet that need.

The English Civil War was therefore about not only who would rule but also what the rules would be and who could supply them.[21] Without authorized regulation—without a legitimate source of rules—everything seemed fair game, and many different rules were possible.[22] As a result, no one was safe, and no one knew his or her place. To Hobbes, this appeared akin to an imagined state of nature, for in the midst of fraternal conflict, there was little time to engage in useful and productive activities, especially if one could never be sure of keeping what one produced or acquired. Moreover, the problem was not only that one might be killed by one's enemies but also that one might be legally dispossessed by one's friends, thrown into the Tower of London, and executed. Henry VIII had done this to the Catholic Church's properties and his various opponents in the sixteenth century. That practice continued well into the seventeenth century. So why even try to maintain practices and appearances?

Hobbes saw, too, that men would no longer accept the authority of the old system, and so he set out to propose a new source of authority in order to meet what he saw as the demand for it.[23] Thus, *Leviathan.* But in offering this solution, Hobbes also found it expedient to assume away many features of recent English society and history that might complicate his story. Under the circumstances, all the trappings of life and society were so much decoration, and so he could argue that reasonable men could use their powers of reason, whatever their particular social and political position and material interests, to restore legitimate authority and order.[24]

Meanwhile, Back on the Island

Let us now return to our group of English schoolboys, who, stranded in the middle of nowhere but having accepted the symbol of authority and the new sovereign, are busy constructing their new society. Sadly, perhaps, Ralph is not Hobbes's Leviathan—he is too good, too golden, and too dependent on Piggy. Jack Merridew, by contrast, knows how to command respect and authority. Jack would be an excellent sovereign. His group of hunters quickly becomes the society's "military force," and following internal discord among the boys, they secede from Ralph's state. Jack becomes the leader of his own "independent" and autocratic state, which, as we shall see, goes to war with

Ralph's democracy.[25] But we are getting ahead of ourselves here and into Waltz. Before going there we need to consider the conditions of economic possibility in the boys' new society.

No society can survive without organizing production, and it cannot produce without a division of labor.[26] But it is not immediately obvious that such organization is necessary on the boys' island. As in John Locke's imaginary state of nature,[27] copious amounts of fruit are available, and for the first day or two after the crash, the boys avail themselves of this bounty (although some suffer for their greediness). Indeed, they could probably survive indefinitely by foraging, with no need to create a social order. So why construct one at all? This is where history begins to matter. Ralph is emblematic of English class society, and Jack, of the British warrior class. Neither can imagine life without social hierarchy, although they have little idea how to construct one. Somewhat ironically, this task is left to Piggy, working-class bursary boy at some nameless and, no doubt, little-respected public school, to devise how society is to be created and what form it will take. Yet, how does Piggy know what must be done? Here, history, socialization, and memory play their roles.

Even in the late 1940s and early 1950s, after a long leveling war and Labour Party rule from 1945 to 1951, British society remained pretty class bound.[28] The public schools, in particular, made a continuing effort to sustain British patriotism and class order. Prior to World War I, and to a significant degree between the wars, many upper-class boys were prepared only for military service—at least until they could be eased into a proper adult role in society. The public schools were thus the training ground not only for "civil manners" but also for loyalty to "king and country" and the officer corps. Unbridled enthusiasm for war led to the slaughter of many of England's upper-class young men in the European trenches between 1914 and 1918, one of the first examples of class suicide. The political compromises necessary to get the working class to fight in World War II and to support the social order without seeking to overturn it seemed destined to put an end to class society—at least until Margaret Thatcher became prime minister and class nostalgia returned, albeit largely among the *nouveau riche*.

But even nationalization, socialization, and taxation under Labour did not eliminate class hierarchy, which had acquired all the trappings of a "natural" order. While dying in 1954, it was not yet dead. The public schools continued to play a role here because the educational system was bifurcated into vocational and academic tracks that largely corresponded to class distinctions. The residue of this dual system continued until as recently as 1988 in the differentiation between "O levels" (ordinary, leading to nonintellectual employment) and "A levels" (advanced, in the twelfth and thirteenth grades, usually leading to college). Unless they were exceptionally bright, working-class students were generally tracked into the former; middle- and upper-class students, into the latter.[29] The public school system feeding the universities, including Oxbridge, offered scholarships to promising working-class students (usually men) but never at the cost of eliminating or ignoring class distinctions.

We might guess that Piggy believes deeply in the new, democratic dispensation and takes politics and the social order with the utmost seriousness. He has been taught of their importance to England, even as his exceptional place in English society has probably been deeply impressed upon him.[30] The working class works, the ruling class rules, but in postwar Britain everyone gets to vote! Moreover, the working class makes things and runs them. By contrast, the ruling class lives on profits and investments and sometimes goes to war, but it has no idea how to make society operate properly. Piggy recognizes that organization is key, but lacking authority, he must rely on Ralph and the conch shell to get the other boys to go along.[31] If they organize, they can produce, and if they can produce, they can also "reproduce" and survive until rescued. Piggy's solution is a form of English postwar "democratic socialism," but even that has its limits.[32]

If Ralph is a bright, gentle, and somewhat brainless member of the ruling class, Jack Merridew is more a bourgeois toff whose only real comparative advantage is class brutality.[33] That he orders his choristers to march along the hot beach dressed in their heavy uniforms and proudly announces his leadership credentials to the rest of the boys only serves to underline his aspirations to privilege and class mimicry. Indeed, it is men like Jack who have repeatedly egged England into war in order to demonstrate their masculinity, and it is probably men like Jack who have now exposed England to atomic annihilation—a truth later suggested when he sets fire to the island in order to capture and kill Ralph.

For now, however, it is Jack who notes that there are pigs on the island and that he and his band of hunters can provide meat, a welcome addition to the monotony of fruit three or more times a day. Ralph can rule, Piggy can make up rules, and Jack will behave as though they do not apply to him. A bargain of sorts is struck (and it is a gendered one, at that; see below). This new society consequently requires three things to survive and even thrive: resources, a household, and rescue. For the first, the little 'uns gather fruit and bring it to the group, while Jack's hunters trap pigs and provide meat. For the second, Ralph oversees construction of shelters with the help of other, older boys, while Piggy teaches the little 'uns about the England some of them are already beginning to forget. For the third, Piggy also supplies the technology—his glasses—to light a signal fire, while the hunters make sure it burns night and day (a task at which they ultimately fail).

From the perspective of the neoclassical economist, there is nothing mysterious about this division. Every man comes to the table with particular skills. Some hunt, some tend to industry, and some care for children.[34] It makes no sense for each boy to do everything. Not only is that an inefficient deployment of skills, but it also results in a suboptimal supply of goods and services.[35] By applying comparative advantage and a division of labor, however, goods and services can be provided at an adequate level, thereby allowing the members of society to engage in activities such as eating, sleeping, writing, reading, praying, and arithmetic, all required for the social reproduction of (class) society. Moreover, those who cannot produce "real goods"—teachers, mothers, and leaders—can nonetheless teach, cook, and lead for the benefit of those who "bring home the bacon."

This bargain breaks down rather quickly, but that is another story. More important here are two points. First, the boys' new society is closely patterned on English class society with all of its brutality, fixed roles, and misogyny. Second, this new society is deeply gendered, and while Golding leaves sexual relations out of the book—something never the case in English public schools[36]—it seems fair to say that Jack thoroughly fucks over the rest of the boys and not by accident—such homoeroticism is a concomitant of masculine domination. Ralph, as noted above, is as a boy of considerable beauty, whereas Jack is presented as dark and brooding.[37] We can imagine Ralph poised on a mountaintop, gazing into the distance, pointing into the future, a fair-haired boy who evokes homoerotic desires in others. (Would it be too much to suggest that the sadomasochism exhibited by Jack's hunters, especially Maurice, represents a none-too-repressed erotic desire for Ralph and those he represents?) Piggy, by contrast, is thoroughly feminized. He cannot see without his "specs." His health is poor. He is fat and nonathletic. He lacks both father and mother. His intellectualism is regarded with disdain as the mark of a weakling. Moreover, he is charged with oversight of the little 'uns, the small children. As the island's only "woman," Piggy seems an inevitable target of gendered violence, especially after the "masculine" hunters engage in terrorism and declare war against the nonmasculine "household" headed by Ralph.

All of this suggests that the absence of authority is not at the heart of organized murder and destruction in *Lord of the Flies*; rather, the cause of the catastrophe is the reproduction of the British social order—what others might call "culture"—as well as its epistemic violence against both the lower classes and women. As Stephen Greenblatt argues,

> The ensemble of beliefs and practices that form a given culture function as a pervasive technology of control, a set of limits within which social behavior must be contained, a repertoire of models to which individuals must conform.

... The most effective disciplinary techniques practiced against those who stray beyond the limits of a given culture are probably not the spectacular punishments reserved for serious offenders ... but seemingly innocuous responses: a condescending smile, laughter poised between the genial and the sarcastic, a small dose of indulgent pity laced with contempt, cool silence.[38]

Golding's boys stand in contrast to men in the state of nature who are imagined to have no sense of history. From a very young age, these boys have been thoroughly socialized into English class society, which they regard as a "natural" formation, and they have brought this history to the island with them along with the "cultural" practices internalized virtually since birth. In the boys' natal society, the division of labor runs in two directions, between men and women, on the one hand, and the upper and lower classes, on the other. In the latter case, the upper class loses no opportunity to brutalize its inferiors; in the former case, the men always have it over the women. On their seemingly Edenic island, the boys create hell, not because there is no one to keep them from doing so but because this is what their elders in England have taught them is right and proper.

The novel's disastrous ending suggests two other points. First, the seemingly modest terms of neoclassical economics—markets, supply, demand, division of labor, and so forth—mask deeply rooted, structural forms of epistemic violence into which each new generation of children is socialized. We are not born good or evil, even though our individual neuropsychology may, under certain circumstances, push us in the direction of "uncivil behavior." More critically, we learn whom to love, whom to hate, and how to act on those emotions not from instinct but from our parents and peers, our preachers and teachers, our media and rituals and language. Most of the time, rules, laws, and the conventions of civil behavior constrain and repress the resulting propensities to acts of violence, even as social violence is structured into everyday, naturalized social relations. The apparently neutral language of "division of labor" masks power relations that can easily become violent, as is readily apparent in rage and violence directed toward low-paid immigrants. This is also one reason why those who rule cultivate hate toward the Other, whether against the enemy outside or the inferior within.[39]

Second, as a result, this division of labor also cultivates precisely that fear that makes liberal society possible. In this respect, anarchy is an always-present tendency in liberalism (of which realism is merely a variant).[40] More to the point, a division of labor fragments social solidarity and fosters individualism and alienation. Although a certain stretching of organic relations of production and reproduction is necessary for liberalism and capitalism to work, the resulting "possessive individualism"[41] tends toward the anarchic condition of underregulated markets in which selfishness and self-interest result in widespread atomization.[42] Fear—of the Other, of different classes, of immigrants—then becomes the glue that holds together liberal society. In this respect, consequently, and as Cynthia Weber notes so astutely, it is fear *in* liberalism that makes possible the supposedly anarchic international states system.[43]

Boys, the Economy, and War

We can be fairly sure that William Golding never read *Man, the State, and War*, although Kenneth Waltz almost certainly read *Lord of the Flies. Man, the State, and War* remains Waltz's opus, and in the fifty years since publication, it has been assigned to hundreds of thousands of college and graduate students. Many of them might not have always understood its arguments or liked the book, but they probably have not forgotten it. Whether such a readership qualifies Waltz's book as a work of "popular culture" is debatable. That its themes are a fiction and are frequently reflected in popular culture is undeniable—"Lost" and "Survivor" are only two of the most recent variants on the state-of-nature theme.[44]

Waltz wrote his dissertation in the early 1950s and revised it later in the decade. He was, like Golding, deeply concerned about the possibility of atomic war with the Soviet Union. The outbreak of the Korean War in 1950 seemed to point toward the imminence of World War III, while the advent of the hydrogen bomb convinced many that such a war would annihilate humanity.[45] Those in positions of power and authority ridiculed such fears and tried to assure an anxious public that thermonuclear war would not mean the end of humanity, but no one was entirely certain what might follow should such a war occur.[46] From his book we can infer Waltz's belief that if he could clarify the sources of war, he might also be able to recommend how to prevent it.[47] In the event, he arrived at a rather gloomy conclusion: wars among states happen because there is nothing to prevent them. He ascribed this to the abiding condition of international anarchy—a.k.a., the state of nature—in which only the state can protect itself from other states ("self-help") and which it must do at all costs if it is to survive. War is one possible result of such efforts, and history suggests that it is a common one.

In *Man, the State, and War*, Waltz is witheringly dismissive of philosophers, policy makers, psychologists, and professors who argue that the causes of war might be found in human nature—the evil in men's minds leads them to aggression against others—or in the structure and practices of the state—dictatorships are evil and rely on war to generate domestic support and obedience. Without a world authority—a parent or superego writ large—nothing prevents individual states from acting out their natural tendencies and inclinations, like unsupervised children in a playground or on an island. War is, thus, inevitable in the absence of properly enforced rules and regulations. These regulators are not international laws, however, but, rather, the threat of destruction and death, and their application when deemed necessary, as conveyed in the original film version of "The Day the Earth Stood Still" (1951), as Klaatu and Gort are about to leave Earth after having been treated rather poorly by their hosts.

Addressing a gathering of scientists, Klaatu tells them, "We of the other planets" have organized a deterrent force, a "race of robots," who "at the first sign of violence . . . act automatically against the aggressor. And the penalty for provoking their action is too terrible to risk. . . . If you threaten to extend your violence [into space], this Earth of yours will be reduced to a burned-out cinder."[48] The causes of specific wars, argues Waltz, might be found in the irrational beliefs and practices of certain individuals as well as the tendencies of some forms of government to fall back on organized violence, but those explanations are best left to historians with the time to pursue what is now, in any case, history.

And history is bunk, as Henry Ford once said.[49] Although *Man, the State, and War* is rich with historical events, figures, and narratives, Waltz, too, seems to regard history as mostly bunk. His states exist in an eternal condition of unchanging diffidence and fear, unable (and not merely unwilling) to create an international society and always opposed to efforts in this direction. To agree to a Klaatu-like solution to the problem of war—whether that solution consists of planetary troopers or interplanetary robots—would turn states into something else (something unmasculine, like Piggy?), and because states value their sovereignty (autonomy) above all else, they could never agree to such a self-transformation. This particular perspective sits uncomfortably next to Hobbes's. He saw no problem in individuals giving up or limiting their autonomy (sovereignty) in return for the elimination of war and the opportunity to "pursue more profitable enterprises." For Waltz, at any rate, such a transformation in states was not only impossible but unnatural.

In the decades since its publication, *Man, the State, and War* has been the object of countless analyses and critiques and the subject of an equal number of scholarly papers and books supporting its structural arguments.[50] My goal here is not, however, to criticize Waltz's argument but, rather, to locate it in *Lord of the Flies* and connect the two books to both neoclassical economics and critical political economy. I do this in two steps. First, I show how certain of Waltz's assumptions appear in *Lord of the Flies* as common principles of neoclassical economics. Then, I show how Waltz's political economy is deeply flawed because he was so dismissive of the importance of history in shaping people and their present.

In the free market, the "rational man" [*sic*] is king.[51] Everyone encounters the market with certain desires and a specific quantity of resources (capital) that can be used to fulfill those desires. Recall that in the discourse of neo-classical economics, an individual's desires are called "preferences." I would prefer to acquire more butter than guns; you would prefer more guns than butter. I can go to a butter fair, while you can go to a gun fair. Once we see the cost of that which we would prefer to have, we can calculate how much fulfilling our preferences requires and decide whether we can afford to buy guns or butter and how much of either or both we can purchase. This act of "rationality" is normally expressed in purely monetary terms—it makes no sense for me to offer undying loyalty or a term of servitude to a seller of either guns or butter, for what is a person to do with such a commitment?[52] And using a gun to steal butter is not a rational act either, at least not in terms of the market. It is simply theft, which hearkens back to something like the state of nature.

Although economists and public policy analysts continually seek to bring more and more aspects of human behavior into the ambit of market relations,[53] it is fairly easy to see that not everything we do falls under the rule or rules of contract.[54] More importantly, perhaps, economic models of rational behavior are difficult to apply to groups.[55] Even when we join a group—be it a church, a political party, a social movement, or a mob—its members' individual desires and goals may be quite different. To be sure, everyone probably shares at least one desire or goal—to pray, vote, buy, demonstrate, riot—but that does not mean that everyone will act in precisely the same way, even under identical circumstances or initial conditions. We cannot speak of the desires or preferences of a group as though it were an individual, and so it is necessary to make a gross simplification. If we want to apply rationality to the group, we must pretend it is a single (or corporate) individual.[56]

This is precisely what Waltz does in *Man, the State, and War*, foreshadowing his later development of structural realism in which the assumption of rationality becomes hardened to the point of crystallization.[57] The state makes choices and acts as though it were a rational individual. Its desires, usually called the "national interest,"[58] apply to the entire body politic, and failure to pursue those interests in a rational fashion is both illogical and dangerous. Because the state exists in a presocial condition, however, it must behave like an individual in the imaginary state of nature. Economists assume that rules and rule protect the individual against depredatory violence by others. Waltz, by contrast, assumes no such thing for states. In his view, they "wake up" every morning to face the exact same world as the day before, one in which nothing can be assumed or learned, and experience is worth nothing.[59] In Waltz's economy of violence, therefore, the state must stockpile sufficient resources so that, should an opportunity for "exchange" present itself—of missiles rather than money—it can outbid the Other and, it is hoped, acquire prestige rather than suffer humiliation (or devastation). The shorthand for this type of exchange is "power," which can be accumulated and used in bargaining with others or coercing them if necessary.

We can see, just barely, such reasoning in *Lord of the Flies.* Once appointed to lead the hunters, Jack has acquired a resource—force—that will give him leverage in his dealings with Ralph. Technically speaking, the force under Jack's control is really the state's, not his. Moreover, the actual application of force is meant to be strictly limited to producing meat, which, in the internal division of labor, can be exchanged for fruit, shelter, fire, socialization, and "manly" respect. Jack is not, however, happy with this arrangement. He desires the glory that, as Ralph's subordinate, is denied to him. Furthermore, bound to both household and state by the division of labor, he and his hunters cannot pursue their preferences in full, even though they possess the resources to fulfill them.

Jack's solution is secession—a state of his own. He takes his hunters, wages a "war of liberation," and declares a second, independent polity on the island. He then rules according to his fantasies and writ over subjects bound to do his bidding. Now, however, the pattern of rational exchange and comparative advantage within society has been broken. Jack's state can trade in meat, but Ralph's has little or nothing to offer in return—except fire, as made possible by Piggy's glasses. Jack's state also has a supply of violence that Ralph's now lacks. Like the mafioso he is, Jack offers Ralph's boys "protection" if they agree to join him and swear fealty. Not everyone is willing to accept this bargain, particularly Ralph and Piggy, who hew to the old forms and norms of production and reproduction. Unable to purchase with threats what he desires, Jack falls back on state terrorism, stealing fire and leaving Ralph's society bereft of its last bargaining chip. At this point, only the idea of Ralph's state remains, and even that threatens Jack, who seeks to eliminate all alternatives by declaring (nuclear) war on Ralph and Piggy.

According to Waltz, in a "world" of two states without a sovereign (adult), nothing will prevent war between them except a "balance of power." When power and prestige are at stake, it is humiliating to truck and barter for one's safety from attack. The economy of violence requires that exchange take not the form of goods and money but, rather, threat, injury, and surrender. To be sure, the victor may realize material gains—land, weapons, people—but these are secondary to status.[60] Jack has little or nothing to gain from destroying Ralph's state other than domination and glory, but that is enough for him. This is a theme oft-repeated in both popular culture and a pattern repeated in international politics: glory is its own reward. History is thought not to matter much. But, in fact, it does.

History Matters

Following the Franco-Prussian War in 1870 and 1871, Germany annexed the French province of Alsace-Lorraine. After World War I, France reclaimed the province. During World War II, Germany reoccupied it, and following that conflict, the territory was returned to France. It is not as if anyone consulted the region's inhabitants about their homeland preferences—they were, in any case, somewhere between being French and German, speaking a local dialect that was neither. Nor can it be said that either France or Germany was substantially better or worse off for the possession or dispossession of Alsace-Lorraine. Why, then, were France and Germany so intent on controlling it?[61] That the two states might have fought so many wars, in part over two provinces of relatively little material significance in the great scheme of things—apologies to any Alsatians or Lotharingians who might be reading this—can hardly be attributed to anarchy, proximity, or threat alone. There was nothing to prevent France and Germany from going to war, but the memory of lands gained and lost, the thrill of victory and the agony of defeat, the desire to "bring home" all those who were members of the ancient parentland were, no doubt, powerful motivators for those wars to which the two countries went.

More to the point, possession was important in terms of whose rules would govern the contested territory and what that might mean for social production and reproduction. When Germany ruled, the people were taught one set of historical "truths" about themselves and others; when France ruled, they were taught another. Although the specific divisions of labor operative in Alsace-Lorraine might not have changed greatly under successive rulers, the regulation and socialization of people almost certainly did. Inasmuch as these histories became the basis for the legitimacy of occupation—pardon me, restoration of ancient territories to the mother-/fatherland—the repeated rewriting of rules and rule, especially in terms of inhabitants' behaviors toward their rulers, made a difference.

In other words, history matters, and history's matters do not simply vanish from one day to the next. History matters not only because of individual and collective memory or the desire for revenge and remuneration but also because it is in the course of everyday history's matters that societies produce and reproduce themselves and within which people's socialization into collective beliefs, memories, and practices takes place. Such socialization is a form of "regulation" or, in a Foucauldian sense, governmentality and self-discipline.[62] In Waltz's world, such things do not count, if they even exist. A state has immediate interests, and if other states threaten these, what happened yesterday, or last week, or even last century says nothing about what could happen tomorrow. The Romans warned, *Si vis pacem, para bellum* ("If you would have peace, prepare for war"). For the moderns, according to this way of thinking, there is no true peace, ever, and one would be a greater fool to imagine it feasible or even possible.

At first reading, *Lord of the Flies* seems to subscribe to this modernist tenet. The Beast, dreamt of by a little 'un, imagined and seen by the older boys, and made material by Jack and his minions, does not merely represent the darkest corners of the id, as a psychological reading might suggest. The Beast is also the *superego*, the authority that appears, at first look, to be absent from the island. Indeed, all of England struggles against The Beast not only during war but all the time. Ironically, and paradoxically, The Beast is both order and disorder, and it is a product of history. It threatens to emerge as violence within society; it brutalizes society in order to stanch such violence. Fear becomes the means of control, the way to prevent too much anarchy. Would such control be necessary were there nothing to fear? This is an old story, one with which we are only too familiar today.

Back in England, this fear of The Beast is foundational to the violence of class society and, perhaps paradoxically, to its liberalism. Constitutionalism has defanged and denatured Leviathan—the sovereign[63]—who no longer holds absolute power over her subjects and cannot induce the order necessary for profitable pursuits through subjects' fears of her threats and violence. The constitutional state holds the power of life and death, but this is a rationalized and bureaucratic power that few truly fear. Thus, to induce fear, something to fear must be imagined: The Beast. Indeed, The Beast is ontological: without fear there can be no order, without order there can be no state or "profitable enterprises," and without the state, life is "nasty, brutish, and short." Or, so we are told.

Yet, The Beast is a figment of the collective imagination, constructed through history. In this respect, it is not amenable to neoclassical economics. Fear of The Beast is irrational, evoked by collective emotions and hysteria.[64] And if fear of The Beast is not to disappear in the relative order of everyday capitalist life, it must be constantly renewed; it must be structured into everyday social relations; it must become the very foundation on which state and society operate.[65] Members of society must act as though The Beast is real, impose on others the reality of The Beast, and suppress all doubts that The Beast really exists. And if and when The Beast inside seems to lose some of its teeth, for whatever reason, there remains The Beast outside, which allows those in power to proclaim, "There is no alternative!"

In *Lord of the Flies*, the presence of Ralph's state evokes the (re)creation of The Beast by Jack and his minions. At home, British class society and its rigidities ensure that upper- and middle-class fears of the lower classes—witnessed during the English Civil War and many times since—support the country's class-based social relations and divisions of labor. Every so often the ruling class finds it expedient to throw the lower classes a few bones, but never so much as to disorder society as a whole. On the boys' island, however, the democratic society and its skeptron promise freedom from The Beast as well as class society and its brutalities—everyone will be equal with an equal right to be political. But such an ideal and utopian society might undermine the orderly, hierarchical regulation internalized by the boys and threaten those who rule, leading to "the world turned upside down," as was said in seventeenth-century England.[66]

Jack becomes the agent who restores the historical "order," although, in doing so, he must also destroy the island and any hope of maintaining that old order (Golding provides a convenient deus ex machina in the arrival of the Royal Navy, which saves the boys from themselves and their own Beast, eliding the fact that such a rescue would not be available to any society or state in a world annihilated by atomic weapons).[67] It is not enough, however, to control the instruments of violence, as Jack discovers—he must also control minds, thoughts, and the conditions of possibility.[68] He and his associates have been taught well in England's public schools. Terror is the best means of exercising control over those who might dream of other ways of life. Drawing on his education, socialization, and naturalized beliefs, Jack recapitulates English history and the destruction of the Diggers, Ranters, Levellers, and Chartists who, in their times, dreamt that things could be otherwise, sought to realize those dreams, and were ruthlessly crushed.[69]

Where is Waltz in all of this? The Beast is present in his world, although there is little indication that when he wrote *Man, the State, and War*, he recognized this. Realism bids us imagine the worst of all worlds and to act as though it were real, while neoclassical economics bids us to regard everyone else as a competitor and think only of our own interests. "Worst-case analysis" is a projection of our imagination. We are urged to prepare for and compete against The Beast. Failure to do so could expose us to our worst fears, and so we prepare for that worst fear in order to avoid it—and, perhaps, cause precisely what we fear. Wars happen, says Waltz, but prudence might prevent them. Nuclear weapons are unfortunate, but as he writes in his later works, our fear of them instills in us a healthy prudence, one that might yet avoid the vengeance of The Beast.[70] Or not—especially if we fail to recognize The Beast within.

It's Not Yet Over, Is It?

Of the three literary works considered in this chapter, *Lord of the Flies* might offer the greatest insights into both social theory and world politics, even if that was not William Golding's intent. Inasmuch as the imprint of English history and class structure are impossible to efface from the boys' subjectivities, the violence and war that kill Piggy and threaten to destroy the island cannot simply result from an absence of authority. By no means natural, the causes of war nonetheless are within us, as individuals who are socialized into society's norms and practices. Thomas Hobbes seemed to recognize these "truths," although accepting them would have led him to other arguments and conclusions. When the time came to make domestic peace in the seventeenth century, England's ruling classes fell back onto old patterns rather than finding less violent ways to restore order: they united to suppress the lower classes, whom they feared more than any Beast outside. Four hundred years later, Kenneth Waltz sought to construct, too, an ahistorical economy of violence in which the rationality of exchange would replace the brutality of war. Yet, at the end of the day, his theory of "permissive causes" offered little more than the banal observation that "stuff happens." Only specific histories could explain specific wars.

More to the point, the brutality and epistemic violence that are so common even in liberal societies are not accidental, a rarely noted lesson taught by *Lord of the Flies*. For Hobbes, fear of the sovereign and not other people made liberalism possible. Ironically, perhaps, in Golding's tale an initial absence of such fear poses a threat to the boys' first society—there is nothing to keep them together, to keep them out of the state of nature in which, as Cynthia Weber notes, there is no fear. Jack Merridew's role, therefore, is not to destroy the liberal peace but to make it possible, even if he must burn the island to save it. Jack draws on culture, history, and socialization in order to do this—as savages, the boys are not primordial; they are British all the way down.

That Kenneth Waltz paid little or no attention to any of this in *Man, the State, and War* is unsurprising; that he and his followers have so steadfastly refused to give up the myth of anarchy suggests that fear of what might follow the beheading of such a truth is greater than even the possibility of atomic annihilation. Such deliberate blindness is endemic to liberal capitalist societies whose upper classes are more fearful of their lower classes than rogue, revolutionary, or revisionist states. The "myth of anarchy" is, in other words, more than just a myth—it is a foundational element in a very real form of social control at the heart of liberalism, based on fear of violence by the lower classes against the social order controlled by the upper classes. At the same time, this order is reified as "politics," even as it systematically prevents anything much more contentious than periodic ratification of that order. Political theory, consequently, tells us that liberal society is the best of all possible worlds; political economy suggests that perhaps it is not.

7

Economy and Gender

WORKS OF POPULAR CULTURE, especially those in search of mass audiences, are always careful about distinguishing between men and women. These instantly recognizable gendering conventions serve not only to maintain the comfort levels of most readers and viewers but also to reinforce hegemonic understandings of gender—how men (or menlike characters) should act; how women (or womenlike) characters should act—and what punishments follow from inappropriate behavior.[1] Even today, when films regularly "bend" such rules in terms of plot and casting—think here of "Brokeback Mountain" (2005)—there is sure to be a media kerfuffle. This is especially true among those who feel somehow threatened by presentations of fluid or labile gendering.[2] For the most part, however, little explicit attention is paid to gendering in most films and novels, even though it is always present. Moreover, as we shall see in this chapter, it is often present in rather unexpected and unobserved ways. For example, "The Dark Knight" (2008) appears to be a shoot-'em-up about superheroes, crime, and the eternal clash of good and evil. It is also a film about men and the market and how both are gendered.[3]

In chapter 6, I pointed out some of the gendered aspects of *Lord of the Flies* and linked them to the boys' household and the division of labor therein. Just as few readers will recognize gender in Golding's novel, neoclassical economics largely fails to address or acknowledge the central role of gender in the production and reproduction of society, economy, and everyday life. The only exception is perhaps in attempts to account for differences in wages and managerial positions between men and women—and these are often attributed to numbers of years of experience, different skill sets, and women's refusal to "play by the rules" (which are gendered as well). Classical Marxism tends toward a similar blindness, focusing on class conflict as the independent variable that determines social and other relations. Yet gendering is omnipresent and not merely in civil society and social life—it is central to all economic systems and processes. Moreover, even though there is a tendency in capitalist societies to regard gender as a "problem" arising from differences between and among men and women, gender literally makes capitalism possible. Indeed, absent a gendered division of labor, production, and consumption, capitalism might not "work" at all.[4]

Of course, much of popular culture is scripted to take advantage of precisely this "normal" division of social roles between genders, especially in order to market cultural goods to one or another prized demographic. The target audience for "Sex in the City" is quite distinct from that for "The Dark Knight," even as both make liberal use of gendering to frame their plots and characters. That distinction is not, however, of particular interest here. Rather, this chapter focuses on the way in which gender appears as a structural feature of economics and political economy in works of popular culture. Consequently, it is as important to examine the roles of men as it is those of women, for we are least likely to perceive gendering with respect to men when we encounter it. In that light, after a brief discussion of what gender means in the context of economy and political economy, I turn to an analysis of "High Noon" (1952), the famous Cold War film starring Gary Cooper as the marshal who saves his small town from its enemies. Cooper's Will Kane is almost never seen as a feminized (or nonmasculine) character—that role is left to his virginal Quaker wife, Amy Fowler Kane, and the film's highly sexualized and sole Latina, Helen Ramirez. She also happens to be the town's capitalist as well as Kane's ex-lover. Without gendering, as we shall see, the film does not—cannot—work as intended. Nor can the masculinized state function properly so as to meet viewers' expectations.

In the third part of this chapter, I examine George Orwell's *Nineteen Eighty-Four* and return to Margaret Atwood's *The Handmaid's Tale* in order to illustrate how the state seeks to control women and their bodies, as well as family and sexual relations, in order to reproduce both citizens and itself and maintain the social order. This theme has appeared in earlier chapters, but I return to it here because, on the one hand, family and sex—often addressed separately—are generally regarded as part of the "private sphere," off-limits to both state and market, even as, on the other hand, they are constitutive elements of the social order so central to the capitalist economy and its gendered state. *The Handmaid's Tale* is, quite clearly, a feminist vision of dystopia, so its dismal treatment of family and sexual relations comes as no surprise. Orwell's dystopian book, by contrast, has been treated historically as an attack on

Soviet-style socialism, although it might also be regarded as a satire on certain tendencies in American society, especially in its prudishness. Moreover, Oceania's efforts to control the private sphere are no less important to the maintenance of the state and order than is its use of terror and torture—perhaps more so, since it is in and from the private sphere that resistance to Big Brother is most likely to emerge.

Finally, I examine the relationships among men, states, and markets through the lens of "The Dark Knight." This most recent Batman film—at least, as of 2009—might not appear to add much to the focus of this chapter, yet it is notable especially for its gendering of the state (a.k.a. Gotham City), its economy, and its characters. The vast majority of comic book superheroes, including women, have conventionally been highly masculinized and even homoerotic objects, although the actual sex act remained largely out-of-bounds (or off the page and screen), for reasons of censorship, "decency," and fear of polluting the minds of the young.[5] This remained the case even when, as during the 1960s, male superheroes like Spiderman began to suffer from "emotional problems."[6] "The Dark Knight" strays from this straight-and-narrow course, although it is also quite discreet about sex.[7] While the film minimizes male competition for women by killing off the primary love object, it nonetheless highlights the state's constant struggle to prevent the male-regulated market from veering off into demasculinized anarchy and chaos. Allegorically, at least, the film raises a number of questions about good and evil and whether, in a market society, such distinctions have any real meaning.

Gendering in Social Life and Popular Culture

Those who study and write about "gender" emphasize that it is not the same as "sex." Strictly speaking, sex is an individual biological attribute linked to species reproduction and survival (although asexual reproduction is not uncommon in the "natural" world). Gender, by contrast, has to do with behavioral attributes and practices associated with, and socially assigned to, stereotyped "men" and "women."[8] For legal and religious purposes—marriage contracts and heterosexual dominance, among other things—many human societies have distinguished historically between male and female, attached a broad range of attributes to each, and usually treated these as distinct, "natural," and "immutable."[9] These differences are, generally speaking, articulated in terms of binaries such as strong/weak, rational/irrational, and so on. When individuals are described in such terms—or characterized in terms of "male" and "female" attributes and behaviors—they are being gendered. Because both men and women can possess gendered attributes not associated with their biological sex, there is no necessary relationship between sex and gender.[10]

The trope of confused or mixed sexual identities can become quite common in societies whose members are uncomfortable with deviations from dominant norms—a number of Shakespeare's works play with such confusions—but generally only in the context of comedy or as a source of tragic outcomes for the confused and bewildered. In Western popular culture, men masquerading as women are often the butt of jokes, mishaps, and misunderstandings ("Mrs. Doubtfire," "White Chicks"), and such cross-dressers are almost always restored to their "proper" biological sex by the end of the story. When women pass for men or behave in a masculine way—or when men do not behave like "men"—some kind of tragic flaw or ending is often in store ("Thelma and Louise," "Brokeback Mountain"). In the former instance, men learn and male viewers and readers are taught that acting like a woman ("nonmasculine") is not only embarrassing but also a threat to ever being taken seriously again as a "man." There is also an implicit warning that society cannot remain "in order" if men act in this fashion on a consistent and widespread basis. The warning issued is that it can be dangerous or even fatal to stray from a socially assigned gender role. That such morality tales often become the subject of cultural and political controversy only serves to underline how threatening nonnormative behaviors appear to some people and societies and to what extent some societies are willing to exercise violence in order to restore the "proper" social order.

The construction of works of popular culture based on such role confusion is not, however, normally about sex; rather, it involves gender.[11] That is, the binary attributes broadly associated with masculinity and nonmasculinity are brought into play,[12] and an author's reliance on the confounding of audience expectations is key to plot. We are so deeply socialized to expect certain specific behaviors from those who are identifiably "men" and "women" that when we see contrary behaviors (men acting like women and vice versa) or appearances (men disguised as women and vice versa), we recognize that certain naturalized conventions are being toyed with or broken. But gendering goes much deeper than mere appearances or plot lines and can be central to those works in which the dramatis personae are all male or appear to epitomize masculinity (such as Marshal Kane in "High Noon").[13] As a general rule, then, films that foreground gender conclude with the reestablishment of "appropriate" roles and social order (although see "My Beautiful Laundrette," 1985, and "The Crying Game," 1992). Structurally, however, this may not happen and is certainly not necessary.

Disciplining gender roles is an important state function inasmuch as their maintenance is basic to capitalism. In 1996, when then U.S. Federal Reserve chairman Alan Greenspan warned of "irrational exuberance" in the stock market, he was speaking not only about investors' greed and potentially poor judgment of risks but also about the broader consequences of undisciplined capitalism.[14] As we shall see in the final section of this chapter, the "free market" is a realm of emotion, illogical and "irrational" choices, and even anarchy. Left to run free and uncontrolled, these can undermine state and society as is increasingly evident in the global fiscal crisis and wild gyrations in stock markets and other financial indicators during 2008 and 2009. Such behavior grows out of uncertainty about the future and broad concerns that the state will be unable to prevent another Great Depression with all that implies for domestic and global peace and order. Thus, disciplining the market is of utmost importance.

Primary to the state's role, however, is control of sexual relations and the making of babies inasmuch as one cannot have a "state" without a "people." This particular "creative problematic" has several crucial elements, at least from the perspective of those who govern or manage the state and its social order. First, a society will not survive for very long if it has no children and also restricts immigration. Although the ruling factions of most countries tend to have relatively few offspring so as not to diffuse familial wealth and power, they have relied historically on the masses for both labor and cannon fodder.[15] Second, and paradoxically, at the same time the rich and powerful also fear the less privileged having too many children since they might seek power, acquire it, and confiscate property.[16] Third, too much sexual license is thought to undermine social order and loyalty to the state and its demands because people are too immersed in themselves. Hence, control of the highly desired sexual act allows the state to reward its followers, who therefore find it in their interest to behave. All of this—evident in both *The Handmaid's Tale* and *Nineteen Eighty-Four*—would seem contrary to common practice in the capitalist societies in which we live today, in which sexual and gender freedom seem to be the rule of the day. Yet, it is precisely the particulars of "social order" that are at issue in contemporary conflicts over teenage mothers, abortion rights, and same-sex marriage, among other matters. In all of this, the state takes a masculinist stance by asserting its "rights" of control over the bodies of its people, just as men have done to women throughout the ages.

Not only is the state masculinized, but so is the capitalist economy. Neoclassical economics tends to elide this point, as noted above and in chapter 6, treating gendered divisions of labor as reflective of "natural" differences in skills and capabilities among men and women rather than the result of structural bias or selection processes in households and waged labor markets. Consequently, gender bias in the workplace is treated in legal and individualized terms, that is, not as a foundational structural element in social relations of production but, rather, as the product of deliberate actions by specific individuals who defy norms and laws and should therefore be punished. Consumption is quite visibly gendered in instrumental terms too, as is evident in films such as "Sex and the City" or ubiquitous cop shows on television with their endless truck commercials, as goods and advertising are pitched to differentiated desires socialized into consumers and cultivated by producers. The example of diamonds is archetypal in this respect.

The gendering—or, rather, masculinization—of both states and markets is of a different order and character. Historically—which is to say, centuries ago—both states and such markets as existed were the literal property of those who ruled. Prices, products, producers, and purchases were all subject to the dictates of state and sovereign. The rise of capitalism was linked to a certain degree of individualization and "deregulation," as the sovereign relaxed his or her grip on the economy; began to allow more individual freedom in terms of occupation, acquisition of wealth and property, and sale of goods and services; and encouraged competition among producers and suppliers. Although there is no particular reason to label "autonomy" or "competitiveness" as specifically masculine attributes—consider the coed nature of the Olympic Games[17]—over the past couple of centuries both became associated with accumulation of political power and wealth, the former through democracy, the latter through increasingly liberalized markets and ideologies associated with them, such as Social Darwinism. While corruption is an ancient problem, contemporary democracy and capitalism seem also to become ethically corrupting if too much "freedom" is permitted. In a hypercompetitive world, however, one engages in any behavior to get ahead, including libel, dirty tricks, theft, pillage, and murder. This, at least, is suggested by "The Dark Knight," in which distinctions between good and evil men have virtually disappeared by the film's end. That women are largely erased from and in the film is indicated by the inexplicable demise of Rachel Dawes halfway through, a plot development that casts the remaining mostly male antagonists in gendered roles, some of which are demasculinized.[18] But more about that later; let us first look at a quintessentially masculine film, "High Noon."

Hah, Noon!

"High Noon" tells a fairly pedestrian story. In the Old West, a town's marshal is preparing to leave his job and start a different, more peaceful life with his new bride. The bad guys he put in jail are returning to wreak havoc on the town, however, and no one is prepared to help the marshal face them down. He must make a final stand to punish the bad guys and save the town, which he does (with a little help from his wife). Released at the height of the Cold War, not long after the invasion of South Korea by the North and almost at the same time as the detonation of the first hydrogen bomb, "High Noon" can be read in several ways. It could be an allegory of World War II and America's role in "rescuing" Europe from its cowardice in the face of German aggression. Alternatively, it might be regarded as an allegory of the Cold War in which Europe refuses to face the Soviet threat and the United States must come to the rescue—but only this once and never again! Finally, some have offered it as an allegory of the fainthearted response of American intellectuals and artists to the rise of McCarthyism.[19] None of these is relevant here, however gendered those narratives might be. Instead, worth noting is the gendering of the characters in the film, particularly Marshal Will Kane (Gary Cooper). Was there ever an actor more masculine than Cooper? With his dark good looks and no-nonsense, unemotional, taciturn character, Kane was a perfect role for Cooper as well as an iconic representation of the state's reliance on no-nonsense masculinity for order. But the plot imposes on Kane a contradiction in his "social being": the man of primitive violence is to be turned into a bourgeois capitalist, albeit not by own choosing.

The film opens with Kane's marriage to the very blond Amy Fowler, a pacifist and a Quaker, who has made him promise to give up shooting—a masculine pastime—and take up shopkeeping—a nonmasculine one. Amy is stereotypically virginal, emotional, and illogical, the last two traits having threatened the social order of Hadleyville, New Mexico, before Kane arrived in town. They could recur if and when he departs. Quakers are, historically, associated with not only peace (and a refusal to pledge loyalty to the hierarchy of the state) but commerce too—this was all they had left after England's Glorious Revolution. They proved very successful at business, both in England and North America (think of William Penn).[20] Although Kane is neither churchgoing nor God-fearing, for love of Amy he has reluctantly agreed to leave town and open a general store in some other, less violent settlement.

But the postwedding celebration is disrupted by a telegram—which always bring bad news—warning that Frank Miller, head of an eponymous gang of four, is returning to Hadleyville on the noon train. He and his buddies seek revenge against Kane for putting Miller on death row some years earlier; now Miller has been released by the folks "up north" (those "folks" are gendered too). Much to Amy's dismay, Kane spurns her pleas to avoid involvement by fleeing the town. He refuses her entreaties and unsuccessfully attempts to mobilize a posse for the coming showdown. Fearing for their safety, none of the townsmen will join Kane, who is forced to face his enemies alone. He manages to kill three. Amy picks up a gun and, working against type, shoots the fourth. Disgusted, Kane throws his badge into the dirt and turns his back on the people of Hadleyville. He and Amy ride out of town to take up their more profitable enterprises and a new life elsewhere.

We might simply treat "High Noon" as another mythic story about good and evil in the Old West, a perennially popular theme not only in popular culture but also in politics (see, e.g., the first "Star Wars" film, "A New Hope," 1977, and "No Country for Old Men," novel, 2005; film, 2007). A good deal more is going on here, however. Not only is Hadleyville a "frontier" town, but it is fast becoming a prosperous middle-class settlement with a promising economic future. Before Kane's arrival, it was a stereotypical site of taverns, cowboys, whores, and casual violence, all forms of disorder associated with sin, carnality, and irrational exuberance. As the desk clerk reminisces to Amy, who has sought temporary refuge in his hotel while she waits for the noon train, Hadleyville was a much more interesting place before Kane cleaned it up. Now it is full of stores and prim God-fearing people, and there is no fun to be had at all. When Kane goes to the local church to seek volunteers for his posse—all the action takes place in real time, over a single hour on Sunday (shades of "24"!)—the pastor criticizes him for not attending services regularly and being married by a justice of the peace. Moreover, as noted above, the good burghers in the pews decide that the impending fight is between Kane and Miller. Not wanting to get involved or injured or to dirty the town's rising reputation, they turn him down.[21]

Kane is consequently torn between two gendered roles. On the one hand, he has promised Amy to become a shopkeeper devoid of star and gun. His greatest challenges will concern what to charge for goods in order to stay in business and making small change for, and small talk with, customers (imagine Gary Cooper engaging in small talk!). In that role, moreover, Kane will be subject to capitalist discipline rather than his own "natural" tendencies to shoot first and ask questions later. He will not be permitted to abuse or kill his customers, and he will no longer hold the monopoly of legitimate violence. On the other hand, Kane does possess a will to order (no pun intended) and the means to achieve it. His version of order is a well-behaved populace that allows women and children to walk the streets without fear. A pacific city-state, moreover, facilitates the practice of orderly capitalism, even though those in charge of maintaining civil peace cannot themselves be practitioners of capitalism.[22] That Kane might be killed in the process of maintaining masculinized law and order, which will make him a hero, matters less than his standing up for that system and protecting those who are nonmasculine (i.e., bourgeois children, women, and men). But Kane cannot be both—there is no room in this film for shopkeepers with guns. Thus, Kane is either the violent state or he is peaceable capital. In chapter 8, we will return to the theme of the violence intrinsic to capitalism and find that even shopkeepers are not wholly peace-loving folk (contemporary films are much more prepared to showcase violence in stores and businesses). Here we only note that this contradiction threatens Kane's social being as well as his union with Amy.[23]

Two other characters in the film also bear scrutiny for their gendering: ex–deputy marshal Harvey Pell and hotel and tavern owner Helen Rodriguez. Rodriguez—the more complex, interesting, and important of the two—is the town's capitalist, owner of both saloon and hotel (in the latter, she is a silent partner). We are left to guess how Helen came by her money, but her dark skin and overt sexuality—in stark contrast to Amy—leave few doubts about its source. In name, appearance, and accent, she is also "Mexican" (no nuance there). Consequently, even if her money is green and gold, in Hadleyville she is a second-class citizen. But she is also the most powerful character in the film. In a curious inversion of stereotypes, Helen is almost Yankee-like in her fiscal perspicacity and ability to close a deal as well as masculinized in her coldness toward others and her decisiveness in a crisis. When she learns that Frank Miller is coming on the noon train, she wastes no time liquidating her investments, packing her belongings, and fleeing to safer investment climes (suggesting an intimate history with Miller too).

By contrast, Harvey Pell is both fool and foil. Before Amy arrived in Hadleyville to take up a teaching job, Helen Rodriguez was Kane's lover. When the film opens, Helen is embroiled in a tempestuous, somewhat one-sided affair with Pell, who worships her (his attitude is not reciprocated). Pell eagerly awaits Kane's departure, intending to succeed him in a second masculine role as marshal. Kane, however, sees Harvey as an irresponsible buffoon. He is eager but easy to push around and incapable of keeping order in Hadleyville. Helen does not think that Harvey can replace Kane either. "You are no more than a boy!" she tells him in withering and emasculating terms, enraging Pell, who becomes all the more determined to become the new marshal and take full control of the state, violence, and Helen. Whereas Kane is split between two roles—one masculinized, the other not—Harvey is clearly nonmasculine and unfit to maintain social order, despite his swagger. Indeed, when the Miller Gang comes to town, Pell is nowhere to be seen. He sits out the fight, expecting to pick up the pieces once Kane is dead. Such a reticent attitude is not good for business or the peace of the bourgeoisie. After Kane's departure, Hadleyville's town fathers will look elsewhere for a new marshal, one closer in temperament to the unemotional Kane.

Babies for the State

There is an abiding myth in American society that both the family and sexual relations are private matters; therefore, the state is not to meddle in them. Practice differs considerably from theory inasmuch as the state is deeply implicated in shaping and regulating both family and sex, whatever their form or practices. By contrast, although few would favor the full commodification of the family, babies, and sexual intimacy, there is little question that the market penetrates deeply and extensively into the household, family, and bedroom. It is all the more surprising, therefore, that vociferous demands for the "right to privacy" are directed primarily against the state, with much less concern where the market is involved. Perhaps this is a holdover from times past when state and church bore major responsibilities for facilitating reproduction of the social order, supporting and sustaining particular class and status hierarchies, and ensuring that property remained in "proper" hands and was not confiscated by the masses. Since the nineteenth century, however, such regulation has had more to do with protecting and sustaining the state itself and the social order that supports it through what Michel Foucault called "governmentality" and "biopolitics," the management of populations through specific political and social strategies and practices.[24] Inasmuch as the market is deeply imbricated in such management practices, it becomes clear that neither capitalism nor the state stays out of the home, family affairs, or intimate relations.

Consider babies. The state's interest in babies is linked to its own survival as well as the operation of the economy in a number of ways. First, of course, babies are bodies, and bodies are labor as well as cannon fodder. Industrial power requires the former as workers; war requires the latter as soldiers. In both instances, the ranks must be kept orderly and regimented so as to maximize both production and destruction. (With nuclear weapons and volunteer armies, there is less demand for masses to die on battlefields, and with technology, automation, and outsourcing, there is less demand for factory labor.) Second, there is a historical regulatory connection between the family ruled by the patriarch and the state ruled by the sovereign, both "fathers of their country" (see the frontispiece of the first edition of *Leviathan*). Hence, just as the ruler of the family has an interest in making babies, particularly male ones, in order to perpetuate the family name and protect property, the ruler of a country has an interest in the making of (especially male) babies in order to perpetuate the kingdom and his family's control. While there may be many fewer kings and queens in the world today than in the past, there is nevertheless a growing concern throughout the world's white dominions about the long-term implications of "too few" babies and a corresponding fear of "too many" babies in the world's other dominions.[25]

Third, state regulation of sexual desire serves imperial interests and ends. In colonized countries especially, the rulers' "rights" to native women are essential to political control, even as assertion of such rights serves to emasculate native men (this along the lines of the nobility's *ius primae noctis* or *droit du seigneur*).[26] Finally, control of the sexual urge is regarded as essential to the maintenance of social order. If people have too much sexual freedom, they might cease to work for the state and spend all of their time in pursuit of pleasure.[27] We might note that the military has an interest, too, in regulating those sexual relations that could reduce combat effectiveness as well as attentiveness in difficult situations.[28] If soldiers are too free to have sex, they might make love and not war. Some fear this, especially if men could have sex with men whenever they wanted.[29] Either way, the social order might collapse.

But sexual desire can also be channeled into other activities of concern to the state, including nationalism and war. George Orwell's *Nineteen Eighty-Four* illustrates these propositions; indeed, the novel offers a wealth of insights into political economy, although here I mention only a few. First, within the ranks of the Outer Party to which Winston Smith and Julia, his lover, belong, marriage, or rather partnering, is closely controlled. As we are told,

> The aim of the Party was not merely to prevent men and women from forming loyalties which it might not be able to control. Its real, undeclared purpose was to remove all pleasure from the sexual act. . . . All marriages between Party members had to be approved by a committee appointed for the purpose. . . . The only recognized purpose of marriage was to beget children for the service of the Party.[30]

Smith's long-dissolved marriage to Katharine was subject to such Party approval. The two separated when no children were forthcoming after fifteen months of performing what his wife called "our duty to the Party." That "duty" was to produce babies, who would be educated according to the norms of the Party, instructed to keep an eye on their parents, and socialized to love only Big Brother.

When Winston first spies Julia at the daily "Two Minutes Hate," she is wearing the sash of the Junior Anti-Sex League, whose mission is to foster "complete celibacy for both sexes."[31] Convinced she is spying on him and intends to betray him to the Inner Party, he develops an immediate dislike for her. Winston is stunned, therefore, to be handed her surreptitious note reading, "I love you." Their relationship progresses from clandestine rendezvous in crowded streets to trips to the country and, finally, assignations in an illegally rented room—under the management and surveillance of the state, as it turns out. In this room, Winston and Julia are trapped by the Thought Police and taken off to the Ministry of Love. There they are tortured, brainwashed to love Big Brother, and eventually executed, still loving only Big Brother (who may or may not be a real person but is certainly the "father" and apocryphal Leviathan of Oceania).

Julia is neither very thoughtful nor self-reflective. By contrast, existential and ontological questions and doubts endlessly plague Winston. Almost in passing Julia explains something that has never occurred to Winston: "sexual privation induced hysteria, which was desirable because it could be transformed into war fever and leader worship." Sex requires energy, which is then no longer available for "marching up and down and cheering and waving flags." Winston realizes that "the sex impulse was dangerous to the Party, and the Party had turned it to account."[32] By extension, that energy can be directed to other tasks, including work and military service. Lest this seem unlikely or of no relevance to capitalism, recall that Henry Ford, among others, ran his company towns with an iron hand, refusing to hire job seekers with suspect familial relations and firing employees who failed to abide by his moral strictures.[33] Workers who sought sex and pleasure outside the properly regulated family could not be relied on to show up for work at the required time, and they were probably alcoholics too.

Ironically, perhaps, in *Nineteen Eighty-Four* the Inner Party does not seek to regulate sexual relations among the proles, those poor, uneducated, and generally undisciplined masses whose multiplication the rich and powerful normally fear. Invoking a kind of pseudosocialist wish for the working classes to unite, Winston writes in his journal, "If there is hope, it lies in the proles."[34] The Party, by contrast, hardly cares for the proles, regarding them as little more than useless mouths to feed and control through bread, circuses, and badly made cooking pots. We are not even told whether the proles work in Oceania's factories—if, indeed, such enterprises even exist—or fight in her armies. As is the case in capitalist societies, opposition to the state arises not among the poor but, rather, the middle classes (the "Outer Party"), who are most conscious about what they lack and what they want.[35] In *Nineteen Eighty-Four*, it is the Outer Party whose privacy is violated by the state. In our society, the invasions are more general, although who actually reads library books (or newspapers) anymore?[36]

The Handmaid's Tale further highlights the state's interest in regulating reproduction. The neo-Puritan Republic of Gilead is experiencing a dearth of babies due to widespread female sterility caused by the poisoning of land, water, air, and food in earlier times. For Gilead's leaders, this is a serious problem—without children to socialize into the state's morality and practices, their society will disappear.[37] Rather than environmental factors, however, they blame feminism and abortion for the birth dearth. At the same time "loose" women—feminists, prostitutes, lesbians, activists—offer a source of fertility that the state can harness to fulfill its needs. As we saw earlier, those who are fertile are sent to reeducation centers, stripped of their names, dressed as handmaids, and assigned to couples unable to have children.

Through "the Ceremony" the state harnesses the labor of husband, wife, and handmaid for its benefit.

Gilead's sexual division of labor is based on biblical sources: handmaids are named after Bilhah, Rachel's handmaid, who bore two sons to Jacob after Rachel could not. As in *Nineteen Eighty-Four*—on which Atwood loosely based her novel—marriage in Gilead is solely for the purposes of procreation, and any other sexual relations are strictly forbidden—in theory at least. Those in high places, such as Offred's master, can slip their fetters without fear of punishment. He takes her to a nightclub where "loose" women in state custody, unable to bear children, are employed to fulfill the fantasies of the society's elite males. Men play a role in the sexual division of labor too. As noted in chapter 3, Offred has an affair with Nick, the driver, hoping that the two might make a baby. Nick is only too happy to oblige, and apparently their endeavor is successful. Offred is spirited away, however, before we discover the ultimate fate of her or her baby.

What are we to make of this "tale"? Do we infer that even when the state takes over the regulation of sex, there remains a market in lust and love; that there is a residue of freedom from social bondage to be found in violating the canons of any society; or that the body can be a site of resistance to the rules and rule of men? Atwood wrote the novel in response to fundamentalist trends she saw in Ronald Reagan's America and posited that if one took these trends to their logical conclusion, a neo-Puritan state was not only possible but already in place. Although the Puritans, as we call them, were deeply engaged in commerce and the market and, by more recent accounts, not at all averse to enjoying sex,[38] they also thought their religion and faith able to control men's appetites and passions. As Nathaniel Hawthorne's *Scarlet Letter* (1850) reminds us, however, the threat of future punishment and promise of future salvation are weak reeds on which to base a social order.

One last point: *Nineteen Eighty-Four* is never explicit about the state's property rights in women's bodies—in theory there is no property in Oceania, just as there are no laws. By contrast, the Republic of Gilead clearly "owns" the handmaids. They are not only property of the state but also "natural resources" to be exploited in the service of state and society. Handmaids can be deployed or destroyed as the state wishes. Through their common dress and demeanor, and as a result of intensive surveillance, their individuality is suppressed, and they are left very little personal freedom, even in the most private of spheres. To be sure, Gilead is hardly a recognizable model of contemporary capitalist society—it is more of a syncretic mix of modernity and neo-Puritanism—but it suggests that bodies and sexuality must be controlled if order is to be maintained. Gileadeans see too much freedom, too much capitalism, too much self-control over the body (especially women's over their own) as

the fatal flaws in the late, great United States whose unbridled licentious-
ness—especially among women—swept it into history's dustbin.

The Joker's on You!

As we saw in *Lord of the Flies*, an absence of women in a film or novel does
not mean an absence of gendering. At first viewing, "The Dark Knight" seems
not to follow this dictum—unless one considers its target demographic:
young males in search of violence-based fantasies. Yet, the relative dearth of
female characters suggests otherwise.[39] Indeed, through its male characters
"The Dark Knight" offers a heavily gendered critique of state and capital
dressed up as a comic book superhero film. Historically, comic books have
been regarded as a lowbrow, lower-class form of fantasy somewhere below
the pulp fiction of the first half of the twentieth century.[40] Comic books were
enormously popular as cheap commodities, earning fortunes for those able
to take advantage of the market (made up mostly of boys and young men).[41]
"The Dark Knight" is based on DC Comics' Batman character but, in keeping
with recent trends in graphic novels, draws on a much darker, film noir tradition. Inasmuch as the film noir of the late 1940s and early 1950s is regarded
as a critique of post–World War II American society and its hypocrisy and
capitalist hunger—and film noir was always heavily gendered—"The Dark
Knight" is something of a not-entirely-nostalgic throwback to an earlier film
genre rather than the cheap comic book.[42]

   The film's primary male characters—there are eight by my count—can
be categorized along three axes: state, capital, and gendering (see table 7.1).
These are not independent axes as, once again, the central conundrum in
Gotham City—a.k.a. Chicago, as Superman's Metropolis is a stand-in for
New York—is the problem of social order, represented here as "crime." The
epistemological problem the film poses, moreover, is quintessentially postmodern. "Crime" cannot be clearly identified as "good" or "evil" and, perhaps invoking the Rolling Stones, "every cop is a criminal."[43] Even the lines of
political authority are opaque. Is the Batman friend or foe? Is the mayor clean
or dirty? What are Harvey Dent's true motives in seeking high office and low
vengeance? Who are the "real capitalists" in Gotham—Bruce Wayne and his
associates or the crime syndicates? Most importantly, who is masculine and
who is not? Bruce Wayne and his alter ego both seem to be manly men, but
are they? The Joker's propensity for violence and mayhem would seem to
mark him as masculine, but what about his devotion to anarchy and disorder,
which suggest otherwise? (And do not forget those scurrilous rumors about
Batman and Robin back in the 1970s.)[44]

Table 7.1.   Primary Male Characters of Batman

Character	Characteristics	Signifier
Bruce Wayne	Rich toff, dark and brooding, appreciates the finer things in life; unable to bond with women; mothered by Alfred	Of capital; desires an orderly life and society; weak masculinity
Harvey Dent	Young, blond, handsome; "Boy Wonder" wants to be a hero and to save Gotham from evil	Of the state; seeks order because that is what the state does; weak masculinity
Lucius Fox	Older, wiser, thoughtful holder of power who enables Wayne and the Batman but tries to regulate them	Of power in the service of capital and functional ends; strong masculinity
Alfred	Older, wiser, experienced; advises Wayne and the Batman on manners and propriety	Of maternal care; ensures ward is fed, dressed, and has a clean handkerchief; nonmasculine
Detective Gordon	Older, experienced family man, but married to his job	Of force in the service of the state; masculine
The Batman	Dark and brooding, muscular, rational and violent, angry and revengeful; believes the means justify the ends (mostly)	Of both rationality and violence; somewhat confused about gender
The Joker	Unattractive, unkempt, emotional, irrational, impulsive, anarchic, sly, and witty; looking for a good time	Of nonmasculine tendencies and the market's propensity to veer off into chaos
Two-Face	Dent out of control, giving full play to emotions through rationalized violence	Of the state's tendencies toward violence when crossed

Crime plagues Gotham City, which wages a constant battle against criminal syndicates, but its council and cops are not entirely clean either (reminding us, of course, of Chicago's and Illinois's political and criminal history, which often have been more or less the same thing). Corruption in high places is not so great a problem since that is just another cost of "doing business," but too much criminal activity of the "wrong" sort is a problem for the city because it scares people and cuts into the profits of legitimate businesses. Still, even garden-variety criminals are capitalists, and they understand basic economics, too. So long as they do not take too much and do not kill too many people, they can be tolerated like fleas on a dog.

Sometimes, however, prominent people get killed, which upsets the "natural" order. As Gotham City's richest resident and greatest booster, archcapitalist Bruce Wayne is less concerned about corruption than the random violence that took his parents' life and that, as the Batman, he is dedicated to fighting. But Wayne hardly projects the image of a crime fighter. He is handsome, stylish, polite to a fault, and sexually repressed. He is also well mothered by his butler, Alfred. Bruce Wayne might be the most eligible bachelor in Gotham, but he is, quite decidedly, unmasculine. (Wayne's refusal to commit to Rachel Dawes, who knows his secret identity, only reinforces our doubts about him.) Hence his need for a makeover: no one would take him seriously without a disguise, since that would sully his image and badly unnerve his investors and bankers.

By contrast, and notwithstanding a dark, brooding, and threatening appearance, the Batman appears hypermasculine and highly sexualized—outfitted in a tight costume that shows every muscle in high definition.[45] Indeed, the Batman is more missile than man, a penis seeking out those dark spaces where criminals incubate their dastardly plans. The Batman's opponents are also masculinized, although they are crude, badly dressed, and unmannered (one might call them "working-class" criminals rather than the Wall Street type). Whereas the Batman uses his masculinity in service of state and capital, imposing order where the latter fear to tread, the criminals pervert their masculinity, engaging in the rape of society, violating its norms, and stealing what is not theirs. Thus, when the Batman arrives, he penetrates the criminals' lair and, symbolically, at least, deflowers them. Nonetheless, we cannot say that the Batman is wholly masculine since, as Bruce Wayne's alter ego, he is also subject to Alfred's motherly care and feeding.[46]

District Attorney Harvey Dent is a mirror image of Bruce Wayne. He is blond, good-looking, outgoing, and, unlike Wayne, sexually available and committed to colleague and fiancée Rachel Dawes. Both a political animal and a bulwark of the state and its monopoly on violence, Dent vows to launch a crusade against crime using all the power and force available to "clean up" the city. Bruce Wayne sees in Dent the Great White Hero that he (Wayne) can never be and hopes that Dent's energy and enthusiasm will carry over into the city's government and police force, restore citizens' faith in both, and bolster the business of Gotham, which is business.

But Dent is not so happy with himself. He envies Wayne for his wealth and polish and the Batman for his heroics. Dent hopes he can prove to Rachel and Gotham that he can also be both polished and heroic and is both and therefore worthy of both her and the city's love. This is an impulsive and irrational desire for which he ultimately pays the price. Moreover, Dent's boyish good looks—not unlike Harvey Pell's in "High Noon"—belie his efforts to project masculinity. Ultimately, in light of Gotham's history and politics, Dent's campaign is dangerous for him and fatal for Rachel. He cannot protect the woman he loves, much less the city he hopes to save.

There are, to be sure, standard masculinized players in the film. Detective Gordon is both rational and powerful, as well as a committed to his nuclear family's safety (as a man should be), but he operates surreptitiously—and looks a bit like a weasel—without ever really showing his hand. One of the few "good cops" in Gotham's police department, Gordon sees through Dent's folly and the Batman's intentions. He is also a "game theorist" par excellence, who seems to intuit how all the players are going to move and how to be in the right place at the right time (I return to game theory in chapter 8). Lucius Fox, Wayne's "technical advisor," also represents an all-knowing, all-seeing "rational power," as evidenced by the bank of television screens on which he watches the city. Fox worries that both Bruce Wayne and the Batman might be engaged in unethical excesses, but he goes along with them, perhaps knowing that he cannot both control their irrational tendencies and keep his job.

Heath Ledger's Joker, however, is the most complex character in the film and not merely because of his Oscar-winning performance. The Joker personifies irrationality and anarchy, both decidedly nonmasculine attributes. Paradoxically, he also represents the spirit of capitalist enterprise and exuberance, which may tend toward chaos and uncontrollable situations. That the Joker is meant to be gender bending is evident in his makeup, which he cannot even apply correctly. Historically, a Joker's made-up face was intended to please and entertain, and modern clowns follow along. But a clown's makeup is always very precise, even as it is exaggerated, demonstrating that however irrational a clown might be in the circus ring, it is all in great fun.[47] Not so in this film.

In 1989's "Batman," Jack Nicholson's iconic Joker was, however evil, a natty dresser, a careful artist, and a meticulous planner as well as highly masculinized and fun loving.[48] By contrast, the Joker of "The Dark Knight" is sloppy, careless, and nonmasculine.[49] As one Internet commentary puts it, "Ledger's Joker is no joke. He is not just 'the bad guy,' the evil villain serving as foil to Batman's hero. His sociopathy is beyond good and evil: it thwarts the very possibility of moral order. . . . It is like a force of Nature, the very principle of chaos."[50] And given both his personal disorderliness and his penchant for disorder, the Joker is most definitely not masculine. As Rebecca Hester has argued,

> The mind/body duality facilitates the perception of the body as an object, as the property of the mind. Despite the claims to universality of this mind/body relationship, however, not all bodies are objectified. White, male bodies are more

valued because they embody what is taken to be the paradigmatic or universal rational mind. In contrast, female and racialized bodies become ever more visible as an unruly threat to society. Their bodies become equated with danger and uncleanliness as opposed to the purity of Anglo, male bourgeois society.[51]

Insofar as the market, too, is a "force of nature," the Joker personifies its essential uncontrollability. He is irrational (really a-rational),[52] seeking destruction for the pure joy it gives him. His penchant for anarchy also characterizes unregulated capitalism—in Karl Marx and Friedrich Engels's classical formulation in *The Communist Manifesto*, "All that is solid melts into air" (see chapter 8)—often without evident purpose or logic, it might be added. The Joker makes this clear in the mesmerizing monologue he delivers to Harvey Dent, who lies in the hospital recovering from his injuries, refusing cosmetic surgery, and plotting his revenge against Gotham. As the Joker puts it, he is a force much like Fortuna (or Mother Nature unleashed), a randomness in the universe that foils the best-laid plans of mice and men but is also, often, the key to great power and wealth:

> Do I really look like a man with a plan, Harvey? I don't have a plan. . . . I *hate* plans. Yours, theirs, everyone's. . . . I show schemers how pathetic their attempts to control things really are. . . . Look what I have done to this city with a few drums of gas and a couple bullets. . . . Introduce a little anarchy, you upset the established order, and everything becomes chaos. *I am an agent of chaos.* And you know the thing about chaos, Harvey. It's fair.[53]

While some have drawn connections between "The Dark Knight," the George W. Bush administration, and regime change in Iraq[54]—a not entirely inappropriate comparison—the Joker is better understood as acting on behalf of a foundational principle of capitalist markets.[55] Schemers pursue rational and predictable strategies with purpose and order in mind, and they exhibit masculine tendencies in this effort, even if they are doomed to be foiled. Chaos and anarchy, by contrast, are associated with unregulated emotions and irrationality, which are regarded as nonmasculine traits. If left unregulated and to their own devices, capitalist markets have an inherent tendency in this direction since the social good is often not the aggregate of individuals' good. As I argue in chapter 6, Hobbes's state of nature is not about presocial humanity but about the consequences of largely unregulated economic and social change in mid-seventeenth-century England—that is why Leviathan went "missing." Chance and risk are concomitants of high rates of return, and whenever there are winners, there are also losers. This is evident in the collapse of global financial markets and all that has followed, except that investors hate Fortuna when it turns against them.

The contradiction, as the Joker seems to frame it, is that planners and their schemes can never wholly control chaos and anarchy. At best, they can only be countered by complementary chaos and anarchy, out of which there might emerge certain discernable patterns and a new order, at least according to chaos theory. I rather doubt that the Joker subscribes to such ideas—there's too much logic and scheming in chaos theory—but that cannot necessarily be said about his opponents. Neither Bruce Wayne nor Harvey Dent is in a position to match the Joker's activities and methods—at least, not until Dent becomes Two-Face, and then he is too logical about seeking revenge. Both Wayne and Dent do seek to contain the Joker through a quintessentially liberal and market-based activity, bargaining, until they discover that negotiation with chaos is not possible. At that point, the Batman must intervene as a complementary agent of chaos and anarchy to suppress, if not eliminate, the Joker. Capitalism can never be fully regulated or contained, but it can be tempered. This is the Batman's mission.

In the scheme of things in "The Dark Knight," is the Batman good or evil? Viewers must judge for themselves, although if we follow the Joker's reasoning, the distinction is meaningless: shit happens. Where it falls is more up to gravity than aim or intent since we cannot control gravity. Recall that under the rules of the old Production Code Administration, films could not show sinners and criminals benefiting or being rewarded for their behavior.[56] Today's films are still subject to such judgments, and audiences tend to dislike movies with morally equivocal endings. Yet, at film's end, now commissioner Gordon calls the Batman "our Dark Knight," suggesting that he will undertake those morally dubious, nonrational actions supposedly forbidden to the police. He will be guided, in other words, by utilitarianism rather than law or ethics, albeit by a utility whose gender is not at all clear. Whether this is meant to point to the torture in which U.S. agents do not engage or the corporate theft that American CEOs do not commit is left to the audience to decide.

We're All Gendered Now

Gendering in popular culture is both very visible and virtually unnoticed. As we have seen in earlier chapters, women who appear either as central or secondary characters almost always confront the structural and instrumental effects of gendered rules and behaviors. When men are involved, gendering is less evident. But if a cigar is often just a smoke, sometimes it is not—especially if it blows up. The lives, experiences, trials, and tribulations of men and women—even when they are in exploding cars or gun battles—are core themes in most films and literature inasmuch as these interest certain audiences.

Indeed, to the extent that gender is also central to capitalism and its political economy, contrasting representations and the commodification of men and women, as well as masculine and nonmasculine, are givens. Viewers and readers seek points of identification and difference with characters in movies and books, which further socializes them into stereotyped roles that depend on what they consume, the work they do, and their fantasies and fears. Also, seeing or reading about normalized roles usually reassures them: things are presented the way they should be and vice versa. It is the rare film or book that truly troubles such hegemonic logics. All of this is, perhaps, too obvious for further comment.[57]

But gender is much more deeply embedded in cultural representations than we might think—even when they seem "normal." Not only is a gendered division of labor central to capitalism, its popular culture, and people's consumption of the latter, but it is also foundational to the very beliefs, practices, and institutions that comprise capitalist society and the state, both materially and representationally. A female cop is no longer regarded as unusual; a bad female cop (or Terminatrix) is. In particular, when a not-masculine figure—whether cop, nurse, or suicide bomber—acts against type, those deeply embedded and gendered expectations are being tapped. Imagine "Wall Street" were the bad guy named Gordana Gekko.

8

Capitalism and Disruption

The bourgeoisie cannot exist without constantly revolutionizing the instruments of production, and thereby the relations of production, and with them the whole relations of society. . . . All fixed, fast frozen relations, with their train of ancient and venerable prejudices and opinions, are swept away, all new-formed ones become antiquated before they can ossify. All that is solid melts into air, all that is holy is profaned, and man is at last compelled to face with sober senses his real condition of life and his relations with his kind.

—Karl Marx and Friedrich Engels, *The Communist Manifesto*

A HALLMARK OF CAPITALISM IS CONSTANT and revolutionary change. This is captured in Karl Marx and Friedrich Engels's famous observation, as well as Joseph Schumpeter's concepts of "creative destruction" and "churn."[1] Constantly changing systems and arrangements of production complicate social relations of reproduction as people move from one job or profession to another and, in so doing, to the ends of the earth and back. This process transforms them and those around them as well as their societies. Yet, for most people such change is a mystifying process, experienced as an individual case of Fortuna when we have the good luck to happen upon a new employment possibility or, perhaps, the bad luck to be fired as a result of misbehavior or not hired due to a lack of connections. Sometimes people are tempted to blame unseen conspiracies, corruption, or vested interests such as bankers, oil companies, sheikhs, the Illuminati, Satan, and liberals.[2] That individual misfortune might be the result of the "normal" operation of social systems or that policy makers (and economists) might view such misfortune as a "benefit" to society is neither conceivable nor very satisfying. Yet that is the way the capitalist economy "works."

Indeed, from the perspective of neoclassical economics, high rates of aggregate economic growth are desirable irrespective of effects on individuals since they offer the highest levels of economic utility to society as a whole (we ignore, for the moment, the benefits and consequences of speculative "bubbles").[3] The inefficient deployment of resources as, for example, in gas-guzzling SUVs, obsolete steel mills, and old computers represents a drag on the economy because other investments and uses could generate greater growth and wealth. Consequently, it is good and socially beneficial that older production technologies be scrapped and replaced by those that foster higher productivity as well as greater profit potential. If, in the course of such change, people lose their jobs, communities are decimated as businesses close, and national economies are undermined, well, that is the cost of "economic progress."[4] As Marx and Engels intimate, however, the social and political consequences not only may be revolutionary but can also trigger violence, wars, and other sorts of political upheavals.

But you might ask, what does this have to do with economics or political economy or capitalism? After all, the maintenance of a social order would seem to fall within the provenance of politics, police, and law. Even in a capitalist society, as Anatole France wrote in *Le Lys Rouge* (1894), "The law, in its majestic equality, forbids the rich as well as the poor to sleep under bridges, to beg in the streets, and to steal bread." That the police rarely have to roust the rich from their nests under bridges or in doorways is surely not of importance to us or our focus in this book. Recall, however, the westward pilgrimage of Bill "D-FENS" Foster across Los Angeles. Even if the causes of his ill-fated journey were to be found in the economy, the task of making sure that he did not threaten either public or family fell to Detective Martin Prendergast, who was neither lawyer nor economist.[5] As we contemplate the turbulence in the global economy following the deflation of the global securitized mortgage bubble, we might wish to reconsider the relationship between the economy and the kinds and degrees of social disorder it sometimes generates.[6]

This chapter focuses, therefore, on the macroeconomic and structural effects of capitalist transformation, creative destruction, and churn—that is, how societies change and are changed, peacefully and violently, as capitalism works its ways on the material world, its social relations, and its belief systems. It is important to understand that neoclassical economics has little to say about this matter, even though instability and uncertainty always pose a risk to rational investment and the profit rate. Still, if there is social disorder, it is not generally treated as a systemic problem but, rather, attributed to disorderly people and their individual problems and therefore best dealt with by police, prosecutors, and prisons. To the extent that effects are farther reaching—causing the death of entire industries, for example, and the disruption of families, neighborhoods, and cities—society must adapt or die. Metaphorically speaking, this is exactly the narrative we see in two of Denys Arcand's films, "The Decline of the American Empire" (1986) and "The Barbarian Invasions" (2003). Both focus on a group of French-Canadian friends who, over the years, drift apart but come back together in the second film as one of them is dying of cancer. That these two films are also a metaphor for the rise and fall of Québécois nationalism, a cycle very much dependent on the changing economic relationship between that province and its large neighbor to the south, the United States, is more backstory than foreground element.[7] Although these films do not precisely reflect American capitalism and political economy, they do depict a society whose "social being" is being reshaped into a doppelganger of the American system.

For societies that feel the winds of capitalist revolution, the problem of social disorder and violence cannot be addressed structurally—to do so is to risk destruction of the basis of capitalist prosperity (and property). Thus, those in charge seek to police and discipline unruly individuals so as to signal to the rest of society the need for order and the risks of disorder.[8] Consequently, the terrorist attacks of September 11, 2001, on New York and Washington, D.C., can be understood, at least in part, as a product of capitalist change and churn, as are the endless replays of terrorism in books (*Terrorist*, by John Updike, 2006), television ("24," 2001–2009), and film ("Live Free or Die Hard," 2007). The fourth in the "Die Hard" series, "Live Free" is the most graphic and least subtle in its reduction of capitalist disorder to "terrorism," depicting a disgruntled bureaucrat who, to feed his ego, decides to teach a lesson to America's electronic infrastructure, its elites, and its bourgeoisie.

We need to be careful, however, in taking a reductionist approach to "disorder" and social disruption inasmuch as this leads to the relentless focus on the individual as the source and cause of violence. As we saw in chapter 7, "The Dark Knight" presents the Joker as a personification of individual culpability: He has no causes or schemes; he just happens! Thus, because we assume that individuals have motives and intentions and act on them, it becomes necessary to extract useful (valuable) information from individuals in order to prevent or avoid future disruptions of the social order. Here we come face to face with two fundamental stimuli that operate in the market: pleasure as expressed through desire and pain as expressed through risk avoidance.[9] To some extent, we have already addressed the pleasure principle in chapter 2, but we have not yet considered the infliction of pain as a fundamental element in the morality and practices of economics and political economy. Is torture, then, a political or economic act? Philosophically speaking, is torture a form of consequentialism, indeed, of economic utilitarianism—the greatest good for the greatest number?[10] Is torture merely an extension of the pain so often inflicted by the operation of markets, especially when they fail? Or are such questions simply hyperbolic nonsense? To answer them, I examine several works in which torture plays an important, if not central, role, including "24," "The Marathon Man" (1976), and "Syriana" (2005).[11]

Finally, could it be said that capitalism is inherently and intrinsically violent? Marx certainly thought so.[12] If so, how might we explain such tendencies? It is useful to recall here the Social Darwinism of the nineteenth century, a conceptually and ethically degraded version of Charles Darwin's theories about evolution mixed with arguments about "nature, red in tooth and claw." This phrase first appeared in Lord Alfred Tennyson's poem "In Memoriam A. H. H."[13] and subsequently became the sound bite for political and social ideas and practices about struggles for survival among nations, states, and businesses.[14] Today, a form of such Social Darwinism is a foundational proposition underlying notions of economic competitiveness as well as "game theory" (and nuclear deterrence). The latter is an economistic approach to explaining interactions between individuals on the basis of nature, information, and stimulus (no history required here). In his 1979 follow-up to *Man, the State, and War*, grandly titled *Theory of International Politics*, Kenneth Waltz went so far as to compare states in the international system to corporations in the market, arguing that both live and die in fierce competition with each other. During the Cold War, game theorists analyzed missile "exchanges" between the United States and the Soviet Union in order to determine the most "efficient" use of thermonuclear warheads (see "WarGames," 1983). If capitalism is "war by other means," then we should not doubt that some sort of violence is deeply embedded in markets. In this penultimate chapter, I return to "Syriana" and "Wall Street" and introduce "WarGames" as illustrations of the final point.

A Great Debate

As we have seen in earlier chapters, except in economics where the neoclassical marginalist view still dominates, one of the perennial debates in the social sciences has to do with people's behaviors and social relations. Why do people act as they do and do what they do? Recall that according to the tenets of "rational choice" theory, individuals are cost-calculating beings always seeking to fulfill their self-interests and preferences in order to maximize satisfaction and pleasure (back to Thomas Hobbes and the Joker again!). Thus, when people make costly or irrational choices, their behavior is attributed to poor information about alternatives and outcomes, which is either the result of "market failure" or deliberate concealment by others.[15] To a significant extent, then, responsibility for choices and consequences follows from what an individual knows and how he or she acts under a given circumstance. Here, scientific knowledge and awareness of personal relations and civil behavior are important. The fact that there might be a broader, social component to the choices available, to the information needed to make a choice, and to the consequences of different choices is largely ignored (or regarded as marginal to explanation). Under such conditions, what is rational for the individual might be catastrophic for society. Flipping houses might be extremely profitable for some, yet in playing a major role in bringing down the economy, disastrous for many.[16]

But as Marx, Engels, and many others have made clear, capitalism is not a static system, and the costs and conditions of production, exchange, and consumption are constantly changing in response to both structural factors and individuals' gaming of the system. When gasoline is cheap (in real terms—and in the United States it is, once again, as cheap as it has ever been), the costs of driving an SUV are tolerable if not exactly low. When gasoline is expensive the use value of large vehicles declines, while smaller, more fuel-efficient cars command a premium in the market. In this respect, individuals respond to the price signal by making a rational choice: get rid of the gas guzzler, drive less, and use alternatives if available. The knock-off effects of such behavior, though, reverberate throughout the entire economy.

Back in the 1980s, American automobile companies bet on large vehicles rather than the smaller ones produced by Asian and European manufacturers, and they built dozens of factories dedicated to producing only SUVs and trucks. Now, because demand for these vehicles has declined (although it is rising again in response to cheap gasoline), General Motors, Ford, and Chrysler have lost vast sums of money, their corporate share values have plummeted,[17] and they have closed factories and dealerships right and left. Indeed, in 2009 both General Motors and Chrysler were forced into bankruptcy. Tens of thousands of their employees are on furlough or without jobs, lacking the income to pay rents and mortgages, travel, buy food and clothing, and so on. In the face of declining demand for their goods and services, local economies decline, businesses downsize or close, and malls empty out. Houses are abandoned, and those that remain occupied are worth less and less. This leads to more unemployed, less business, and more disruption.

The impacts do not end there. Less travel means lower fuel-tax collections, which finance highway construction and repair. Construction workers lose their jobs. Fewer people drive to tourist destinations, and they spend less if they go, causing tourism-dependent businesses to suffer and close. Housing developments built far from urban centers on the premise that residents can afford to drive to jobs in and around cities are abandoned. Not only does housing construction decline, but all the companies supplying materials also experience effects. Finished but unsold houses put downward pressure on the value of all nearby real estate, making it more difficult for those who re-main solvent to sell their houses and move closer in to the city. Property-tax revenues, which pay for education and social services, decline. More layoffs follow. The cycle continues. Eventually, as gasoline consumption declines, its price goes down too, and people may begin to drive more and move back out to edge cities. In the interim, however, much damage has been done.[18] Similar processes take place when the economy recovers and booms: new types of production and goods and new forms of labor can also have disruptive effects on the social order as some people and groups find their incomes growing, and others find them in decline.

These are both examples of "creative destruction."[19] Writing in the 1930s, Joseph Schumpeter recognized that consumers and industries do not auto-matically dispose of older goods when newer ones become available in the market. The incentives to replace products and production methods arise within the operation of capitalism as new, more efficient technologies, prac-tices, and goods generate higher profits for those who first deploy them and decreasing profits and growing losses for those who do not. In this process of replacement, moreover, older systems must be junked—or sold to devel-oping countries—so that they do not constitute a drag on productivity and growth. Depending on circumstances, those employed in connection with the now-obsolete arrangements might have or acquire the skills required for employment in new industries, or they might not and be laid off. New workers with appropriate training and skills may replace old ones, at higher salaries, or older, experienced workers willing to work for low wages may be hired.[20] In other words, for an economy to grow at a high rate, stuff must be destroyed so that new stuff can be made, sold, and bought, while "redun-dant" workers are fired so newly skilled ones can be hired. Creative destruc-tion reinvigorates capitalism, and all this is for the "good." The resulting "churn," or turnover, in employment is simply a cost of doing business. And people can find new jobs or move to where the jobs are available. At least that is how the story goes.[21]

But is the overall result socially beneficial or not? Is it good for the public welfare? From the neoclassical perspective, this is the wrong question. Rather, we should determine (1) whether there is aggregate growth in a society's economy, and (2) whether anyone is worse off as a result of this growth. In the first instance, growth reflects the more efficient deployment of financial, technical, and human capital (skills), which should, in the longer run, improve overall living standards throughout the economy. If the short-term effects lead to new distributional inequities of concern to society, they should be addressed through market mechanisms such as lower tax rates on the poor, income tax rebates, "welfare-to-work" programs, and skills training rather than direct redistribution of wealth from rich to poor.[22] In the case of churn, people thrown out of work need to acquire new skills and capabilities that allow them to reenter the job market through finding work in different occupations. Protecting obsolete industries in order to maintain employment only leads to further job and income losses (and "free trade" is a much better way to keep costs down and foster new industries).

In the second instance, the best social policies are those that "lift all boats," whether dinghies or yachts—at least, so the former are not swamped in the wake of the latter. In technical terms, this is called "Pareto optimality," a condition in which those who are worst off do not experience any negative effects as a result of economic policies and changes. Such a goal is, however, more a theoretical objective than a realistic outcome because it is difficult to fine-tune policies and practices so as to ensure that no one is negatively affected. More to the point, those who are well-off and stand to benefit from economic change are disinclined to compensate the less well-off, especially when policies do not produce the hoped-for results.[23]

From a more critical perspective—although not, strictly speaking, a Marxian one—such economic change does not take place in a political or social vacuum. Those in positions of power and authority who are able to change the organization of the political economy through norms, laws, regulations, and various forms of influence are also wont to pursue policies and practices that generally benefit them and their well-off colleagues and supporters.[24] The latter two are also much more likely to vote as well as make substantial donations to electoral campaigns than those who are less well-off or without power. The political trade-off then becomes whether to protect older industries in order to protect jobs if those workers tend not to vote and will not vote for particular elites. Or should help go to those who will vote and contribute to those who make the policies? The tendency is, therefore, to put responsibility for their future on affected individuals rather than to attempt to remedy structural inequities that generate industrial decline, job loss, and class impoverishment. But "reskilling" is not always that easy. If too many people in one place are retrained for similar occupations, the need for all of them may not exist, and they might remain unemployed.[25]

Down and Out in Los Angeles and Sheffield

To better understand how creative destruction and churn work, let us return to "Falling Down." Recall that Bill Foster has lost his job in the defense industry, where he had been "protecting us from the Communists." In fact, Foster is a victim of the West's victory over communism as well as the technological, political, and economic change that made it possible, although he is thoroughly mystified by what has happened to him and his city. The end of the Cold War, although often attributed to Ronald Reagan's forthright rhetoric and massive U.S. defense spending,[26] is better understood as the "sweeping away" of what seemed for so long to be fixed and frozen. In short, the Soviet economy was not organized to deal with the gale-force winds of change that began to blow through the Eastern Bloc during the 1970s. Relative to the West, the "Communists" were falling farther and farther behind both economically and technologically—this was before China's opening to the market, which the Soviets later regarded with great suspicion and trepidation. The Communists produced shoddy goods—remember the "Yugo paradox," whereby the poorly made Yugoslavian car competed with the well-made South Korean Hyundai—in inadequate quantities to meet consumer demand, and were unable to modernize or generate the internal resources needed to finance both military and consumer production at the same time. We need not further pursue this argument here.[27] Here, we are interested in its effects on the U.S. defense industry for two reasons.

First, one initial American reaction to the end of the Cold War was to reduce military spending. For four decades the United States contracted with U.S. defense corporations, many of which were located in Southern California, to design and build vast and often baroque war-fighting platforms and projectiles—missiles, submarines, aircraft carriers, nuclear warheads, and space stations.[28] Once the Soviet Union fell apart, these military forces far exceeded any conceivable needs. It made sense to cut back on such projects. The defense corporations reacted logically to reduced budgets and began to shut down facilities and factories and look for new fields to conquer.[29] Presumably, Bill Foster was fired as a result of this process—in a moment, we'll look more closely at his consequent behavior. Second, the microelectronics revolution of the 1970s and 1980s tended to make many earlier Cold War skills obsolete. Tasks that once required large cadres of engineers, scientists, and mathematicians to test new designs could now be simulated on desktop computers. Calculators replaced slide rules; computer code and modeling replaced algebra and geometry. As Foster puts it in the film, "I'm overeducated, underskilled. . . . Maybe it's the other way around. I forget. And I'm obsolete. I'm not economically viable."

We see how Foster is "compelled to face with sober senses his real condition of life and his relations with his kind," as Marx and Engels put it. A job counselor might have advised Foster to find a new job—any job—and to go back to school—perhaps at night or on weekends—to learn the skills he would need to participate fully in the new post–Cold War world. Real estate would be a good bet. That this might not be the best advice is not immediately evident. Thousands of newly minted engineers are coming out of American universities, not to mention Chinese and Indian ones. They already possess those new skills and will accept starting wages much lower than Foster's salary in his last posting. Moreover, it is not always easy to learn the new tricks required to find a new job. Certainly, a certificate and transcript from a community college does not guarantee a job interview, much less a job. It must occur to Foster, placing his too-late breakfast order at Whammyburger, that he could someday find himself standing in the manager's place—but Foster is overeducated for even that degree of complex decision making.

Others might go quietly. Foster refuses to accept either change or Fortuna (and we see that he had something of a bad temper to begin with, or maybe he is just a misunderstood and angry white male).[30] He has had no hand in spinning the wheel or throwing the dice, so why should he suffer when the vagaries of history turn up losing numbers for his bosses? Foster wants only "to go home," where he imagines the "fixed, fast frozen relations" still apply, where he remains employed, if not as an anti-Commie engineer at least as a husband and father—although he has been made redundant in that department too. And he brooks no resistance in his westward progress toward home, even if the world through which he moves has melted away and is hardly recognizable to him. Are we meant to sympathize with Bill Foster's plight? Given his violent outbursts, one might not think so. Yet, the violence done to him by an economic system that has used and disposed of him cannot be denied. Moreover, Foster's fate and final disposition bring to mind William Jennings Bryan's peroration against the gold standard at the 1896 Democratic National Convention in the midst of a similar period of economic change: "You shall not press down upon the brow of labor this crown of thorns. You shall not crucify mankind upon a cross of gold." At the end of the film, floating lifelessly in the water off the Venice pier with arms extended as in a crucifixion, it would seem Foster has been sacrificed to a new god.

To be sure, change is not always such a bummer. "The Full Monty" offers a rather more optimistic, if irreverent, view of creative destruction, churn, and "reskilling." This narrative revolves around a group of six British steelworkers who have lost their jobs as Sheffield's once-vibrant steel industry closes down during the 1970s (who has not heard of "Sheffield steel"—aside from you?). In this instance, we are led to assume that mill technology has become outdated and inefficient and the cost of Sheffield steel too high to compete in the global market.[31] This, at least, is what happened to the industry in the American Northeast—in what came to be called the "Rust Belt"—during the 1970s and 1980s, as new steel-making technologies and practices rendered obsolete the open-hearth, century-old, energy-intensive furnaces of Pennsylvania and its environs. Moreover, the new mills that opened elsewhere in the United States required many fewer workers with different skills.[32] Where new jobs appeared in the Rust Belt, they tended to be low-paying service positions. So it is in and around Sheffield.

As the film opens in 1972, two of the six protagonists are in an abandoned factory wrestling with a steel beam they hope to sell for scrap. Unsuccessful in their efforts and joined by another friend as they walk down the street, the three observe a queue of women outside of their "local" (pub) waiting to enter a performance by the Chippendales,[33] a (franchised) male striptease act (we are not informed of the prior employment status of these performers). Deciding that they can strip as well as the next guy, the three put together a similar act—calling it "Hot Metal"—and promise to do the "Full Monty" and disrobe completely. At first the men get cold feet, but told that the performance is sold out, they strip and are, of course, a great hit with the mostly female, screaming audience. Presumably, the six now have a new occupation for which they have the requisite skills and equipment and which will more than pay their bills. (We need not go into gender implications here, need we?)

What, if anything, is the economics lesson of this British film? Perhaps it is that everyone has hidden skills that, if recognized and properly deployed, can fill some kind of occupational niche (or, perhaps, that burger flipping is less embarrassing than stripping?). One must simply be entrepreneurial and seize the day. Or perhaps the lesson is that service industries have replaced metal bashing and that, in this instance, the demand for striptease is not easily satisfied by out-of-town imports (although the Internet more or less puts paid to that argument). Bringing Starbucks to town does not work either: how many coffee shops does one town need? Maybe the lesson is that everyone should "smile and be happy" because the economy is so flexible and accommodating, at least for the six buddies and for the present moment.

It is difficult to argue, however, that Sheffield will now become the striptease capital of the world or acquire some sort of comparative advantage in producing male strippers, if only because there is a virtually endless global supply of men (and women), many of whom are willing to "think globally, strip locally."[34] To put the point another way, most service industries are focused primarily on local production and delivery. Aside from call centers and the like,[35] such services are not amenable to large-scale offshoring unless some kind of nonperishable good is involved, such as books, bodies, or phone calls. We are not told what befalls those who are not so flexible.

"All the Churches Emptied Out"

"Globalization" is a contested term—it has many definitions and generates many disagreements. I take it to mean, most fundamentally, the compression of space and time and the ever-deeper penetration of capitalist beliefs and practices into the everyday lives of people around the world.[36] As "fixed, fast frozen relations" are disrupted, destroyed, and deconstructed, people respond in a variety of ways. Some accept the changes; others resist them. At the extreme, violence can erupt in unpredictable ways. But globalization cuts both ways and, depending on how we understand and respond to it, also offers great opportunities for those who are well placed and able and willing to take advantage. The objective here is not, however, to offer yet another disquisition on economics and political economy. Rather, I want to perform a dissection and deconstruction.

The objects of my attention here are Denys Arcand's two Québécois films mentioned in the introduction to this chapter. The first is "The Decline of the American Empire," which is generally described as a "comedy." Eight friends associated with the Department of History at the Université de Montréal gather together for dinner and a long-running conversation about their (joint) sexual activities and exploits. Released in 1986, the film reflects on the recent history of Quebec and, in particular, the rise of Québécois nationalism during the 1970s and 1980s.[37] For more than two hundred years, since the British defeat of France and ceding of French Canada to British rule in what Americans call the French and Indian War and Europeans the Seven Years War (1756–1763), the Anglican, English-speaking community of both Canada and Quebec dominated Catholic French Canadians ("Québécois"). Poorer and more working-class, French-speaking Québécois were generally discriminated against, and their culture was rather systematically demeaned and even suppressed. These conditions began to change during the 1960s for reasons political, religious, and economic.

In 1968, the Parti Québécois was established with the goal of declaring the province's independence from the Canadian Confederation. In 1976, the party won Quebec's provincial elections and began the process of separating from Canada, which included passing legislation to make French the primary public language of Quebec.[38] The law alienated English speakers, who began to leave the province. It also motivated new immigrants to Canada to go to other parts of the country. This reinforced the role and power of the French language and its speakers in Quebec's political and social affairs. The exodus of English speakers also had economic consequences as various niches in the province's division of labor were abandoned and subsequently occupied by French speakers.

The second factor generating social change was the growing secularization of the French community, in part a result of the Second Ecumenical Council of the Vatican (Vatican II, 1962–1965), which greatly liberalized Catholic doctrine and practice. Vatican II also seemed to shift matters of conscience from church rulers to the individual, permitting a certain freedom in personal matters (an interpretation that Popes John Paul II and Benedict XVI have both tried to squelch). Vatican II and growing prosperity also had a significant effect on the French Canadian birth rate, which plummeted over the following decades as contraception became acceptable and widely used and as women entered the labor force. Smaller families, rising mobility, and general well-being meant that many members of the French-speaking community, especially the bourgeoisie and intelligentsia, saw their standard of living rise, and they became much more cosmopolitan and internationalized. Finally, Quebec as a whole became more important as a business center and experienced general economic growth due to resources, wealth, and financial services. One could say that the rise of the French Canadian community, especially in Montreal, also opened up certain international language opportunities in Europe that were unavailable to English-speaking Canadians from other parts of Canada.[39]

By 1986, as we shall see, such comparative advantages were already on the wane, but during the heady days of Parti Québécois rule, young French Canadians believed that the sky was the limit. More to the point, the shadow cast over Quebec by the United States was fading, a result of the economic crisis of the 1970s, the spike in energy prices, and the American defeat in Vietnam.[40] Whereas during the 1950s or even the 1960s Washington would never have tolerated a sovereign Quebec, by the following decade, independence did not seem impossible. Thus, the title of the first film—"The Decline of the American Empire"—is not so much about the United States' waning influence as about the liberation of the Québécois from their centuries of subordination in Canada and to the English-speaking world. The ongoing conversation about sex among the friends is as much about collective political freedom as individual lust.

Not until "The Barbarian Invasions," however, do we discover the fate of the eight friends and their dreams of a free, sovereign Quebec. Over the period between 1986 and 2003, they have drifted apart, grown older, changed jobs, moved, and experienced all the other things that happen to people. What emerges, however, are two distinct, yet linked, narratives. In this film, the focus is on Rémy Girard, a University of California, Berkeley–trained professor of American history tenured at the Université de Montréal. Only in his mid-fifties, Rémy discovers that he has terminal cancer and not long to live. Ingloriously replaced in the classroom by his graduate teaching assistant—the students do not seem to care very much who teaches them—Rémy undergoes medical examination and treatment in one of Montreal's overcrowded and run-down public hospitals.

Deeply concerned for him (and not wanting to take responsibility), Rémy's ex-wife Louise summons their estranged son Sébastien from London to care for his father. Sébastien, a wildly successful investment banker, speaks English fluently. He uses his wealth and influence to have his father installed in a decent, refurbished room—on an abandoned floor of the hospital—to be examined by doctors with functioning, up-to-date equipment—in Vermont—and to be treated for his pain—with marijuana. The last is procured through the help of Sébastien's childhood friend, Nathalie, who has remained in Quebec, speaks only French, and although gainfully employed, is a heroin junkie. Sébastien also summons the old circle of friends to attend to Rémy. Eventually, close to death and with the assistance of a nurse from the (Catholic) hospital, Rémy takes an overdose of morphine. He dies peacefully in the lakeside house where he and his group of friends spent so much time talking about freedom, food, and fooling around.

In addition to the history described above, the backstory to this narrative runs roughly as follows. In 1967, French president Charles de Gaulle visited Montreal. While speaking to a large crowd, he famously announced *Vive le Québec!* ("Long live Quebec!"), followed by *Vive le Québec libre!* ("Long live free Québec!"). Needless to say, de Gaulle's cry for freedom was extremely popular in Montreal as well as an inspiration to the rising nationalist movement. The rest of Canada did not, however, take it either lightly or as a friendly gesture. By the time of "The Barbarian Invasions," Rémy and his friends, ardent advocates of Québécois independence during the movement's early years, have settled into somewhat less idealistic and more prosaic lives. But they have regrets. After returning from his studies in the United States, Rémy, in particular, was determined to ensure that Quebec not repeat the imperialist errors of its neighbor to the south.

Did he succeed? Students in his class are clearly bored and little interested in either the follies of American imperialism or the struggle for Quebec's independence. They might not be as rich as the Americans, but a modicum of prosperity and the general failure of the movement have inured them to the national struggle. Like Sébastien, many of them look to Europe, where they can become wealthy and part of the new cosmopolitan global class. Those who have stayed behind, like Nathalie, have little to look forward to except long years of banal living followed by terminal decline. Moreover there is nothing comparable to the Catholic religion, nationalist fervor, or sexual freedom, now displaced by the lust for money. As a priest complains when he asks Sébastien's wife, Gaëlle, to assess the monetary potential of a basement full of discarded Catholic statues and reliquaries, which she says have only sentimental value, "In 1966, all the churches emptied out in a few weeks. No one can figure out why" (see the discussion of Vatican II, above, for the answer).

All of this change has taken place under the shadow of the United States, which, after the end of the Cold War, became wealthier and more powerful than ever before. Swept up by the irresistible forces of globalization and lured by the siren call of capital, Quebec and its bourgeoisie gave up nationalism in return for material rewards. But if Arcand's film is to be believed, the province was destined never to achieve the heights of prosperity and efficiency visible across the border even in places as poor and rural as Vermont, where Rémy must go for his medical tests. Quebec will always remain lower in the global economic hierarchy, a supplier of raw materials and labor to the rich, especially those south of the border. Moreover, the province is now so tightly linked to the United States that they will rise or sink together. This is evident in that the film is set in late 2001 after the attacks on the World Trade Center and Pentagon, which seem to represent "the barbarian invasions" of the film's title. Yet, it is never entirely clear who are the "barbarians"—and the film's title clearly refers to more than one "invasion"—or exactly what the consequences of the American invasion might be for Quebec and French Canada. If Rémy somehow personifies Québécois nationalism, his death at age fifty-one no doubt signifies the end of that dream.

What does any of this have to do with economics or political economy? For neoclassical economists, the rise and fall of Québécois nationalism bears little relationship to its economy except, perhaps, as a disincentive to foreign investment. A more important consideration would be the province's comparative advantages in the global economy. These are to be found in its vast supplies of hydropower—Quebec provides electricity to New England and New York State—labor specialization, and tourism. Those who speak only French or limited English can find work in domestic social services; those with the requisite language skills and social capital can emigrate to other places—New York, London, Paris—where they might command premium salaries. And, of course, "French Canada" is an attraction for the inhabitants of "English North America," who can come and spend money for an "exotic" experience—$2.3 billion in 2006[41]—that is nonetheless close to home and offers familiar electrical outlets. There is little to add to this story.

For the critical political economist, by contrast, these are merely superficial features. Nationalism is never merely a social or political phenomenon. It is also about national autonomy, one of whose most important elements is control of the economy. This point was given voice in the eighteenth and nineteenth centuries by Alexander Hamilton in the United States and Friedrich List in what was not yet unified Germany, reaching its apotheosis in the centralized economies of both the Axis and Allies in World War II.[42] Although both old and new states struggled to assert their economic independence during the two decades following the end of that war, this was a losing battle.[43] Ironically, perhaps, Québécois nationalism emerged in the twilight of that era when globalization was already beginning to erode the option of national economic autonomy. In 1968, of course, no one could foresee what might happen three decades later—even as late as 1989, the dream of economic independence remained an attractive one. By the time the 1990s were over, and notwithstanding 9/11, neither Quebec nor Canada as a whole had much hope of keeping the United States at arm's length. Rémy's decline and death, made tolerable by Sébastien's wealth, is about more than merely nationalism.

Free Living and Hard Dying

Although globalization has done its work on Quebec without much in the way of violence, the results of capitalism's work are not always peaceful. For some—the young, restless, and well-educated—flight to other places was once an alternative. In other times and places, however, easy escape is hardly possible. Societal mores define acceptable beliefs and behaviors while peer pressures from family, community, and friends discipline individuals—for the most part—and set them on the bourgeois path. Mobility is never precluded, but as with Nathalie in "The Barbarian Invasions," it is easier to minimize struggle and go with the flow. The disruption of social relations by capitalist flux, however, undermines and overturns such constraints. People can change their social positions, their identities, and their beliefs and practices more easily as a result of change and churn. As an example, consider the following story: "DUBAI, United Arab Emirates—In his old life in Cairo, Rami Galal knew his place and his fate: to become a maintenance man in a hotel, just like his father. But here, in glittering, manic Dubai, he is confronting the unsettling freedom to make his own choices."

Here, Galal, twenty-four, drinks beer almost every night and considers a young Russian prostitute his girlfriend. But he also makes it to work every morning, not something he could say when he lived back in Egypt. Everything is up to him, everything: what meals he eats, whether he goes to the mosque or a bar, who his friends are. "'I was more religious in Egypt,' Mr. Galal said, taking a drag from yet another of his ever-burning Marlboros. 'It is moving too fast here. In Egypt there is more time, they have more control over you. It's hard here. I hope to stop drinking beer; I know it's wrong. In Egypt, people keep you in check. Here, no one keeps you in check.'"[44] This is a different form of liberation than might be found in *Québec libre*. Dubai is highly individualized, and behaviors unthinkable in Egypt are mundane and acceptable in the former.[45] Not everyone is as seemingly sanguine as Rami Galal about such social instability (and he is, by now, probably back in Egypt). In some, however, it generates other feelings, behaviors, reactions—and there is little or nothing to constrain them from acting these out. It is worth repeating that the majority of the 9/11 hijackers were well-educated, middle-class Saudi men repulsed by the corruption and license they saw at home, which was facilitated, if not fostered, by their country's ever-deeper integration into the global economy led by the United States. They found something they could do to strike out against the primary agent of that disruption and did it.[46]

It is not my intention here to explain or excuse terrorism by reference to economism; nor am I arguing that capitalism or hedonistic materialism "cause" terrorism. The germane question is, rather, what relationship, if any, exists between such organized violence and the political economy within which it takes place? Curiously, although "the market" is always offered as a site of peaceful relations among people—and, indeed, many maintain that economic exchange fosters peace rather than war[47]—the market can also be regarded as a site of epistemic violence manifest in deeply embedded forms of domination that do injury to some even as they benefit others. I will further explore this point in the final section of this chapter; here, I return to the theme of capitalist disorder and terrorism as seen in "Live Free or Die Hard."

After three films in which he more or less saves everyone, Detective John McClane is old, tired, and largely washed-up, made obsolete by the technology—computers, cell phones, databases, forensics—available to the young whippersnappers who now dominate both police and government.[48] But apparently he is still needed. "Live Free or Die Hard" depicts an "electronic Pearl Harbor," the much-feared cyberterrorist attack on the United States' vital infrastructures, including communications, finance, and power systems. Everything goes down: phones, radios, televisions, computers, electricity, and even gasoline pumps.[49] The conventional version of this story is that we need fear only our enemies "outside," who have the mobilized capacity to succeed in such an endeavor. While there have been a few coordinated attacks on various websites and online institutions—and there is evidence that other countries have suffered from such mischief as well—it is always difficult to determine the source of such attacks and who might support them.[50] Experience suggests, moreover, that it is often amateur "hackers" who seek to penetrate the computer systems of secrecy-fetishizing agencies such as the

U.S. Department of Defense and the CIA, which themselves have the capacity to seriously sabotage other countries' electronic networks.[51]

Who, after all, possesses the knowledge, funds, and mobilizing skills to engineer an "electronic Pearl Harbor"? It is not necessarily hackers, who tend to be highly individualistic and generally waste their time trying to break into impenetrable systems. They need someone to organize them. In "Live Free or Die Hard," one Thomas Gabriel does the organizing—notice, moreover, that his surname implies the "Last Trump" announcing Armageddon and the End of Days. Gabriel is a former employee of the National Security Agency (NSA), whose website tells us that its "core missions are to protect U.S. national security systems and to produce foreign signals intelligence information"[52] (the NSA is also the best funded of the United States' fifteen to twenty-odd intelligence agencies).[53] Despite repeated warnings about U.S. vulnerability to cyberattacks, Gabriel is fired, rather than lionized and promoted, after he demonstrates how to hack into the computer system of the North American Aerospace Defense Command. With the help of Mai, a young Asian American woman highly skilled in both electronic and martial arts—and who, we are to presume, here represents a warning about China as our "real" enemy[54]—Gabriel seeks revenge by launching a "real" electronic Pearl Harbor.

As a result, all who rely on the Internet and electronic communications in order to manage and mobilize responses to an emergency, including the FBI, CIA, NSA, and other alphabetic agencies, find themselves helpless when "jacked out" of the Web by Gabriel and his minions. McClane, by contrast, has a leg up. He is not dependent on the electronic infrastructure and can still deploy his two primary attributes, wits and strength, in battle. McClane seeks out and destroys the cyberattack's mastermind, albeit only with the help and capabilities of Matt Farrell, one of Gabriel's unwitting and witless hired hands. Unknowingly tasked to help facilitate the attack, Farrell is the only one of a dozen or so who survives assassination by his employer. Thus, by the end of the film, McClane "wins" because he and Farrell are the only ones who still have guns. I will not belabor here the sheer implausibility of McClane's feats of physical derring-do—as opposed to the average filmgoer, film heroes always survive the most violent events because otherwise the film would be very brief. Instead, I will focus on the character of the "terrorist" responsible for disrupting America's capitalist order.

Thomas Gabriel, whose facial expressions suggest he is probably mad as well as a megalomaniac,[55] is another example of an individual who breaks the fetters of social discipline in order to foster disorder and does it simply because he can. But what, exactly, does Gabriel want? As it turns out, he is after money, not power, and apparently has acquired the wherewithal to move billions of dollars from various bank accounts into his own. An unremarked irony here is, perhaps, that any wealth Gabriel purloins from the electronic infrastructure is as virtual as that which he has caused to vanish with his online machinations. After all, as we are learning from the current economic crisis, banks are not required to have more than about 10 percent of their capital in easily accessible form, while other financial institutions hold even less. And, as noted earlier in this book, such "liquid" assets are not in the form of "real" paper money or bullion, either, but exist only as electronic data in the computers of various institutions. Inasmuch as more than $10 trillion in investments have vaporized since late 2007, we might wonder whether Gabriel actually works for Wall Street rather than himself.

The Price of Pain

During the first few seasons of "24,"[56] Agent Jack Bauer faced a world of relentless and unending threat and danger, all in the effort to protect his country from death, devastation, and derision. As we have been told repeatedly since 2001, moreover, the business of detecting and preventing terrorist attacks depends heavily on information, on knowing who intends to attack where and when (a.k.a. "intelligence," although "Burn after Reading" [2008] largely puts paid to the idea that "information is power"). For the most part, the collection of such information requires dogged police work, "sigint" (signals intelligence), and "humint" (human intelligence). All are very labor intensive and quite boring—akin to searching for needles in haystacks—and in the case of humint, which requires working the streets, very problematic and quite dangerous for those who do not speak the local language or know the local culture and its social relations. This is not the stuff of which high-energy, one-hour television programs are made. Thus, Bauer has routinely engaged in the torture of suspects who are associated with "Big Men" or appear to be planning nefarious deeds (and he has been tortured in return). For the most part, of course, the recipients of his attentions reveal clues that lead (or do not, in some instances, as a nuclear detonation in Los Angeles reminds us) to the explosive devices or terrorist plotters of concern. While Bauer plies a rough justice, it nonetheless seems to save some (privileged) lives.[57]

Torture hardly seems like a form of market exchange, and it almost certainly has nothing to do with capitalism, does it? Yet, a closer look reveals something interesting about the practice. Torture does involve exchange, a trade of pain for information. Going further, torture can even be understood as the application of Sigmund Freud's "pleasure principle"; to wit, human beings continuously seek pleasure (benefits) and try to avoid pain (costs). Although one might more commonly associate pleasure with sex, drugs, and rock 'n' roll, we can also imagine an auction as the idealized version of such a "market." One experiences pleasure from a winning bid, pain from a failed one. Torture, in a sense, replicates this logic: a cessation of pain (i.e., pleasure) in return for a winning bid (useful information), and resumption (i.e., greater pain) for a failed bid (useless or no information).

Pursuing such tortured logic further, we might also ask about the marginal rate of return on such pain. That is, at what point does the infliction of pain no longer result in any information whatsoever? Clearly, too much torture can kill, at which point an informant loses both exchange and use value. Thus, torture should be applied until just before the victim suffers irreparable damage and death. Here, we should recall the caution expressed by President George W. Bush's advisers in the U.S. Justice Department, who proposed that at the limit "physical torture 'must be equivalent in intensity to the pain accompanying serious physical injury, such as organ failure, impairment of bodily function, or even death.'"[58] In other words, any torture resulting in serious bodily injury to or death of a suspect would exceed the benefits that might result from information obtained and should therefore not be applied. Thus, waterboarding only simulates drowning, and by this calculus it is acceptable (even if not legal under the U.S. Uniform Code of Military Justice).

We can apply the logic of game theory[59] here, as well, and the torture scenes in "Syriana," in which CIA operative Robert Barnes is subject to the attentions of Iranian agents, are rooted in such calculations. Recall from the discussion of the film in chapter 4 that Barnes has been ordered to assassinate Prince Nasir (who seeks to democratize his oil-rich emirate, a.k.a., Kuwait). The torture is applied after Barnes comes too close to discovering that a diverted U.S. missile, in transit through Iran, is meant to kill Nasir (think here of the Iran-Contra scandal). Confiding to the wrong person that he is en route to the emirate by way of Lebanon, Barnes falls into the hands of America's Lebanese confederates. He is saved, at the last moment, by a member of Hezbollah—most definitely not an American ally.

It is never entirely clear why Barnes is tortured. Is it tit for tat—a reward for his earlier activities in Iran? Is it to extract information from him? Or is it to warn him off his mission to save Nasir? In the event, Barnes tries to warn the prince, but both are killed when the latter's motorcade is blown up in the desert. A little bit of knowledge is a dangerous thing. Barnes knows only a piece of the much greater plot that unfolds in the film. As little as he knows, however, it is still too much. In the competitive world of espionage, deals are rarely what they appear to be, and the marginal cost of a life in the larger scheme of things is close to zero. This is especially the case when that larger scheme involves oil and fabulous wealth.

The price of pain is made painfully evident in "Marathon Man," which falls back on the old trope of Nazi villains at large in New York City. Thomas "Babe" Levy unwittingly becomes involved in an attempt by dentist Christian Szell to recover a stash of diamonds that belonged to the latter's recently deceased brother. Viewers are led to presume that Szell's sibling was a German war criminal who stole the diamonds from Jews about to be gassed in concentration camps. In one of the film's pivotal scenes, Szell ties Levy to a chair and probes his mouth with a sharp dental pick in search of cavities (reminding us to floss daily or pay the costs). Szell repeatedly asks, "Is it safe?" The question stumps Levy. "Is what safe?" he asks. Szell then proceeds to dig the pick into the cavities he finds in Levy's mouth, a process so painful that even one of the dentist's thugs looks away. When it becomes clear that Levy knows nothing—or, at least, will not respond to the question in the required way—Szell puts clove oil on his teeth to deaden the pain. By then, however, Levy has pretty much lost consciousness. Although we might dread a visit to the dentist, most checkups do not involve the type of game theoretic exchange described here. Still, for those with sensitive teeth and nasty memories, the pain and pleasure involved are all too familiar.

Is Capitalism Intrinsically Violent?

The neoclassical economist scoffs at such a question. Markets are sites of exchange, and capitalist markets are sites of efficient exchange. The laws of supply and demand set a mutually acceptable price for goods that, if it does not necessarily maximize either profit for the seller or utility for the purchaser, at least satisfies both. Bargaining and negotiation (a.k.a. haggling) over the price of an item requires more time but is simply a way of more closely matching individual preferences. If an exchange degenerates into overt violence, it is no longer a market, inasmuch as price is replaced by pain and, we might assume, trade by theft.

According to Marx, however,

> Primitive accumulation plays approximately the same role in political economy as original sin does in theology. . . .The discovery of gold and silver in America, the extirpation, enslavement and entombment in mines of the indigenous population of that continent, the beginnings of the conquest and plunder of India, and the conversion of Africa into a preserve for the commercial hunting of blackskins, are all things which characterize the dawn of the era of capitalist production. These idyllic proceedings are the chief moments of primitive accumulation.[60]

The language of the market reeks of potential, if not necessarily realized, violence. Capitalist markets can do violence to people's security and well-being, but this is all to the long-term good.[61] "Creative destruction" seems an oxymoron and almost certainly does not seem an act of creation to those who suffer its consequences. "Churn" does not sound quite so bad, but it fails to convey either certainty or stability. The very word "competition" points, on the one hand, to sports and, on the other, to biology, both of which can be prone to violence. When Kenneth Waltz invokes the model of the market to describe international anarchy,[62] he has in mind that competition is necessary for the survival of both states and corporations. Those that fail to compete successfully die, but even those that do compete might die too. Because sports competitions are not meant to lead to death, we must assume that the biological metaphor is relevant to Waltz.[63] At the extreme, success in the market might include "killing off" competitors through a variety of stratagems, such as dumping of excess production, theft of proprietary information, and even assassination. The desperate businessperson may be willing to use desperate tactics to save what he or she has left.

But such scenarios involve resort to instrumental rather than structural or epistemic violence. Can we go further, therefore, in our analysis? Is there violence implicit in the very process of capitalist exchange? As a rule, markets rely on the regulation of the relative power of parties to an exchange who have some notion that an agreed-on price is "fair." Depending on circumstances, buyer or seller may exercise an implicit threat against the other not to sell or buy at either a "fair" price or any price at all. Given the absence of alternatives, the party in greater need must then accept the coercion implicit in the exchange. Imagine a starving peasant trying to buy food from a rich grain merchant who is in a position to set a price for his product and refuse to sell for less. The peasant has the much-vaunted "freedom of choice" to seek food elsewhere, but he or she might die in the exercise of such liberty. Everything may have a price, but not everyone is able to meet it.[64]

We can observe a more compelling account of the violence inherent in exchange in the film "WarGames" (1983). Released during the height of the second Cold War and the Reagan administration's nuclear saber rattling, the film involves another young hacker, David Lightman, who manages to break into the mainframe computer of a California video game company. There, he finds an intriguing filename, "global thermonuclear war," that connects him to the military supercomputer, WOPR, which controls the United States' nuclear missiles. David plays the game with WOPR, which proceeds to launch a simulated attack on Las Vegas and Seattle, one that the country's military defense systems briefly mistake for the real thing. But after David disconnects,

WOPR continues to play the game in search of the solution that will allow it to "win" a nuclear war. When it finally discovers a winning game, WOPR will launch a real attack on the Soviet Union (it is a masculine computer). Ultimately, WOPR's creator must intervene to convince the computer that there is no "winning" solution in the game. The computer learns that "the only winning move is not to play."

But during the sequence preceding this conclusion, the computer runs through a myriad of "games," in which the two competitors "exchange" missiles. The consequent level of death and destruction determines whether the benefits of attack are worth its costs. This is, of course, no less than the substance of nuclear deterrence theory, an economistic approach to nuclear war that rests on "rational" calculations by parties to a hypothetical exchange of missiles.[65] Although deterrence practice is meant to prevent war, its theorization involves the ever-more convoluted imagining of a purported series of attacks that must be deterred. The fear that one's opponent might not be deterred or believe threats leads to all kinds of complex scenarios and twisted policies and mandates new practices that might increase the likelihood of war.

These kinds of calculations led Herman Kahn to write his books *On Thermonuclear War*, *Thinking about the Unthinkable*, and *On Escalation* in the 1960s.[66] In the first, he argued that not only would the survivors of such a war not "envy the dead" but also that "we can imagine a renewed vigor among the population with a zealous, almost religious dedication to reconstruction." Indeed, such people are not only the stuff of fiction or "Dr. Strangelove" (1964). At a university-organized seminar on nuclear weapons in 1983, I encountered a professor with a similar mind-set (he shall remain nameless here). He spoke about the application of economic models to the problem of efficiently targeting nuclear missiles against the enemy's cities. When challenged about the morality of his research, the professor protested that he was merely exploring ways to make nuclear deterrence more "robust." Epistemic violence, however imaginary, was required to prevent real violence, or so went his consequentialist argument. The problem here is that if we become too familiar with imaginary attacks, we might not flinch when the real thing is looming. And that would be all, folks![67]

We seem to have strayed far from either economics or political economy with this last discussion, yet we should not ignore the fact that the tools of "rational-choice" economics are being applied here. If game theory and econometric modeling can be as easily applied to exchanges of death as to doughnuts, does this not suggest something worrisome? Moreover, a social system that actually pays and rewards individuals for such lines of work—the rationalization of epistemic violence and the hardening of attitudes toward instrumental violence—is almost certainly one whose tendencies lean toward war rather than peace.

Conclusion

We should be careful not to overemphasize the disorder triggered by capitalist economics under normal dynamic conditions. Without delving too deeply into theory, however, unregulated markets evidently have considerable chaotic potential. Why some economies might degenerate into violence and others not, even under very similar conditions, is not subject to generalization. As with the causes of particular wars, Waltz reminds us, specifics matter. Popular culture offers specifics but builds on generalizations, which is why it is a poor guide to what can or will happen in the future. All the same, popular culture, especially film, revels in seemingly senseless violence—why are the car chase and inevitable crash and explosion so necessary to a box-office success?—although this is no more than the logical extension of the norm to its extremes. If fast driving is what everyone dreams about when, like Bill Foster, they are stuck in traffic, perhaps the vicarious thrill of seeing fast driving and the violence it can engender might be even more fulfilling—not to mention much safer—than the real thing. But the fact that such violence is so ubiquitous in film and fiction says something less than uplifting or promising about the society and culture in which we live.

9

Through a Mirror, Darkly

CYPHER: If he had told us the truth . . .
TRINITY: That's not true, Cypher. He set us free.
CYPHER: Free? You call this free?

—"The Matrix"

Things are seldom what they seem, skim milk masquerades as cream.

—*H.M.S. Pinafore*

I HAVE HAD TWO OBJECTIVES IN THIS BOOK. The first is pedagogic, using film and fiction to teach about basic concepts and propositions from critical political economy and mainstream neoclassical economics, illustrating how such texts can be used to teach about these matters. The second is didactic, offering a critique of the many naturalized, normalized, and mystifying social arrangements that characterize contemporary postindustrial society, examining the role of popular culture in offering and reinforcing "common sense" and "conventional wisdoms," and focusing in particular on late-twentieth- and early-twenty-first-century Anglo-American capitalism.[1] In particular, in pursuit of the second objective, the application of concepts from critical political economy arises from my understanding of how cultural products and texts, their content and their framing, can mediate the "regulation" of people and societies—"governmentalization" in Foucauldian terms.[2] All of this is, perhaps, too obvious, but it bears repeating that in a social environment characterized by high degrees of commodification and consumption, not only are we what we buy, eat, use, destroy, and excrete, but we are also how we imagine ourselves to be. "Deconstructed from the texts" is not quite as sexy as "ripped from the headlines," but it is not all that different.

My goal in this final and mercifully brief chapter is not, however, related to either of these broader objectives; nor is my intent polemical. Notwithstanding the critical approach and textual interpretations offered in this book, I do not regard popular culture as a source of, or incitement to, revolutionary social action or transformation.[3] A recognition of the extent to which we are ensnared in the iron web—or Matrix, if you will—is, perhaps, a first step toward transformative and emancipatory ends. Here, however, it is worth contemplating filmmakers' apparent intentions in recent biopics of supposedly revolutionary characters such as Che Guevara ("Che: A Revolutionary Life," 2008), on the one hand, and popular (and populist) rabble-rousing attacks such as those directed by Michael Moore ("Roger and Me," 1989; "Fahrenheit 9/11," 2004), on the other. It is probably safe to say that no one has ever funded the production of a text or film whose explicit purpose was the destruction of the means of production of that text or film.[4]

Moreover, in writing this text about texts, I also have a faint hope that the former might be adopted as a course text—it is always a (nonrevolutionary) pleasure to receive a royalty check in the mail, however small it might be—thereby not only enabling students to see, however dimly, through what is reflected by the silver screen but also to enhance what they might see when they go to the movies or read novels. Perhaps in this way I might contribute to both their education and pleasure. I could, of course, simply "publish" my text on the Internet and offer it for free, subject to one of the growing number of anticopyright schemes available today. Whether that would result in wider adoption or greater effect is difficult to say. Information certainly flows more freely today than in earlier times, a change noticeable even within my lifetime and academic career—but, then, a flood can be as dangerous and damaging as a drought, and there is no way to tell whether today's informational inundation is more likely to drown us in opaque confusion or let us float away in transparent clarification.

In other words, I do not and cannot stand outside of the social time and context in which I observe, analyze, live, and write. I am a teacher, a writer, a consumer, a citizen, a cynic, and an idealist as well as individual who has studied and dreamt of other times and places. Some of these times and places are fact; others are fantasy. Some are in the future, some the past, and others the present. But my studies of them have always been from a standpoint rooted in the politics, economics, and sociality of late-twentieth- and early-twenty-first-century America. What I produce is, as Robert Sullivan argued (see chapter 1), less than a conscious "mirror [of] the economically determined social structure of [our] era," even as I am "trapped within the ideological confines of [our] time." Moreover, like Thomas (Neo) Anderson, I am something of a prisoner of this particular matrix. In contrast to Neo, however, no one will ever offer me a blue pill or a red pill or the chance to wake from the "the world that has been pulled over our eyes to blind [us] from the truth." Knowing the "truth" might free us to some degree, but it will not free us from the world as it is today.

In many ways this is regrettable, and it reminds us, again, of Margaret Thatcher's TINA dictum: "There is no alternative." She, of course, was considered, and considered herself, not only a high ideologue but also the paradigmatic pragmatist devoted to passing out the blue pills that would maintain the social discipline so necessary to neoliberal capitalism and its flourishing. Unfortunately, her inability to imagine alternatives also blinded her to the plots and conspiracies cooked up among her friends, colleagues, and competitors that led ultimately to her downfall. Too enamored of her reflection in the mirror, too obtuse to see through it, however dimly, Thatcher could not recognize that even she, the "Iron Lady," was trapped in the iron web and subject to its dictates and ironies. Are we then better or worse off for being aware of our social being and all its contradictions?

The extent to which we seek to ignore those contradictions and to feel good about being trapped might be best mirrored in Danny Boyle's immensely popular "Slumdog Millionaire," which won eight Academy Awards in February 2009. Ostensibly, that film is a "rag-to-riches" story, a retelling of the Horatio Alger myth in which a slick plot and Fortuna turn an impoverished boy from the slums of Mumbai into a widely hailed millionaire.[5] While Jamal Malik's life is a string of horrific and vivid illustrations of the condition of the poorest of the poor and most oppressed of the oppressed in India (and Jamal is Muslim, to boot), the American audience for whom the film was made must not be allowed to feel too badly about either those conditions or the United States' possible role in their creation.[6] How else to avoid losing money on the film, then, but by conjuring up a miraculous conclusion, albeit one whose probability is infinitesimal (or, as it is expressed in calculus, "the limit as x approaches zero")? Put another way, this film is an "opiate for the masses" (which is not only a phrase from Marx but also the name of a Phoenix-based rock band).

"The Matrix" is not guilt free in this respect either. Audience members are led to fear that alien, omniscient, and technologically advanced Others control both individual and human destiny (and who is to say they are wrong, even now?). Those Others could be very human, or they could be machines or corporations or states or . . . who knows what? Rather than being repulsed and staying away, however, we film consumers flock to them in droves, eager and willing to buy the product, largely oblivious of our own imprisonment in a Matrix of our own making that we support only too happily with our currencies.[7] As consumers of a slyly self-knowing exposé of our collective condition and observers of a film full of special effects that not only sell a product but also incite us to break out of the iron web in which we are trapped, we are being inducted into a kind of false consciousness that tells us to pay no attention to our own alienation. In the brilliant reflection of Neo's adventures, both "real" and virtual, we see such truth only dimly through the screen. Of the many special effects in "The Matrix," this last one might be the greatest of them all.

Notes

Chapter 1: Political Economy, Capitalism, and Popular Culture

1. Throughout this book, film and television titles are enclosed in scare quotes (" "), while book titles appear in italics. Where I cite both book and film, I use italics. Also, because detailed film and novel plot synopses are now widely available on the Internet (see both the Internet Movie Database at www.imdb.com and Wikipedia at http://en.wikipedia.org/wiki/Main_Page), I provide only brief summaries, at most, throughout this book.

2. The "rational actor" model is foundational to neoclassical economics. It posits that individuals with complete information will always seek to maximize their self-interest, defined usually in terms of income or some comparable indicator. See chapters 4 and 5 for more details.

3. "Neoclassical economics" is often conflated with liberal economics and capitalism, although the three are not, strictly speaking, identical. See below and chapters 2 and 4.

4. See, e.g., Barbara Slavin and Milt Freudenheim, "For the Tories, None but 'Tina,'" *New York Times*, October 18, 1981, http://query.nytimes.com/gst/fullpage.html?sec=health&res=9F06E3DA1339F93BA25753C1A967948260&scp=4&sq=%22there%20is%20no%20alternative%22%20thatcher&st=cse (accessed March 2, 2009).

5. Michael Hardt and Antonio Negri, *Empire* (Cambridge, MA: Harvard University Press); Michael Hardt and Antonio Negri, *Multitude: War and Democracy in the Age of Empire* (New York: Penguin, 2004).

6. Max Weber, *The Protestant Ethic and the Spirit of Capitalism*, trans. Talcott Parsons (New York: Scribner's, 1958), 181. The original German term is *stahlhartes Gehäuse*, which others have translated as "steel-hard cage."

7. Robert Sullivan, "Karl Marx (1818–1883)," The Victorian Web, 1988, revised 2007, www.victorianweb.org/philosophy/phil2.html (accessed December 27, 2008).

8. Films critical of capitalism, such as those of Michael Moore, consequently tend to play on viewers' resentments rather than highlighting the contradictions and structures that produce the absurd situations that he showcases so provocatively.

9. I do not want to make too much of the Wachowski brothers' critique of capitalism in "The Matrix"; Zion, as it appears in the first film's sequels, is closer to a liberal, multicultural utopia than an anticapitalist revolutionary society.

10. Eric R. Wolf, *Europe and the People without History* (Berkeley: University of California Press, 1982), ch. 3.

11. The literature is vast; for a brief introduction, see, e.g., E. Roy Weintraub, "Neoclassical Economics," in *The Concise Encyclopedia of Economics*, Library of Economics and Liberty, 2002, www.econlib.org/library/Enc1/NeoclassicalEconomics .html (accessed March 2, 2009).

12. *Naturalization*, as I use the term here, implies that we take something to be "natural," or outside of our control, even if that something is "social" and can be changed.

13. Or in Karl Polanyi's words, "Laissez-faire was planned; planning was not." *The Great Transformation*, new ed. (Boston: Beacon, 2001), 147.

14. Originally "economics" was known as "political economy," a usage dropped during the later nineteenth century. Today, the term *positive political economy* is associated with rational choice and game theory. In Robert Cox's terms, "critical political economy," which is on offer in this book, is "concerned with the historically constituted frameworks or structures within which political and economic activity takes place. It stands back from the apparent fixity of the present to ask how the existing structures came into being and how they may be changing." See Robert Cox, "Critical Political Economy," in *International Political Economy: Understanding Global Disorder*, ed. Robert Cox and Bjorn Hettne (London: Zed Books, 1995).

15. Peter Drahos, with John Braithwaite, *Information Feudalism: Who Owns the Knowledge Economy* (London: Earthscan, 2003). Power is much more nuanced than this statement suggests; see, e.g., Michael Barnett and Raymond Duvall, eds., *Power and Global Governance* (Cambridge: Cambridge University Press, 2005); and Ronnie D. Lipschutz, with James K. Rowe, *Globalization, Governmentality and Global Politics: Regulation for the Rest of Us* (London: Routledge, 2005).

16. "Common sense" comprises the "diffuse, unco-ordinated features of a general form of thought common to a particular period and a particular popular environment," and "its most fundamental characteristic is that it is a conception which, even in the brain of one individual, is fragmentary, incoherent and inconsequential, in conformity with the social and cultural position of those masses whose philosophy it is." *Selections from the Prison Notebooks of Antonio Gramsci*, ed. and trans. Q. Hoare and G. Nowell Smith (London: Lawrence and Wishart, 1971), 330n, 419. See also Mark Rupert, *Producing Hegemony: The Politics of Mass Production and American Global Power* (Cambridge: Cambridge University Press, 1995).

17. The 1960s TV series "The Prisoner" explored the mysteries of imprisonment and order. On "Lost," see J. Wood, *Living Lost: Why We're All Stuck on the Island* (New

Orleans, LA: Garrett County Press, 2007). On "Survivor," see Matthew J. Smith and Andrew F. Wood, eds., *Survivor Lessons: Essays on Communication and Reality Television* (Jefferson, NC: McFarland and Company, 2003).

18. Note that this song originated as an advertising jingle for Coca-Cola and was only subsequently turned into a hit song. The commercial can be found on YouTube at www.youtube.com/watch?v=ib-Qiyklq-Q (accessed May 26, 2009).

19. Is this an allusion to Robert McNamara, president of the Ford Motor Company before becoming John F. Kennedy's secretary of defense?

20. We might, however, impute morality to the agents "behind" the bottle or to the effects of the bottle's contents on the drinker, be they chemical or flammable. The bottle is an object, not a subject. See chapter 2.

21. Patricia Cohen, "Jean Baudrillard, 77, Critic and Theorist of Hyperreality, Dies," *New York Times*, March 7, 2007, www.nytimes.com/2007/03/07/books/07baudrillard .html (accessed March 9, 2009). An interesting critique of "The Matrix" and Baudrillard can be found in Richard Hanley, "Simulacra and Simulation: Baudrillard and *The Matrix*," Philosophy and the Matrix, November 20, 2002, http://whatisthematrix .warnerbros.com/rl_cmp/new_phil_fr_hanley2.html (accessed March 2, 2009).

22. For a discussion of how norms of war are internalized through everyday socialization, see Vivienne Jabri, *War and the Transformation of Global Politics* (Houndsmill, Basingstoke, UK: Palgrave Macmillan, 2007).

23. Ronnie D. Lipschutz, *Cold War Fantasies: Film, Fiction and Foreign Policy* (Lanham, MD: Rowman & Littlefield, 2001). It is instructive to note that the most popular foreign films are those that integrate common tropes and ideas found in American life; increasingly, successful foreign films and television shows are being remade for specifically American audiences (often with disappointing results). Even so, commercial success is by no means guaranteed.

24. The film "Roman Holiday" (1953), starring Audrey Hepburn and Gregory Peck, was filmed on location in Rome rather than on a Hollywood set precisely so that the audience could see the city.

25. Tom Zaniello, *The Cinema of Globalization: A Guide to Films about the New Economic Order* (Ithaca, NY: Cornell University Press, 2007); Cynthia Weber, *Imagining America at War: Morality, Politics, and Film* (London: Routledge, 2006).

26. Timothy Murray, *Like a Film: Ideological Fantasy on Screen, Camera and Canvas* (London: Routledge, 1993).

27. Charles C. Moul, *A Concise Handbook of Movie Industry Economics* (Cambridge: Cambridge University Press, 2005); Jason E. Squire, ed., *The Movie Business Book* (New York: Simon and Schuster, 2006).

28. Well, this is not precisely correct. Right-wing scold David Horowitz seems to think I am a dangerous ideologue. Would that this were the case. See David Horowitz and Jacob Laksin, *One-Party Classroom: How Radical Professors at America's Top Colleges Indoctrinate Students and Undermine Our Democracy* (New York: Random House, 2009).

29. This is the notion that beliefs and ideas influence practices and outcomes, and vice versa; see Anthony Giddens, *Social Theory and Modern Sociology* (Cambridge, UK: Polity Press, 1987).

30. I understand a *discourse* as an integrated, although not always internally consistent, framework of normative beliefs, associated practices, and material infrastructures. This definition differs somewhat from that, in particular, of Michel Foucault and others. The basic notion here is that people subscribe to the particular beliefs and causal arguments of a discourse and act on them. Their action produces and reproduces a material base that feeds back to confirm the validity of the beliefs, arguments, and practices. A discourse thus generates "truths," although it is not a generator of the Truth, whatever that might be. See Stuart Hall, "The West and the Rest: Discourse and Power," in *Modernity: An Introduction to Modern Societies*, ed. Stuart Hall et al., 184–227 (Cambridge: Polity, 1995).

31. Sullivan, "Karl Marx."

32. According to Bruno Latour, *actant* is "a term from semiotics [that refers to] . . . any entity that modifies another entity in a trial." See Bruno Latour and Catherine Porter, *Politics of Nature: How to Bring the Sciences into Democracy* (Cambridge, MA: Harvard University Press, 2004), 237. To put this more clearly, it is something that causes an agent to act, for example, a light pole in the path of a car causes the driver to swerve (we hope).

33. George Simmel, *The Philosophy of Money*, trans. Tom Bottomore and David Frisby (London: Routledge and Kegan Paul, 1978).

34. Actually, there is considerable debate about this point. Some historians argue that forms of capitalism appeared much earlier in human history than fourteenth- to fifteenth-century Europe, although investment and speculation were not characteristics of those systems. See Max Weber, *General Economic History*, trans. F. H. Knight (1923; rpt. New York: Collier-Macmillan, 1961).

35. Nicholas G. Onuf, *World of Our Making: Rules and Rule in Social Theory and International Relations* (Columbia: University of South Carolina Press, 1989).

36. "But in the short run some of us can't get buried [in the ground] because of the credit crunch"; see Paul Krugman, "In the Long Run We Are All Dead," *New York Times*, October 12, 2008, http://krugman.blogs.nytimes.com/2008/10/12/in-the-long-run-we-are-all-dead (accessed January 27, 2009). What Keynes actually said was, "The long run is a misleading guide to current affairs. In the long run we are all dead."

Chapter 2: Money and Desire

1. One exception is a "cap-and-trade" system designed to commodify the "right to pollute." See Ronnie D. Lipschutz, *Global Environmental Politics: Power, Perspectives, and Practice* (Washington, DC: CQ Press, 2003).

2. My discussion of "money" here is fairly impoverished and mainstream. In fact, money is very complex. See, e.g., Jane I. Guyer, "Cash Economies" (December 2007 draft paper for the conference titled "Rethinking Economic Anthropology: A Human Centered Approach," London School of Economics, January 11–12, 2008), www.rethinkingeconomies.org.uk/web/d/doc_87.pdf (accessed March 10, 2009). For a

more detailed and nuanced discussion, see Jane I. Guyer, *Marginal Gains: Monetary Transactions in Atlantic Africa* (Chicago: University of Chicago Press, 2004); and Viviana Zelizer, *The Social Meaning of Money* (Princeton, NJ: Princeton University Press, 1997).

3. See, e.g., George Simmel, *The Philosophy of Money*, trans. Tom Bottomore and David Frisby (London: Routledge and Kegan Paul, 1978).

4. John F. Chown, *A History of Money: From AD 800* (London: Routledge, 1994); Alan Ryan, *Property* (Minneapolis: University of Minnesota Press, 1987).

5. A "hard" currency can be exchanged for other currencies and vice versa; a "soft" currency can generally be used only in the country of issue. But hard currencies can become soft, and vice versa, too. See Guyer, "Cash Economies."

6. For photos of nontraditional uses of hyperinflated currencies, see www.bits ofnews.com/images/graphics/economy/weimar2.jpg (accessed January 2, 2009). On Zimbabwe, see Sebastien Berger, "Zimbabwe Hyperinflation 'Will Set World Record within Six Weeks,'" *Telegraph,* November 13, 2008, www.telegraph.co.uk/news/world news/africaandindianocean/zimbabwe/3453540/Zimbabwe-hyperinflation-will-set-world-record-within-six-weeks.html (accessed March 10, 2009). In Neal Stephenson's *Snow Crash*, discussed in chapter 5, such hyperinflation has happened in the United States, whose currency is virtually worthless. Trillion-dollar bills are called "Meeses," while quadrillion-dollar bills are "Gippers." Those who do not recognize the allusions should look up *Snow Crash* on Wikipedia.

7. Michael Thompson, *Rubbish Theory: The Creation and Destruction of Value* (Oxford: Oxford University Press, 1979).

8. Of course, goods cost something to mine, make, or manufacture, but it is generally assumed that going through the effort of making a thing takes place in response to some kind of demand or desire for it. As we shall see, demand often must be created.

9. Edward Jay Epstein, "Have You Ever Tried to Sell a Diamond?" *The Atlantic,* February 1982, www.theatlantic.com/doc/198202/diamond (accessed February 1, 2009).

10. There is considerable debate over whether the world has reached, or is about to reach, "peak oil," the point at which global oil production begins to decline. See Kenneth S. Deffeyes, *Hubbert's Peak: The Impending World Oil Shortage* (Princeton, NJ: Princeton University Press, 2001). According to Michael Klare, the Energy Information Administration (EIA) of the U.S. Department of Energy has now gone over to the "peak oil" side; see "Goodbye to Cheap Oil," Tomdispatch.com, June 11, 2009, http://tomdispatch.com/?month=2009-6 (accessed June 21, 2009). The EIA report is "International Energy Outlook 2009," EIA, May 27, 2009, www.eia.doe.gov/oiaf/ieo/highlights.html (accessed June 21, 2009).

11. Ronnie D. Lipschutz, *The Constitution of Imperium* (Boulder, CO: Paradigm, 2008), ch. 6.

12. A "reserve currency" is a hard currency that is internationally accepted as legal tender, freely exchangeable for other currencies, and in sufficient supply to meet demand for it outside the country that prints or creates it.

13. "Big Winner from Plunge in Sterling," *New York Times*, October 27, 1992, http://query.nytimes.com/gst/fullpage.html?res=9E0CE1D7143EF934A15753C1A964 958260&scp=3&sq=soros%20pound&st=cse (accessed March 10, 2009).

14. A 1963 episode of *The Twilight Zone*, "I Dream of Genie," has the lamp's finder deciding that none of the conventional wishes produce happiness. He therefore wishes himself to become the genie, which allows him to give others happiness.

15. This is the title of an early Chaplin film (1917). "Living the Life of Riley" was a popular equivalent expression during the twentieth century and was based on the nineteenth-century poems of James Whitcomb Riley, who extolled the virtues of an orderly and prosperous home life. Some argue, however, that the phrase came from the Reilly clan of County Cavan in Ireland, which lived well and minted its own money (see the entry in Wikipedia, http://en.wikipedia.org/wiki/The_Life_of_Riley).

16. Mick LaSalle, *Complicated Women: Sex and Power in Pre-Code Hollywood* (New York: Thomas Dunne, 2000).

17. In fact, this was the "second" Gulf war, the first being that between Iran and Iraq during the 1980s.

18. In order to avoid some of the inconveniences of having to actually move large sums of coin and bullion, merchants and traders developed letters of credit, which allowed accounts to be settled locally. But national money supplies depended on the quantity of gold or silver in circulation and storage. See Liaquat Ahamed, *The Lords of Finance: The Bankers Who Broke the World* (New York: Penguin, 2009).

19. Joseph A. Ritter, "The Transition from Barter to Fiat Money," *American Economic Review*, March 1995, http://research.stlouisfed.org/wp/1994/94-004.pdf (accessed February 1, 2009). A typical dismissal of fiat money can be found in Darryl Schoon, "The United States Fiat Money and the Federal Reserve System," Financial Sense University, June 23, 2008, www.financialsense.com/fsu/editorials/schoon/2008/0623.html (accessed February 1, 2009).

20. This is not to suggest that only states were in the business of creating money; generally speaking, only states or their authorized agents were legally permitted to do so. Today, "money" is created every time you use a credit card—even though it will eventually become "real" if and when you pay the bill.

21. In fact, reductions in the U.S. federal funds rate to a "range" between 0 and 0.25 percent in late 2008 means that it is now possible for large enterprises to borrow money almost for "free"—although banks are not very willing to make loans to even the most solvent of debtors. This has more to do with banks' uncertainties about whether or not they are solvent than an absolute scarcity of money for lending.

22. In brief, Keynesian economics involves stimulating economic growth through injection of funds into circulation (as opposed to using interest rates to manage the money supply).

23. See, e.g., Charles P. Kindleberger, *Keynesianism vs. Monetarism: And Other Essays in Financial History* (London: Taylor and Francis, 2006).

24. That is, that part of the economy that is surveyed and measured; private interest rates (i.e., from loan sharks, "payday-loan" operators, and credit card issuers) are generally much higher than public ones. See William F. Maloney, "Informality Revisited," *World Development* 32, no. 7 (2004): 1159–78.

25. See Federal Reserve Bank of San Francisco, "U.S. Monetary Policy: An Introduction," 2004, www.frbsf.org/publications/federalreserve/monetary/Monetary-Policy.pdf (accessed March 10, 2009).

26. An excellent and comprehensive online survey of the causes and consequences of this "Great Recession" can be found at David Hendrickson, "The Overall Idea," *Cause for Depression*, October 30, 2008, https://lodgeus.com/cgi-bin/nph-gowingo.cgi/000010A/http/pictorial-guide-to-crisis.blogspot.com (accessed March 10, 2009).

27. A useful distinction can be made here between "liquid money" and "capital." The former denotes that which is available for spending at short notice; the latter, funds for, or tied up in, longer-term investments, including various forms of paper, goods, skills, and technology. I tend to conflate the two here.

28. Oddly, this is related to John Locke's argument about property: that into which one puts labor. Locke also argued, however, that anything created by a servant is owned by the master. Similarly, anything created or done "for hire" belongs to the employer who pays for the labor and not to the employee. See the discussion of intellectual property in chapter 3.

29. Jonathan Nitzan and Shimshon Bichler provide a much deeper and thought-provoking look into the money and value question in *Capital as Power* (London: Routledge, 2009).

30. Other difficulties would also arise were everyone in a capitalist system to receive identical wages whatever their work. These are not addressed here.

31. In the old Soviet Bloc and other places, setting wages based on some standard metric led to what we might regard as paradoxical outcomes—tram drivers being paid more than college professors—and various forms of corruption as people sought to increase their incomes.

32. The closure of retailers across a wide range of goods and services in 2008 and 2009 illustrates what happens when consumers refuse to spend or to pay posted prices. The lengths to which businesses will go in order to cover at least some of their costs can be seen in Jack Healy, "Desperate Retailers Try Frantic Discounts and Giveaways," *New York Times*, January 3, 2009, www.nytimes.com/2009/01/03/business/media/03marketing.html (accessed January 3, 2009).

33. Blue chips are the highest denomination in poker, and a blue-chip stock is assumed to be a safe and reliable investment whose value will remain relatively stable while it pays out regular dividends.

34. Note here that the share price of the stock or security may not actually reflect the "true" value of the underlying asset or company. Since share price is the aggregate of buyers' and sellers' estimates of the future flow of *profits* to the enterprise, a low or declining estimate will drive down the share price to a point below the material value of that fraction of the company represented by the share.

35. In fact, asset inflation and asset bubbles are fairly common throughout the history of capitalism; see, e.g., Peter M. Garber, *Famous First Bubbles* (Cambridge, MA: MIT Press, 2000); and Maureen O'Hara, "Bubbles: Some Perspectives (and Loose Talk) from History," *Review of Financial Studies* 21, no. 1 (2008): 11–17.

36. Susan Strange, *Mad Money* (Manchester, UK: Manchester University Press, 1998).

37. Is there not something curious about this locution, especially if the money "at work" was made from the work of others?

38. Susan Strange, *Casino Capitalism* (Manchester, UK: Manchester University Press, 1997).

39. The Khan Academy (www.khanacademy.org/#Credit Crisis) offers a series of very useful short videos on the current financial crisis. See also Hendrickson, "The Overall Idea," *Cause for Depression*.

40. "Glengarry Glen Ross" (1992), based on a play by David Mamet, offers insights into real estate boiler rooms, which are not that dissimilar from other financial boiler operations.

41. Gekko was apparently modeled on three well-known speculators of the time: Ivan Boesky, Carl Icahn, and Michael Milken. Only Icahn has not been indicted, tried, and jailed for fraud. At this writing, a sequel called "Wall Street 2: Money Never Sleeps" is due in theaters in 2010.

42. But see Robert Solow, "Trapped in the New 'You're on Your Own' World," *New York Review of Books*, November 20, 2008, 79–81.

43. J. M. Brown, "Renowned Soquel Author John Robbins Says He Lost Life Savings in Madoff Scheme," *San Jose Mercury News*, January 23, 2009, www.mercury news.com/ci_11536788 (accessed February 2, 2009); Gerald Strober, *Catastrophe: The Story of Bernard L. Madoff, the Man Who Swindled the World* (Beverly Hills, CA: Phoenix Books, 2009).

44. The term *bonfire of the vanities* refers to the fifteenth-century Italian practice of burning objects deemed to figure in the commission of sin, such as books, pictures, mirrors, clothing, cosmetics, and so on. Here, of course, it means something slightly different.

45. See, e.g., "Bonds," AARP.org, www.aarp.org/money/financial_planning/session six/bonds.html (accessed March 11, 2009); and Clifford Smith, "Bonds," *The Concise Encyclopedia of Economics*, www.econlib.org/library/Enc/Bonds.html (accessed March 11, 2009).

46. Bonds are ranked on the basis of the reliability of revenue flows to, and likelihood of repayment by, the issuer. A triple-A bond is the gold standard; a D-rated bond is pretty much worthless. See, e.g., Glenn Yago, "Junk Bonds," *The Concise Encyclopedia of Economics*, Library of Economics and Liberty, 2008, www.econlib.org/library/Enc/JunkBonds.html (accessed January 3, 2009). As to how bonds are rated, see Timothy J. Sinclair, *The New Masters of Capital: American Bond Rating Agencies and the Politics of Creditworthiness* (Ithaca, NY: Cornell University Press, 2005).

47. Tom Wolfe, *The Bonfire of the Vanities* (New York: Farrar, Straus and Giroux, 1987), 229.

48. Louise Story, "On Wall Street, Bonuses, Not Profits, Were Real," *New York Times*, December 17, 2008, www.nytimes.com/2008/12/18/business/18pay.html (accessed January 3, 2009).

49. Thompson, *Rubbish Theory*.

50. "Just deserts" is that which is justly (or legally) deserved.

51. Scott Carney, "Why a Kidney (Street Value: $3,000) Sells for $85,000," *Wired*, May 8, 2007, www.wired.com/medtech/health/news/2007/05/india_trans

plants_prices (accessed January 5, 2009); D. A. Budiani-Saberi and F. L. Delmonico, "Organ Trafficking and Transplant Tourism: A Commentary on the Global Realities," *American Journal of Transplantation* 8, no. 5 (May 2008): 925–29.

52. Andrew Blankstein and Charles Ornstein, "2 Men Charged in Sale of Donated Bodies," *Los Angeles Times*, March 8, 2007, http://articles.latimes.com/2007/mar/08/local/me-willed8 (accessed February 3, 2009).

53. The possibility of cultivating organs from stem cells or even clones has also been proposed. See Kazuo Ishiguro, *Never Let Me Go* (New York: Knopf, 2005), and the film "The Island" (2005).

54. Fred Hirsch, *Social Limits to Growth* (Cambridge, MA: Harvard University Press, 1976).

55. "A Diamond Is Forever," *San Francisco Chronicle*, November 28, 2008, A30.

56. For anyone puzzled by "Lexi" and "Camrus," note that I am simply applying rules of singular and plural here.

57. Moreover, a commercial pedicure can also lead to serious health problems. See, e.g., Lawrence K. Altman, "Microbe in Salon Footbath Is Suspected in Boil Outbreak," *New York Times*, April 27, 2001, http://query.nytimes.com/gst/fullpage.html?sec=hea lth&res=9404E7DA1339F934A15757C0A9679C8B63&scp=2&sq=pedicure%20infect ion&st=cse (accessed January 6, 2009).

58. Kenneth Arrow, "The Economics of Information: An Exposition," *Empirica* 23, no. 2 (1996): 119–28; quote is on 125.

Chapter 3: Bodies and Possessions

1. This is not to argue that markets are not as old as human civilization. Forms of capitalism have appeared throughout history, but they have never been oriented toward accumulation for investment and future returns. It is the process of accumulation of capital for reinvestment and further accumulation that is unique. See Ellen Meiksins Wood, *The Origin of Capitalism: A Longer View* (London: Verso, 2003). For a fascinating discussion of the trans–Indian Ocean economy prior to Western colonization, see Amitav Ghosh, *In an Antique Land: History in the Guise of a Traveler's Tale* (New York: Knopf, 1993).

2. Eric R. Wolf, *Europe and the People without History* (Berkeley: University of California Press, 1982); Kees van der Pijl, *Nomads, Empires and States: Modes of Foreign Relations and Political Economy*, vol. 1 (London: Pluto, 2007).

3. Helen Macbeth, Wolf Schiefenhövel, and Paul Collinson, "Cannibalism: No Myth but Why So Rare?" in *Consuming the Inedible: Neglected Dimensions of Food Choice*, ed. Jeremy MacClancy, C. Jeya Henry, and Helen Macbeth, 198–204 (Providence, RI: Berghahn Books, 2007); Carlos Fausto, "Feasting on People: Eating Animals and Humans in Amazonia," *Current Anthropology* 48, no. 4 (August 2007): 497–530.

4. Organic agriculture and the local food movement try to overcome the mystification of food production, notwithstanding incessant pressures to "eat globally" year round.

5. "Commodity fetishism" refers to the "value" that commodities, including money, seem to have in lieu of the social relations and labor that actually inhere in the things themselves. It appears, however, that the term *body fetishism* is more generally used to apply to the "cult of the body," especially as related to health and fitness and among homosexual men.

6. Bonnie English, *A Cultural History of Fashion: From the Catwalk to the Sidewalk* (Oxford: Berg, 2007).

7. David Harvey, "The Body as an Accumulation Strategy," *Environment and Planning D: Society and Space* 16, no. 4 (1998): 401–21.

8. Paco Underhill, *Why We Buy: The Science of Shopping* (New York: Simon and Schuster, 1999); Malcolm Gladwell, "A Reporter at Large: The Science of Shopping," *The New Yorker,* November 4, 1996, www.gladwell.com/pdf/shopping.pdf (accessed March 12, 2009); and Lizabeth Cohen, *A Consumer's Republic: The Politics of Mass Consumption in Postwar America* (New York: Vintage, 2004).

9. The notion of "bare life" is from Giorgio Agamben, developed in *Homo Sacer: Sovereign Power and Bare Life,* trans. Daniel Heller-Roazen (Stanford, CA: Stanford University Press, 1998). In this instance, I use the term to refer to minimal consumption for basic survival.

10. This is not for lack of trying, however: both oxygen bars in Los Angeles and Tokyo and transferable carbon-emission permits as part of "cap-and-trade" schemes involve putting a price on air; see Ronnie D. Lipschutz, *Global Environmental Politics* (Washington, DC: CQ Press, 2003).

11. Michael Thompson, *Rubbish Theory: The Creation and Destruction of Value* (Oxford: Oxford University Press, 1979).

12. See, e.g., Gillian Tett, "Time Is Nigh to Put the True Value of CDOs Out in the Open," *Financial Times,* February 27, 2008, www.ft.com/cms/s/0/8f75443a-0470-11de-845b-000077b07658.html (accessed March 13, 2009).

13. In George Orwell's *Nineteen Eighty-Four,* Winston Smith is out in the street when he hears a commotion from nearby and thinks the proles are "breaking loose at last!" It turns out that he is witness to a fight among several women over the last of a limited supply of poorly made saucepans (New York: New American Library, 1983), 60–61.

14. Kenneth Arrow, "The Economics of Information: An Exposition," *Empirica* 23, no. 2 (1996): 119–28.

15. Matt Richtel, "A Sea of Unwanted Imports," *New York Times,* November 18, 2008, www.nytimes.com/2008/11/19/business/economy/19ports.html (accessed December 29, 2008).

16. See "Being Made Redundant," Direct Gov (UK), www.direct.gov.uk/en/Employment/RedundancyAndLeavingYourJob/DG_10026616 (accessed March 13, 2009). Note that this information is also available in Welsh at www.direct.gov.uk/cy/Employment/RedundancyAndLeavingYourJob/DG_10026616CY.

17. This is one reason why oligopoly—a few as opposed to many firms in a market—is preferred (if monopoly or cartel is illegal or impossible). Output is easier to manage, and thus supply and price can be better controlled.

18. Amy Dru Stanley, *From Bondage to Contract* (Cambridge: Cambridge University Press, 1998).

19. The individual without skills is nonetheless assumed to possess bodily strength that can be used for tasks that require nothing but human "horsepower." This does not, of course, take into account the weak, infirm, or unwilling—whom the English called the "deserving poor" but whom Americans always tend to regard with suspicion.

20. Jim Holt, "The Way We Live Now: 3–28–04; The Human Factor," *New York Times*, March 28, 2004, http://query.nytimes.com/gst/fullpage.html?res=9507EEDF 1730F93BA15750C0A9629C8B63 (accessed December 29, 2008). On the economic "value" of a human life, see, e.g., Kathleen Kingsbury, "The Value of a Human Life: $129,000," *Time*, May 20, 2008, www.time.com/time/health/article/0,8599,1808049,00. html (accessed March 13, 2009); and Peter Dorman, *Markets and Mortality: Economics, Dangerous Work, and the Value of Human Life* (Cambridge: Cambridge University Press, 1996). To calculate the "value" of your life, see the Human Life Value Calculator at www.lifehappens.org/life-insurance/human-life-value.

21. According to an apocryphal calculation by the long-defunct U.S. Bureau of Chemistry and Soils, the mineral content of the human body is worth about $5. But the composition by dehydrated weight of the body suggests that, in fact, we are composed primarily of hydrogen and carbon, neither of which is worth very much; see Michael Onken, "What Is the Elemental Composition of the Human Body?" MadSci Network, June 28, 2000, www.madsci.org/posts/archives/2000-06/962225341 .Bc.r.html (accessed December 29, 2008).

22. Marshall D. Sahlins, "The Original Affluent Society," in *Stone Age Economics* (1972; rpt. London: Routledge, 2004), 1–4.

23. van der Pijl, *Nomads, Empires and States*.

24. Mark Rupert, *Producing Hegemony: The Politics of Mass Production and American Global Power* (Cambridge: Cambridge University Press, 1995).

25. The locus classicus on individualism is C. B. Macpherson, *The Political Theory of Possessive Individualism: Hobbes to Locke* (Oxford: Oxford University Press, 1962).

26. See chapter 2, note 56 about Lexi and Camrus.

27. Caution! Men at work! Dare I point out that if men are out driving trucks, there is probably more work for the women left at home?

28. See, e.g., Sumiko Higashi, "*Invasion of the Body Snatchers*: Pods Then and Now," *Jump Cut* 24–25 (March 1981): 3–4, www.ejumpcut.org/archive/onlines says/JC24-25folder/InvasionBodySntch.html (accessed March 13, 2009).

29. Edward W. Younkins, "Rousseau's 'General Will' and Well-Ordered Society," *Le Québécois Libre* 156 (July 15, 2005), www.quebecoislibre.org/05/050715-16.htm (accessed March 13, 2009).

30. Recall that after 9/11, President George W. Bush encouraged American citizens to go shopping: "I ask your continued participation and confidence in the American economy." Address to the Nation, NewsAIC.com, September 20, 2001, http://newsaic. com/res92001.html (accessed February 4, 2009). On the emergence of the citizen-consumer, see Charles F. McGovern, *Sold American: Consumption and Citizenship,*

1890–1945 (Chapel Hill: University of North Carolina Press, 2006), and the citations in note 8, above.

31. Alison Brysk and Gershon Shafir, eds., *People Out of Place: Globalization, Human Rights and the Citizenship Gap* (New York: Routledge, 2004).

32. See Jonathan Nitzan and Shimshon Bichler, *Capital as Power* (London: Routledge, 2009).

33. Stanley, *From Bondage to Contract.*

34. As Rousseau put it, "The first man who, having enclosed a piece of ground, bethought himself of saying This is mine, and found people simple enough to believe him, was the real founder of civil society. From how many crimes, wars and murders, from how many horrors and misfortunes might not any one have saved mankind, by pulling up the stakes, or filling up the ditch, and crying to his fellows, 'Beware of listening to this impostor; you are undone if you once forget that the fruits of the earth belong to us all, and the earth itself to nobody'" (J. J. Rousseau, *Discourse on Inequality,* "The Second Part," 1754, www.constitution.org/jjr/ineq_04.htm [accessed June 15, 2009]).

35. See, e.g., Andrew Reeve, *Property* (Houndsmill, Basingstoke, UK: Macmillan, 1986); Alan Ryan, *Property* (Milton Keynes: Open University, 1987).

36. Stanley, *From Bondage to Contract.*

37. See, e.g., Diane Johnson, "In Love with Jane," *New York Review of Books* 52, no. 11 (June 23, 2005): 20–23.

38. For a discussion of the complexities of inheritance in earlier times, see, e.g., Gerald Harriss, *Shaping the Nation: England 1360–1461* (Oxford: Clarendon Press, 2005), 98–106, 136–48.

39. Stanley, *From Bondage to Contract.* This remains the case throughout much of the world even today.

40. Offred actually escapes to Canada, although why and with whose help is not made clear; see the "Historical Notes" section at the end of the book. Margaret Atwood, *The Handmaid's Tale* (New York: Anchor, 1998), 297–311.

41. See, e.g., Susan Harding, *The Book of Jerry Falwell* (Princeton, NJ: Princeton University Press, 2000).

42. Utopias and dystopias are never really about the future; they are always commentaries on society as it exists at the time of writing. See Ronnie D. Lipschutz, *Cold War Fantasies: Film, Fiction and Foreign Policy* (Lanham, MD: Rowman & Littlefield, 2001), 30–34.

43. American states retain this right in the form of capital punishment.

44. Margaret Davies and Ngaire Naffine, *Are Persons Property? Legal Debates about Property and Personality* (Aldershot, UK: Dartmouth-Ashgate, 2001), 79.

45. In chapter 8, I consider the violence inherent in the capitalist system and its practices and suggest that it might not be the "peaceful" realm we are conditioned to imagine it is. The "iron web" here is meant as an allusion to Max Weber's "iron cage." Recall that the original German term is *stahlhartes Gehäuse,* sometimes translated as "steel-hard cage."

46. This is hardly imaginary: the Department of Defense's Total Information Awareness office, subsequently renamed the Information Awareness Office, is tasked

with sifting through the myriad of electronic traces left by people in the global communications network in order to detect "dangerous" patterns; see also Ronnie D. Lipschutz, "Imperial Warfare in the Naked City: Sociality as Critical Infrastructure," *International Political Sociology* 3, no. 3 (September 2008): 204–18.

47. Herbert Marcuse, *One-Dimensional Man* (Boston: Beacon Press, 1964).

48. Mary Ann Tétreault and Ronnie D. Lipschutz, *Global Politics as If People Mattered*, 2nd ed. (Boulder, CO: Rowman & Littlefield, 2009), ch. 2.

49. This was, for a long time, the argument against extending the electoral franchise to those who did not own property: if the poor could vote, they would immediately confiscate the property of the rich. As we now know from experience, the poor do not seem to recognize this power—if, indeed, it exists. See, e.g., Thomas Frank, *What's the Matter with Kansas?* (New York: Holt, 2004).

50. Louise Amoore, "Vigilant Visualities: The Watchful Politics of the War on Terror," *Security Dialogue* 38, no. 2 (2007): 215–33.

51. Lyrics as recorded by Woody Guthrie, RCA Studios, Camden, NJ, April 26, 1940, released on "Dust Bowl Ballads," transcribed by Manfred Helfert. © 1958 Sanga Music Inc., New York, NY, at www.geocities.com/Nashville/3448/pretty.html (accessed February 5, 2009).

52. It should be pointed out that for those living in many parts of the world, such total deletion is more and more difficult, if not impossible, since the sheer number of recording and accounting devices that normally collect traces of anyone who comes within their purview makes it almost certain that such traces will be collected and stored.

53. The dream of dematerialization and disembodiment is central to Christian theology and what happens following death as well as after Armageddon.

54. The irony here is that in the absence of appropriate software, files "erased" or "deleted" are not actually eliminated from the recording medium and can often be recovered if necessary.

55. See note 46 above.

56. Recall that John Locke also argues that an employer owns the labor of his servant, a practice that continues today in "work for hire," by which whoever pays a wage owns that which the employee writes or makes.

57. Alan Hunt, "The Governance of Consumption: Sumptuary Laws and Shifting Forms of Regulation," *Economy and Society* 25, no. 3 (August 1996): 410–27.

58. Fred Hirsch, *Social Limits to Growth* (Cambridge, MA: Harvard University Press, 1976).

59. Nestor M. Davidson, "Property and Relative Status," *Michigan Law Review* 197, no. 5 (2009): 757–817.

60. Harvey, "The Body as an Accumulation Strategy."

61. Anthony Giddens, *Modernity and Self-identity: Self and Society in the Late Modern Age* (Stanford, CA: Stanford University Press, 1991); Stephen Greenblatt, "Culture," in *Critical Terms for Literary Study*, ed. Frank Lentricchia and Thomas McLaughlin, 2nd ed., 225–32 (Chicago: University of Chicago Press, 1995).

62. van der Pijl, *Nomads, Empires and States*; Benedict Anderson, *Imagined Communities*, 2nd ed. (London: Verso, 1991).

63. See, e.g., Arnold van Gennep, *The Rites of Passage*, trans. Monika Vizedom and Gabrielle L. Caffee (1908; rpt. London: Routledge, 2004).

64. I don't mean to single out bicyclists here, but they are very visible, especially in terms of machines and clothing.

65. The local yellow pages list some twenty-four bike shops in the "greater" Santa Cruz area, whose population is less than two hundred thousand.

66. See, e.g., Avelle, at www.bagborroworsteal.com, or From Bags to Riches, at www.frombagstoriches.com/rentbag/pc/index.asp (both accessed on March 13, 2009).

67. Recall the U.S. Army's "Army of One" advertisements from 2001 to 2006.

68. The script of "Fight Club," including this exchange, can be found at www.imsdb.com/scripts/Fight-Club.html (accessed June 25, 2009).

69. The food riots of recent years are motivated mostly by higher prices for basic staples, on the one hand, and shortages of those staples as a result of hoarding in the face of low official prices, on the other. As is often the case, the problem is distributional and involves people's lack of income, not absolute local or global food scarcity. But see Javier Blas, "Number of Hungry Worldwide Tops 1bn," FT.com, June 19, 2009, www.ft.com/cms/s/0/f6496490-5cca-11de-9d42-00144feabdc0.html (accessed June 21, 2009).

70. In a classic line that should give shivers to academics, Sol says, "I used to be respected. I was a professor!"

71. As noted earlier, cannibalism was probably a rarity in human societies; see Macbeth, Schiefenhövel, and Collinson, "Cannibalism"; Fausto, "Feasting on People."

72. On the first point, Simon believed that human ingenuity and innovation could solve any problem; on the second, he argued that resources were becoming more plentiful, as indicated by a decline in their cost, and that, should a resource become absolutely scarce and expensive, substitutions would be discovered. See Julian L. Simon, *The Ultimate Resource 2* (Princeton, NJ: Princeton University Press, 1998).

73. A more recent discussion of a nonsocialist cornucopian utopia can be found in Bill Joy, "Why the Future Doesn't Need Us," *Wired* 8, no. 4 (April 2000), www.wired.com/wired/archive/8.04/joy.html (accessed May 20, 2009).

74. Karl Polanyi, *The Great Transformation*, new ed. (Boston: Beacon Press, 2001), 3.

75. Need I add that this is much like Jonathan Swift's "A Modest Proposal?" See the text at http://art-bin.com/art/omodest.html (accessed May 28, 2009).

Chapter 4: Development and Motion

1. Aristotle, *Metaphysics*, Book 1, Part 4, trans. W. D. Ross, http://classics.mit.edu/Aristotle/metaphysics.1.i.html (accessed March 16, 2009).

2. In some ways, neoclassical economists are closer to molecular (micro) biologists, while critical theorists more resemble ecological and evolutionary (macro) biologists and even ecologists. An interesting discussion which contrasts micro and macro

explanations for human behaviors is Robert Caruana, "A Sociological Perspective of Consumption Morality," *Journal of Consumer Behaviour* 6 (2007): 287–304.

3. Adam Smith, *An Inquiry into the Nature and Causes of the Wealth of Nations*, ed. Edwin Cannan, 5th ed. (London: Methuen and Company, 1904), I.2.1. Smith's argument that it is "natural" to truck and barter is another example of how such claims become so deeply embedded and naturalized that they are rarely, if ever, questioned. There is nothing in human biology to prove conclusively that exchange in markets is "natural" behavior.

4. Smith, *Wealth of Nations*, I.1.3.

5. David Ricardo, *On the Principles of Political Economy and Taxation*, 3rd ed. (London: John Murray, Albemarle-Street, 1821).

6. See, e.g., Jagdish Bhagwati, *Free Trade Today* (Princeton, NJ: Princeton University Press, 2003).

7. Such trade does not actually take place because, as a general rule, coal-mining companies do not manufacture televisions in order to obtain coal, although it is not impossible that different divisions of the same company might do both. Indeed, much of international trade involves movement of similar products, such as automobiles, which differ in quality, style, and reliability.

8. An excellent and insightful set of articles by Katherine Boo examines these various factors; see "The Churn: Creative Destruction in a Border Town," *The New Yorker*, March 29, 2004, 62–73; "The Best Job in Town: The Americanization of Chennai," *The New Yorker*, July 5, 2004, 54–69. Both articles can be found on the Internet.

9. The first version of this chapter was written when oil was peaking at around $150 per barrel; the penultimate version, when the price had collapsed to around $40 per barrel. As I edit in June 2009, the price has risen to around $70 per barrel. None of this really has had very much to do with relative scarcity. The spike of 2008 and the collapse of 2009 are due to the rise and fall of demand because of the economic downturn as well as speculative activity in oil futures.

10. During its history, the Organization of Petroleum Exporting Countries has had trouble controlling oil production and the price of oil. Arab oil-producing countries, who control the vast majority of the world's oil, have tried to embargo shipments to the West—most notably in 1973 and 1974—but only with limited success. For a long and sometimes-turgid history of global oil politics, see Daniel Yergin, *The Prize: The Epic Quest for Oil, Money and Power* (New York: Simon and Schuster, 1991). A more recent interesting and focused history is Robert Vitalis, *America's Kingdom: Mythmaking on the Saudi Oil Frontier* (Stanford, CA: Stanford University Press, 2006). There seems not to have been anything published comparable to Anthony Sampson's *The Seven Sisters: The Great Oil Companies and the World They Shaped* (New York: Bantam, 1980) since the mid-1970s, although the Internet is rife with useful (and sometimes accurate) material.

11. On the "resource curse" see Andrew Rosser, "The Political Economy of the Resource Curse" (working paper 268, Institute of Development Studies, University of Sussex, United Kingdom, April 2006), www.ids.ac.uk/ids/bookshop/wp/wp268.pdf (accessed March 16, 2009); and Dwyer Gunn, "Navigating the Natural Resource

Curse," *New York Times*, May 26, 2009, http://freakonomics.blogs.nytimes
.com/2009/05/26/navigating-the-natural-resource-curse (accessed May 26, 2009).

12. Michael Watts, *Silent Violence: Food, Famine and Peasantry in Northern Nigeria* (Berkeley: University of California Press, 1983).

13. See, e.g., Kenneth S. Deffeyes, *Hubbert's Peak: The Impending World Oil Shortage* (Princeton, NJ: Princeton University Press, 2001).

14. Matthew Paterson, *Automobile Politics* (Cambridge: Cambridge University Press, 2007).

15. See, e.g., Kingsley Dennis and John Urry, "The Digital Nexus of Post-Automobility," Department of Sociology, Lancaster University, United Kingdom, at www.lancs.ac.uk/fass/centres/cemore/word%20docs/Digital%20Nexus%20of%20Post-Automobility.pdf (accessed June 11, 2009).

16. Edward Said, *Orientalism* (New York: Pantheon, 1978).

17. Adam Hochschild, *King Leopold's Ghost: A Story of Greed, Terror, and Heroism in Colonial Africa* (New York: Houghton Mifflin, 1998).

18. See, e.g., Aijaz Ahmand, *In Theory: Classes, Nations, Literatures* (London: Verso, 1992); and Said, *Orientalism*.

19. Harry Turtledove's *Colonization* series, which pitches invading lizards intent on colonizing Earth against valiant humans, offers an interesting, if long and turgid, gloss on this fear.

20. Gilbert Rist, *The History of Development from Western Origins to Global Faith* (London: Zed, 1997).

21. Joseph E. Stiglitz, *Globalization and Its Discontents* (New York: Norton, 2002); Amartya Sen, *Development as Freedom* (New York: Knopf, 1999). See also John Isbister, *Capitalism and Justice: Envisioning Social and Economic Justice* (Sterling, VA: Kumarian Press, 2001).

22. It is also worth noting that such explanations draw heavily on nineteenth-century Social Darwinism, which posited the existence of "superior" races and nations and their domination over "inferior" ones. Today, racialism has been replaced by economism. This point is addressed in chapter 8.

23. Rist, *History of Development*; Wolfgang Sachs, *The Development Dictionary: A Guide to Knowledge as Power* (London: Zed Books, 1993).

24. Note that this explanation is not universally accepted. Moreover, there is at least some indication that those countries that have done the best in the development race have had special access to American aid, investment, and consumers.

25. See, however, the warnings about the consequences of excessive domestic investment in Keith Bradsher, "Data Shows China Relies More on Growth at Home," *New York Times*, June 11, 2009, www.nytimes.com/2009/06/11/business/global/11yuan.html (accessed June 11, 2009).

26. This is reminiscent of what I call the "Yugo paradox," after a cheap, poorly made car built in, and exported from, Yugoslavia during the 1980s. The car eventually proved to be no competition for the South Korean Hyundai, which cost about the same but was far better built and more reliable.

27. See, e.g., Edmund Burke, "Ninth Report from the Select Committee (of the House of Commons) Appointed to Take into Consideration the State of the Admin-

istration of Justice in the Provinces of Bengal, Bargar, and Orissa–&c. (25 June 1783)," in *The Works of the Right Honorable Edmund Burke*, vol. 2 (London: Holdsworth and Ball, 1834).

28. Although one might argue that this surplus value is akin to a "rent" paid by the worker for the use of the capitalist's means of production, much as one might rent a trencher in order to dig a sewer trench, which would then be "owned" by the person who did the digging, not the owner of the trencher.

29. Karl Polanyi, *The Great Transformation*, new ed. (Boston: Beacon Press, 2001).

30. According to Waldron H. Giles, PhD, in 2006 the current value of African American slave labor amounted to $20.3 trillion. See "Slavery and the American Economy," *ChickenBones: A Journal*, February 17, 2006, www.nathanielturner.com/slaveryandtheamericaneconomy.htm (accessed March 16, 2009). Depending on one's assumptions—10 hours of work per day for 300 days per year, 500,000 slaves, 200 years of slavery, $8/per hour wage, plus accrued interest at 5 percent over 150 years—this seems plausible, if perhaps too low.

31. "Blood diamonds" are sometimes also called "conflict diamonds." According to the United Nations, "Conflict diamonds are diamonds that originate from areas controlled by forces or factions opposed to legitimate and internationally recognized governments, and are used to fund military action in opposition to those governments, or in contravention of the decisions of the Security Council." From United Nations Department of Public Information, "Conflict Diamonds: Sanctions and War," United Nations, March 21, 2001, www.un.org/peace/africa/Diamond.html (accessed March 16, 2009). This might be too narrow a definition, however, since legal governments have also been known to sell diamonds to fund their very bloody violence and wars.

32. See Greg Campbell, *Blood Diamonds: Tracing the Deadly Path of the World's Most Precious Stones* (New York: Basic Books, 2002).

33. "Background," KimberleyProcess.com, www.kimberleyprocess.com/background/index_en.html (accessed March 16, 2009). Note that when I first consulted the website, at www.kimberleyprocess.com/faqs/index_en.html, during the summer of 2008, it was reported that conflict diamonds represented less than 0.1 percent of the world's supply. About 130 million carats (57,000 pounds) of diamonds are mined every year, so the "rough value" of conflict diamonds is currently around $90 million. The "street value" (i.e., retail) is much higher—somewhere around $1 billion or more.

34. A considerable amount of diamond cutting is now done in Asia, where labor costs are quite low; see Aravind Adiga, "Uncommon Brilliance," *Time*, April 12, 2004, www.time.com/time/magazine/article/0,9171,610100,00.html (accessed May 29, 2009); "Diamonds Lose Their Lustre, Forcing Layoffs in India," *Economic Times* (India), March 29, 2009, http://economictimes.indiatimes.com/News/News-By-Industry/Jobs/Diamonds-lose-their-lustre-forcing-layoffs-in-India/articleshow/4329717.cms (accessed May 29, 2009).

35. The economic crisis has had a serious impact on the Central Selling Organization's control of the global diamond market. For recent analyses of the state of

the diamond trade, see Julia Werdigier, "Diamond Sales, and Prices, Plunge," *New York Times*, February 20, 2009, www.nytimes.com/2009/02/21/business/21diamonds .html (accessed May 29, 2009); and Andrew E. Kramer, "Russia Stockpiles Diamonds, Awaiting the Return of Demand," *New York Times*, May 11, 2009, www.nytimes .com/2009/05/12/business/global/12diamonds.html (accessed May 29, 2009).

36. See, e.g., Paul Lubeck, Michael Watts, and Ronnie Lipschutz, "Convergent Interests: U.S. Energy Security and the 'Securing' of Nigerian Democracy," Center for International Policy, February 2007, www.ciponline.org/NIGERIA_FINAL.pdf.

37. Edward Hooper, *The River: A Journey to the Source of HIV and AIDS* (Boston: Little, Brown, 1999).

38. Of course, the relative costs might turn out to be quite different if drug trial failures, lawsuits, and other costs are taken into account. Although the U.S. "alien torts" law permits foreigners to sue American corporations in American courts for negligence, it is both expensive and difficult to file, pursue, and win such a case. More generally, corporations must be sued in the jurisdiction in which the illegal act has taken place, and it is often even more difficult to get just compensation under those circumstances.

39. Similar arguments can be made about conservation of biodiversity and bio-prospecting for drugs and other potential products in developing countries; see, e.g., Joe Jackson, *The Thief at the End of the World: Rubber, Power, and the Seeds of Empire* (New York: Viking, 2008).

Chapter 5: Technology and Alienation

1. An early story of the alienation generated by technology is E. M. Forster, "The Machine Stops," first published in *The Oxford and Cambridge Review*, in November 1909. The story can be found on the Internet at www.acidlife.com/subconscio/the_ machine_stops_e.m.forster.pdf (accessed March 17, 2009). Interesting discussions of the relationships among history, technology, and capitalism can be found in Merritt Roe Smith and Leo Marx, eds., *Does Technology Drive History? The Dilemma of Technological Determinism* (Cambridge, MA: MIT Press, 1994).

2. Karl Marx, "Estranged Labour," *Economic and Philosophical Manuscripts of 1844*, at www.marxists.org/archive/marx/works/1844/manuscripts/labour.htm#05 (accessed May 29, 2009, emphasis in the original). It is worth noting that "alienation" also means the transfer of legal title from one owner to another.

3. Karl Polanyi, *The Great Transformation*, new ed. (Boston: Beacon, 2001).

4. That such bidding does occur can be seen in the exchange value of human eggs and surrogate mothers on the open market. Figures from the Internet suggest that the former runs somewhere in the neighborhood of $15,000; the latter, from $55,000 to $140,000.

5. Cyborgs are best known, perhaps, as the "Borg" in "Star Trek," but they also appear in many other places. They have become well known in literature and the humanities through Donna Haraway, "A Cyborg Manifesto: Science, Technology, and

Socialist-Feminism in the Late Twentieth Century," in *Simians, Cyborgs and Women: The Reinvention of Nature* (New York; Routledge, 1991), www.stanford.edu/dept/ HPS/Haraway/CyborgManifesto.html (accessed March 17, 2009), 149–81.

6. Tracy Kidder, *The Soul of a New Machine* (Boston: Little, Brown, 1981). For a utopian view, see Ray Kurzweil, *The Age of Spiritual Machines: When Computers Exceed Human Intelligence* (New York: Viking, 1999).

7. The term *westward the course of empire* originates from a 1726 poem by Bishop Berkeley and is the title of at least two well-known works of art, one by Emanuel Leutze (1861), the other by Frances Flora Bond Palmer (1868), later immortalized in print form by Currier and Ives.

8. Leo Marx, *The Machine in the Garden: Technology and the Pastoral Idea in America* (Oxford: Oxford University Press, 2000); Marshall Berman, *All That Is Solid Melts into Air: The Experience of Modernity* (London: Verso, 1983); Smith and Marx, *Does Technology Determine History?*

9. Eric R. Wolf, *Europe and the People without History* (Berkeley: University of California Press, 1982); Kees van der Pijl, *Nomads, Empires and States: Modes of Foreign Relations and Political Economy*, vol. 1 (London: Pluto, 2007); Robert B. Reich, *The Work of Nations: Preparing Ourselves for 21st-Century Capitalism* (New York: Vintage, 1991); Elizabeth Shove, *Comfort, Cleanliness, and Convenience: The Social Organization of Normality* (Oxford: Berg, 2003).

10. Bruno Latour, *Science in Action: How to Follow Scientists and Engineers through Society* (Cambridge, MA: Harvard University Press, 1988).

11. The very term *natural* is problematic, inasmuch as it used to describe those things we deem to not be "cultural" as well as those features of human behavior that appear (or are) deeply and biologically ingrained. A sense of the tension inherent in the term and its uses can be found by comparing William Cronon, ed., *Uncommon Ground: Rethinking the Human Place in Nature* (New York: W. W. Norton, 1996), with Michael E. Soulé and Gary Lease, eds., *Reinventing Nature? Responses to Postmodern Deconstruction* (Washington, DC: Island Press, 1995).

12. Interestingly, the term *alien* is also applied to invasive species, both plant and animal, that did not originate in those places where they have nonetheless become well established.

13. I need note only the plethora of books and films on the topic, including *War of the Worlds,* "Independence Day," and "The Day the Earth Stood Still," as well as Samuel Huntington's *Who Are We? The Challenge to America's National Identity* (New York: Simon and Schuster, 2004); and Peter Brimelow, *Alien Nation: Common Sense about America's Immigration Disaster* (New York: Random House, 1995).

14. Friedrich A. Hayek, *The Road to Serfdom* (Chicago: University of Chicago, 1944).

15. E. H. Carr, *The Twenty Years Crisis, 1919–1939: An Introduction to the Study of International Relations* (London: Macmillan, 1940); Norman Angell, *The Great Illusion: A Study of the Relation of Military Power in Nations to Their Economic and Social Advantage* (London: W. Heinemann, 1912).

16. James von Brunn is the individual who shot up the Holocaust Museum in June 2009; see Devlin Barrett and Eileen Sullivan, "'Lone Wolf' Terrorists Elusive Targets

for Police," *Houston Chronicle*, June 13, 2009, www.chron.com/disp/story.mpl/ap/
washington/6477680.html (accessed June 14, 2009). See also Department of Homeland Security, Extremism and Radicalization Branch, Homeland Environment Threat
Analysis Division, "Rightwing Extremism: Current Economic and Political Climate
Fueling Resurgence in Radicalization and Recruitment," Federation of American Scientists, April 9, 2009, www.fas.org/irp/eprint/rightwing.pdf (accessed June 14, 2009).

17. Terry McDermott, *Perfect Soldiers: The 9/11 Hijackers: Who They Were, Why
They Did It* (New York: HarperCollins, 2005); Jonathan Yardley, "The 9/11 Hijackers," *Washington Post*, May 1, 2005, www.washingtonpost.com/wp-dyn/content/
article/2005/04/28/AR2005042801315.html (accessed August, 21 2009).

18. Barbara Surk, "Dubai Announces Guidelines for Public Behavior," *San Francisco
Chronicle*, March 17, 2009, www.sfgate.com/cgi-bin/article.cgi?f=/c/a/2009/03/17/
MNN916G84P.DTL&hw=dubai&sn=001&sc=1000 (accessed March 17, 2009).

19. Latour, *Science in Action*.

20. Another popular trope in film and fiction is the engineered microbe or virus
that "gets loose" and wreaks havoc on innocent civilian populations, turning them
into zombies or even worse. That list includes "28 Days" (2000), Richard Preston's
The Cobra Event (1998), and "Resident Evil" (2002). For reassurance that the United
States is on top of such things, see David E. Sanger and Thom Shanker, "Pentagon
Plans New Arm to Wage Cyberspace Wars," *New York Times*, May 30, 2009, www
.nytimes.com/2009/05/29/us/politics/29cyber.html (accessed June 1, 2009); and David
E. Sanger and John Markoff, "Obama Outlines Coordinated Cyber-Security Plan,"
New York Times, May 29, 2009, www.nytimes.com/2009/05/30/us/politics/30cyber
.html (accessed June 1, 2009).

21. Such fears are reminiscent of the opening narration to television's original
"Outer Limits": "There is nothing wrong with your television set. Do not attempt to
adjust the picture. We are controlling transmission. If we wish to make it louder, we
will bring up the volume. If we wish to make it softer, we will tune it to a whisper. We
will control the horizontal. We will control the vertical. We can roll the image, make
it flutter. We can change the focus to a soft blur or sharpen it to crystal clarity. For the
next hour, sit quietly and we will control all that you see and hear."

22. See, e.g., Thayer Watkins, "An Introduction to Cost-Benefit Analysis," Department of Economics, San Jose State University, www.sjsu.edu/faculty/watkins/cba.htm
(accessed March 17, 2009).

23. See, e.g., Slavoj Žižek, "The Matrix, or the Two Sides of Perversion," in *Enjoy
Your Symptom! Jacques Lacan in Hollywood and Out*, 2nd ed. (New York: Routledge,
2001), 213–34; and Christopher Grau, ed., *Philosophers Explore the Matrix* (Oxford:
Oxford University Press, 2005).

24. I should note that a more recent viewing of "The Matrix" suggests that the film
might also be a satire, along the lines of Orwell's *Nineteen Eighty-Four* as a satire of the
United States rather than a critique of the Soviet Union. Perhaps what follows should
therefore be read with a certain degree of ironic reflexivity.

25. As Ron Suskind reported on a conversation with a Bush administration aide,
"The aide said that guys like me were 'in what we call the reality-based community,'
which he defined as people who 'believe that solutions emerge from your judicious

study of discernible reality.' I nodded and murmured something about enlightenment principles and empiricism. He cut me off. 'That's not the way the world really works anymore,' he continued. 'We're an empire now, and when we act, we create our own reality. And while you're studying that reality—judiciously, as you will—we'll act again, creating other new realities, which you can study too, and that's how things will sort out. We're history's actors . . . and you, all of you, will be left to just study what we do.'" "Without a Doubt," *New York Times*, October 17, 2004, http://query .nytimes.com/gst/fullpage.html?res=9C05EFD8113BF934A25753C1A9629C8B63 (accessed March 17, 2009).

26. See, e.g., the concluding volume of C. S. Lewis's Narnia series, *The Last Battle* (New York: HarperCollins, 1994).

27. Paranoia is, of course, a constant presence throughout American life and politics. The locus classicus on this theme is Richard Hofstadter, *The Paranoid Style in American Politics and Other Essays* (Cambridge, MA: Harvard University Press, 1966). See also Ronnie D. Lipschutz, "From 'Culture Wars' to Shooting Wars: Cultural Conflict in the United States," in *The Myth of "Ethnic Conflict,"* ed. Beverly Crawford and Ronnie D. Lipschutz, 394–433 (Berkeley: University of California, Berkeley, Institute of Area Studies Press, 1998).

28. The mysterious "They" also turn up in the 1955 film "Kiss Me Deadly," in which private eye Mike Hammer pursues a valuable "whatsit" wanted by everyone else; see Ronnie D. Lipschutz, *Cold War Fantasies: Film, Fiction, and Foreign Policy* (Lanham, MD: Rowman & Littlefield, 2001), 75–77.

29. See, e.g., the "Resident Evil" video game series. We should not disregard the "vaporization" of trillions of dollars from the stock, securities, and real estate markets that, in many instances, also has radical consequences for the identities of those who have lost money.

30. Polanyi, *The Great Transformation*, 3.

31. It is worth noting that William Z. Foster (1881–1961) was for many years general secretary of the Communist Party of the United States of America.

32. Lipschutz, "From 'Culture Wars' to Shooting Wars."

33. In 1972, presidential candidate George McGovern's slogan was "Come home, America!"

34. This recalls Colonel Trout's rejoinder to CIA agent Murdock, about the Vietnamese jungle, in "Rambo: First Blood Part II" (1985): "What some people call hell, he [Rambo] calls home."

35. Angela M. Gulick, "The Handmaid's Tale: More Than *1984* with Chicks," Pacific Rim Studies Conference, February 1996, www.cngl.uaa.alaska.edu/gulick/ HTML/pubthtpr.htm# (accessed March 10, 1998).

36. Such travels into an imagined future were very popular during the late nineteenth century; see, e.g., Edward Bellamy, *Looking Backward: 2000–1887* (1888; rpt. Oxford: Oxford University Press, 2007).

37. Foster's efforts to take well-marked paths and means, such as a city bus, to his destination are repeatedly frustrated. He has no choice but to go to ground and through, rather than around, the people and obstacles in his way.

38. Lizzie Francke, "Deadbeat While Male," *New Statesman and Society*, May 29, 1993, 31–32.

39. See, e.g., Arthur Dudley Vinton's *Looking Further Backward: Being a Series of Lectures Delivered to the Freshman Class at Shawmut College by Professor Won Lung Li (successor of Prof. Julian West)* (Albany, NY: Albany Book Company, 1890); and Floyd Gibbon's *The Red Napoleon* (New York: J. Cape and H. Smith, 1929).

40. It is interesting, perhaps, that Dick's artificial humans and animals were more clockwork than blood and guts; he seems not to have anticipated fully the biotechnological revolution or cloning, as such; see Shelley Hurt, "Science, Power, and the State: U.S. Foreign Policy, Intellectual Property Law, and the Origins of the World Trade Organization, 1969–1994" (PhD diss., Department of Political Science, New School for Social Research, 2009).

41. Racism is alive and well in 2019, even if the replicants are all Anglo-Saxon.

42. In Dick's novel, virtually all living animals have become extinct, so those that remain are very expensive and provide status to their owners. In the film, there are hints that the same has happened to animals (see, e.g., Zhora's snake), but this point is never made very clearly.

43. See, e.g., Nestor M. Davidson, "Property and Relative Status," *Michigan Law Review* 197, no. 5 (2009): 757–817; and John W. Schouten and James H. McAlexander, "Subcultures of Consumption: An Ethnography of the New Bikers," *Journal of Consumer Research* 22, no. 1 (June 1995): 43–61.

44. On the economic "value" of a human life, see, e.g., Kathleen Kingsbury, "The Value of a Human Life: $129,000," *Time*, May 20, 2008, www.time.com/time/health/article/0,8599,1808049,00.html (accessed March 13, 2009); and Peter Dorman, *Markets and Mortality: Economics, Dangerous Work, and the Value of Human Life* (Cambridge: Cambridge University Press, 1996).

45. Alison Brysk and Gershon Shafir, eds., *People Out of Place: Globalization, Human Rights, and the Citizenship Gap* (London: Routledge, 2004).

46. Louis J. Kern, "Terminal Notions of What We May Become: Synthflesh, Cyberreality, and the Post-Human Body," in *Simulacrum America: The USA and the Popular Media*, ed. Elisabeth Kraus and Carolin Auer, 95–106 (Rochester, NY: Camden House/Boydell and Brewer, 2000).

47. Stephenson's Baroque Cycle, consisting of three very long volumes, is an epic of the "first" round of globalization, as England emerged from its Glorious Revolution to become the economic fulcrum of the world. A combination of historical fact and imaginative fiction, it is well worth reading all the way through.

48. This was a theme, too, in Frederik Pohl and Cyril M. Kornbluth, *The Space Merchants* (New York: Ballantine, 1953).

49. Neal Stephenson, *Snow Crash* (New York: Bantam Spectra, 1993), 116.

50. Julian L. Simon, *The Ultimate Resource 2* (Princeton, NJ: Princeton University Press, 1998).

51. Kenneth Arrow, "The Economics of Information: An Exposition," *Empirica* 23, no. 2 (1996): 119–28.

52. Peter Drahos, with John Braithwaite, *Information Feudalism: Who Owns the Knowledge Economy?* (London: Earthscan, 2003).

53. Chris Sprigman, "The Mouse That Ate the Public Domain: Disney, the Copyright Term Extension Act, and *Eldred v. Ashcroft,*" FindLaw.com, March 5, 2002, http://writ.news.findlaw.com/commentary/20020305_sprigman.html (accessed March 18, 2009).

54. David Barboza, "Chinese Court Convicts 11 in Microsoft Piracy Case," *New York Times,* December 31, 2008, www.nytimes.com/2009/01/01/business/worldbusiness/01soft.html (accessed December 31, 2008).

55. Carol S. Robb, *Equal Value: An Ethical Approach to Economics and Sex* (Boston: Beacon, 1995).

56. Arguably, the knowledge commons cannot suffer from crowding or "tragedies," unlike a physical commons of the sort deplored by Garrett Hardin and others.

57. The very notion in this instance of "labor" is debatable inasmuch as such data are subsequently processed by software that can hardly be said to be "working" in a Lockean or even a mental sense. Do computers have rights?

58. According to Ray Kurzweil, "Within a quarter century, nonbiological intelligence will match the range and subtlety of human intelligence. It will then soar past it because of the continuing acceleration of information-based technologies, as well as the ability of machines to instantly share their knowledge. Intelligent nanorobots will be deeply integrated in our bodies, our brains, and our environment, overcoming pollution and poverty, providing vastly extended longevity, full-immersion virtual reality incorporating all of the senses (like 'The Matrix'), 'experience beaming' (like 'Being John Malkovich'), and vastly enhanced human intelligence. The result will be an intimate merger between the technology-creating species and the technological evolutionary process it spawned." *The Singularity Is Near: When Humans Transcend Biology* (New York: Viking Press, 2005). See http://singularity.com/themovie/future .php (accessed March 18, 2009).

59. These acronyms refer to random access memory and read only memory.

60. This is the central conceit of William Gibson's *Neuromancer* (New York: Ace, 1984).

61. Neal Stephenson, *The Diamond Age, or, A Young Lady's Illustrated Primer* (New York: Spectra, 1995). Stross projects the implications and consequences of the "Singularity" in this and other of his books, such as *Singularity Sky* (New York: Ace, 2005) and *Accelerando* (New York: Ace, 2005).

62. Rebecca Hester, *Embodied Politics: Health Promotion in Indigenous Mexican Migrant Communities in California* (PhD diss., Department of Politics, University of California, Santa Cruz, 2009), ch. 6.

63. Colin Gordon, *The Foucault Effect: Studies in Governmentality,* ed. Graham Burchell, Colin Gordon, and Peter Miller (Chicago: University of Chicago Press, 1991), 44.

64. Michel Foucault, *The Birth of Biopolitics: Lectures at the Collège de France, 1978–1979,* ed. Arnold Davidson (New York: Palgrave Macmillan, 2008), 226.

Chapter 6: States and Regulations

1. Well, almost everyone: There are seven to ten million copies in print, and films based on the novel were released in 1963 and 1990.

2. Gayatri Spivak coined the term *epistemic violence* to refer to the silencing of the subaltern by the postcolonial discourses of colonial power. More generally, it refers to forms of oppression and silencing through various textual and discursive practices, such as the law, and is mediated through language, text, descriptions, and internalized norms directed against oppressed "Others." See Gayatri Spivak, *In Other Worlds: Essays in Cultural Politics* (New York: Routledge, 1988), 204; and Jörg Meyer, "The Concealed Violence of Modern Peace(-Making)," *Millennium* 36, no. 3 (2008): 555–74. For an extended exploration of epistemic violence in world politics, see Heather M. Turcotte, *Petro-sexual Politics: Global Oil, Legitimate Violence and Transnational Justice* (PhD diss., Department of Politics, University of California, Santa Cruz, 2008).

3. Cynthia Weber has done so in chapters 2 and 7 of *International Relations Theory: A Critical Introduction*, 2nd ed. (London: Routledge, 2005). While I am indebted to Weber's analysis, my approach is somewhat different from hers. She focuses primarily on deconstructing the "anarchy myth" and its twentieth-century history in the world, especially as presented in Waltz and illustrated in the 1963 film production of *Lord of the Flies*. Later in her book, writing critically of Alex Wendt's constructivist approach to anarchy, Weber identifies herself as a "poststructuralist" and in the chapter on neo-Marxism attacks the ahistoricity of much "postmodern" theorizing. Here, by contrast, history matters. In this chapter, I focus not on films but on books and their histories as well as the origins of myths and practices in the historical specifics of contemporary Anglo-American capitalism, especially as it has shaped what we call the "international states system" and the theories thereof.

4. See Kenneth Neal Waltz, *Man, the State, and the State System in Theories of the Causes of War* (PhD diss., Columbia University, 1954); see http://academiccommons .columbia.edu: 8080/ac/handle/10022/AC:P:910 for bibliographic details (accessed June 26, 2009).

5. As suggested below, Waltz's theory is highly economistic and derivative of liberalism, a point later made about neorealism in Richard K. Ashley, "The Poverty of Neorealism," *International Organisation* 38, no. 2 (Spring 1984): 225–86.

6. Indeed, the only extended citation of Hobbes appears on page 85 of *Man, the State and War*, in the chapter on the second image.

7. Ronnie D. Lipschutz, *After Authority* (Albany: State University of New York Press, 2000), chs. 5 and 6.

8. Ludwig von Mises, *Human Action: A Treatise on Economics* (New Haven, CT: Yale University Press, 1949); Friedrich A. Hayek, *The Road to Serfdom* (Chicago: University of Chicago Press, 1944); Milton Friedman, *Capitalism and Freedom* (Chicago: University of Chicago Press, 1962).

9. R. B. J. Walker, *Inside/Outside: International Relations as Political Theory* (Cambridge: Cambridge University Press, 1992).

10. C. S. Lewis, *The Lion, the Witch, and the Wardrobe* (London: Geoffrey Bles, 1950); see also London Metropolitan Archives, "The Evacuation of Children from the County of London during the Second World War, 1939–1945," Information Leaflet No. 10, November 1997, www.cityoflondon.gov.uk/NR/rdonlyres/590652BD-6D2A-44B4-BA83-E0136C22915C/0/LH_LMA_evacuation.PDF (accessed June 17, 2009).

11. British "public schools" equate to "elite" or "private" schools in the United States. "State schools" in the United Kingdom are the equivalent of public schools in the United States.

12. The novel does not explain the cause of the crash, although there is mention of a storm (metaphor, anyone?). Peter Brook's 1961 film version intimates that the boys' plane is attacked by enemy fighters (the film was released in 1963).

13. Christine Di Stefano, "Masculinity as Ideology in Political Theory: Hobbesian Man Considered," *Women's Studies International Forum* 6 (1983): 638.

14. Nicholas G. Onuf, *World of Our Making: Rules and Rule in Social Theory and International Relations* (Columbia: University of South Carolina Press, 1989).

15. *Scepter*: an ornamental staff held by a ruling monarch as a symbol of power; from the ancient Greek (*skeptron*) for "staff, stick, baton," from (*skepto*) "to prop, to support, to lean upon a staff." From www.allwords.com/word-sceptre.html (accessed June 26, 2009).

16. William Golding, *Lord of the Flies* (New York: Perigee, 1954), 19.

17. Golding, *Lord of the Flies*, 22.

18. R. H. Tawney, *The Agrarian Problem in the Sixteenth Century* (1912; rpt. New York: Harper & Row, 1967). Here is where we might find the "origins" of English society, as the rulers of various Anglo-Saxon territories elected a "high king," who eventually acquired the authority to allocate property and authorize property rights. Is this, then, a case of "anarchy" transforming itself into "society"?

19. See, e.g., Christopher Hill, *The World Turned Upside Down: Radical Ideas during the English Revolution* (London: Maurice Temple Smith, 1972).

20. *Leviathan, or the Matter, Forme and Power of a Commonwealth Ecclesiasticall and Civil*, ed. Michael Oakeshott (New York: Collier, 1962), ch. 17.

21. Onuf, *World of Our Making*.

22. Hill, *The World Turned Upside Down*.

23. As a Royalist, Hobbes had little faith in the order of the Commonwealth, although after *Leviathan* was published, he was forced to make peace with Cromwell's government.

24. A similar disregard for history and social status is present in John Rawls's "original position," which tends to render his thought experiment somewhat pointless. See John Rawls, *A Theory of Justice*, rev. ed. (Cambridge, MA: Harvard University Press, 1999).

25. This action also foreshadows both international terrorism and the rise of "rogue" states, as Jack and his boys engage in uncivil behavior, asymmetric violence, and guerrilla warfare. Indeed, it is his state that deploys the "atomic bomb" against Ralph's nonnuclear society.

26. V. Spike Peterson, *A Critical Rewriting of Global Political Economy: Integrating Reproductive, Productive and Virtual Economies* (London: Routledge, 2003), ch. 3. For

insights into the processes of social organization, see Eric R. Wolf, *Europe and the People without History* (Berkeley: University of California Press, 1982); and Kees van der Pijl, *Nomads, Empires and States: Modes of Foreign Relations and Political Economy*, vol. 1 (London: Pluto, 2007).

27. John Locke, "On the State of Nature," *Second Treatise on Civil Government*, Book II, chapter 2, www.lonang.com/exlibris/locke/loc-202.htm (accessed June 16, 2009). See also Barry Hindess, "Locke's State of Nature," *History of the Human Sciences* 20, no. 3 (2007): 1–20.

28. Arthur Marwick, *British Class Society since 1945*, 4th ed. (London: Penguin, 2003); W. G. Runciman, "How Many Classes Are There in Contemporary British Society," *Sociology* 24, no. 33 (August 1990): 377–96.

29. Carole Leathwood and Merryn Hutchings, "Entry Routes to Higher Education—Pathways, Qualifications and Social Class," in *Higher Education and Social Class—Issues of Exclusion and Inclusion*, ed. Louise Archer, Merryn Hutchings, and Alistair Ross, 137–54 (London: Routledge, 2002), 138–40.

30. In particular, Piggy's speech, manners, and lack of parents mark him off from the other "properly socialized" boys. Note that, at least initially, the boys' uniforms, with their colors and insignia, would have indicated which school they attended and provided information about their families' status.

31. On this point, see the speculations of Dr. Groteschele, the scholar of nuclear war in *Fail Safe*, about who will emerge victorious from the ruins of World War III. The survivors, he claims, will be the most malevolent prisoners kept in solitary confinement and file clerks in the vaults of large insurance companies, the latter protected by the best insulator in the world, paper. Then, "The small group of hardened criminals and the army of file clerks will war with one another for the remaining means of life. The convicts will have a monopoly of violence, but the file clerks will have a monopoly of organization. Who do you think will win?" (Harvey Wheeler and Eugene Burdick, *Fail Safe* [New York: Dell, 1963], 120.)

32. Does this say something about the British government while Golding was in the earlier stages of writing the novel? Most of the members of Clement Atlee's postwar Labour government were not from the working class. One of the few who were, Aneurin Bevan, did not attend public school, although he later won a scholarship from the South Wales Miners' Federation to attend the Central Labour College in London. Bevan did not wear "specs." Nor do we know whether he was raised by his auntie or had "asthmar."

33. See, e.g., Scott Poynting and Mike Donaldson, "Snakes and Leaders: Hegemonic Masculinity in Ruling-Class Boys' Boarding Schools," *Men and Masculinities* 7, no. 4 (2005): 325–46.

34. We might note here that the neoclassical economist never inquires into how such skills have been acquired or how the division is decided. Apparently, both come "naturally."

35. See the discussion of Adam Smith's pin factory in chapter 4 .

36. Jeffrey Richards, *Happiest Days: The Public Schools in English Fiction* (Manchester, UK: Manchester University Press, 1991); Abigail Wills, "Delinquency, Masculinity and Citizenship in England, 1950–1970," *Past & Present* 187 (May 2005): 157–85.

37. This contrast is emphasized much more clearly in the 1963 film.

38. Stephen Greenblatt, "Culture," in *Critical Terms for Literary Study*, ed. Frank Lentricchia and Thomas McLaughlin, 2nd ed., 225–32 (Chicago: University of Chicago Press, 1995), 225–26.

39. Vivienne Jabri, *War and the Transformation of Global Politics* (Houndsmill, Basingstoke, UK: Palgrave Macmillan, 2007); Jonathan X. Inda, *Targeting Immigrants: Government, Technology, and Ethics* (Oxford: Blackwell, 2006), ch. 1; Walker, *Inside/ Outside*.

40. See, e.g., Onuf, *World of Our Making*, 166–68.

41. C. B. Macpherson, *The Political Theory of Possessive Individualism: Hobbes to Locke* (Oxford: Clarendon Press, 1962).

42. Karl Polanyi, *The Great Transformation*, new ed. (Boston: Beacon, 2001). See also the film "Fight Club."

43. Weber, *International Relations*, ch. 2. This is not the same as Judith Shklar's "liberalism of fear." If I understand Shklar's argument correctly, she seemed to believe that constitutionalism could prevent abuse by the state and the powerful. I am suggesting here that liberal society cannot exist without fear and that constitutionalism does nothing more than legalize fear. See Judith Shklar, "The Liberalism of Fear," in *Liberalism and the Moral Life*, ed. Nancy Rosenblum, 21–39 (Cambridge, MA: Harvard University Press, 1989) .

44. "Lost in Space" and "Gilligan's Island" are two other variants. See Cynthia Weber, *International Relations Theory*. On "Lost," see J. Wood, *Living Lost: Why We're All Stuck on the Island* (New Orleans: Garrett County Press, 2007). On "Survivor," see Matthew J. Smith and Andrew F. Wood, eds., *Survivor Lessons: Essays on Communication and Reality Television* (Jefferson, NC: McFarland and Company, 2003).

45. See, e.g., John Lewis Gaddis, *Strategies of Containment* (New York: Oxford University Press, 1982); Morton Halperin, *Limited War in the Nuclear Age* (New York: Wiley, 1963); Stanley Sandler, *The Korean War: No Victors, No Vanquished* (Lexington: University Press of Kentucky, 1999), 229–30.

46. The literature on the short- and long-term impacts of thermonuclear war, both fictional and not, literally exploded during the 1950s. Among the many examples of the former, Neville Shute's *On the Beach* (New York: William Morrow, 1957) was one of the most pessimistic; of the former, Herman Kahn's *On Thermonuclear War* (Princeton, NJ: Princeton University Press, 1960) was one of the most optimistic (several of Robert Heinlein's books for boys were also quite upbeat, while Pat Frank's 1959 *Alas, Babylon* [Philadelphia: Lippincott] suggested that nuclear war could be survived). See also Nancy Ainsfield, *The Nightmare Considered: Critical Essays on Nuclear War Literature* (Madison: Popular Press/University of Wisconsin Press, 1991). And we should not forget Stanley Kubrick's "Dr. Strangelove, or How I Learned to Stop Worrying and Love the Bomb" (1964).

47. In this, his company was Henry Kissinger, *Nuclear Weapons and Foreign Policy* (New York: Harper and Row, 1957), and Kahn, *On Thermonuclear War*, among many others. It is interesting to note that in a 2003 interview at the University of California, Berkeley, Institution of International Relations, Waltz disclaimed any predictive or management potential arising from theories such as his. See "Conversations

with History: Kenneth Waltz," YouTube, February 10, 2003, www.youtube.com/watch?v=F9eV5gPlPZg (accessed June 23, 2003).

48. Taking a leaf from Hobbes and liberalism, Klaatu also points out that this arrangement leaves the people for whom he speaks "free to pursue more profitable enterprises." The entire speech can be found at http://history.sandiego.edu/GEN/film notes/klaatu.html (accessed June 25, 2009), and the script with the speech at www.imsdb.com/scripts/Day-the-Earth-Stood-Still,-The.html (accessed June 25, 2009).

49. "History Is Bunk, Says Henry Ford," *New York Times*, October 29, 1921, http://query.nytimes.com/mem/archive-free/pdf?_r=1&res=990CE3D8103CE533A2575AC2A9669D946095D6CF (accessed March 6, 2009). He also told the *Chicago Tribune*, "History is more or less bunk. It's tradition. We don't want tradition. We want to live in the present, and the only history that is worth a tinker's damn is the history that we make today." Ralph Keyes, *The Quote Verifier: Who Said What, Where, and When* (New York: St. Martin's, 2006), 89–90.

50. See, e.g., Franke Wilmer, *The Social Construction of Man, the State and War* (New York: Routledge, 2002).

51. Patricia Cohen, "Ivory Tower Unswayed by Crashing Economy," *New York Times*, March 4, 2009, www.nytimes.com/2009/03/05/books/05deba.html (accessed March 5, 2009).

52. Jonathan Nitzan and Shimshon Bichler, *Capital as Power* (London: Routledge, 2009).

53. Gary Becker's work is symptomatic of this effort.

54. So-called behavioral economists study what, for the rest of us, seems like common sense: humans don't always act according to the tenets of "economic rationality." This does not mean, however, that they are irrational. See Elizabeth Kolbert, "What Was I Thinking?" *The New Yorker*, February 25, 2008, www.newyorker.com/arts/critics/books/2008/02/25/080225crbo_books_kolbert (accessed March 6, 2009).

55. Mancur Olson, *The Logic of Collective Action* (Cambridge, MA: Harvard University Press, 1965).

56. This fiction was incorporated into American law by the Supreme Court's decision in *Santa Clara County v. Southern Pacific Railroad* (1886).

57. Kenneth Waltz, *Theory of International Politics* (New York: McGraw-Hill, 1979).

58. H. W. Brands, "The Idea of the National Interest," *Diplomatic History* 23, no. 2 (January 1999): 239–61; Peter Trubowitz, *Defining the National Interest: Conflict and Change in American Foreign Policy* (Chicago: University of Chicago Press, 1998).

59. Robert Axelrod's "tit-for-tat" research and arguments were meant to counter ahistorical reasoning such as Waltz's, although he, too, assumed no social history prior to "first contact." See Robert Axelrod, *The Evolution of Cooperation* (New York: Basic, 1984); and Alex Wendt, "Anarchy Is What States Make of It: The Social Construction of Power Politics," *International Organization* 46, no. 2 (Spring 1992): 391–425. For a popular-cultural take on the notion of "learning," see "Groundhog Day" (1993).

60. A. F. K. Organski and Jacek Kugler, *The War Ledger* (Chicago: University of Chicago Press, 1981).

61. In fact, the longer-term history of the region shows that Alsace-Lorraine was transferred back and forth between Germanic and French states a number of times prior to 1871.

62. Michel Foucault, *Discipline and Punish: The Birth of the Prison*, trans. Alan Sheridan (New York: Vintage, 1979); Michel Foucault, "Governmentality," in *The Foucault Effect: Studies in Governmentality*, ed. Graham Burchell, Colin Gordon, and Peter Miller, 87–104 (Chicago: University of Chicago Press, 1991).

63. Carl Schmitt, *Political Theology: Four Chapters on the Concept of Sovereignty* (Chicago: University of Chicago Press, 2006).

64. To be sure, the market is often driven by fear of loss, as is evident in the economic crisis of 2008. This might also be irrational, but that is a calculated irrationality (if such a thing can be said to exist).

65. See the "Two Minutes Hate" episode in Orwell's *Nineteen Eighty-Four* for an illustration of this point.

66. Hill, *The World Turned Upside Down*.

67. Shute's *On the Beach* best illustrates this point.

68. George Orwell put it best, and most cynically, in *Nineteen Eighty-Four*: "He who controls the present, controls the past. He who controls the past controls the future." But such control assumes a "rewriting" of history in people's minds and subjectivities, which is not so easy.

69. Hill, *The World Turned Upside Down*.

70. Kenneth Waltz, "The Spread of Nuclear Weapons: More May Be Better," Adelphi Papers 171 (London: International Institute for Strategic Studies, 1981).

Chapter 7: Economy and Gender

1. Mick LaSalle, *Complicated Women: Sex and Power in Pre-Code Hollywood* (New York: Thomas Dunne, 2000); and Geoffrey O'Brien, "When Hollywood Dared," *New York Review of Books* 56, no. 11 (July 2, 2009): 6–10.

2. Judith Butler, *Gender Trouble: Feminism and the Subversion of Identity* (London: Routledge, 1999).

3. As we shall see below, *gender* is not the same as *biological sex*—and "The Dark Knight" has very few female characters.

4. Women provide a great deal of unpaid labor in the household, which subsidizes wage-paying capitalism. Depending on how one values such unpaid work, the subsidy might amount to $20 trillion or more per year on a global basis (compared to a formal global domestic product of $50 to $70 trillion per year).

5. Frederic Wertham, *Seduction of the Innocent: The Influence of Comic Books on Today's Youth* (New York: Rinehart, 1954); and David Hadju, *The Ten-Cent Plague: The Great Comic-Book Scare and How It Changed America* (New York: Farrar, Straus and Giroux, 2008). For a recent discussion of films from the precode era, see O'Brien, "When Hollywood Dared." R-rated superhero films, such as "Watchmen" (2009), tend to foreground the homoerotic element as well as sexual activity.

6. Peter Parker/Spiderman's "emotional problems" had mostly to do with women and guilt (as distinct matters) and were never very interesting.

7. For the moment, I ignore the question of whether Batman was/is "straight" or "gay."

8. See, e.g., V. Spike Peterson, *A Critical Rewriting of Global Political Economy: Integrating Reproductive, Productive and Virtual Economies* (London: Routledge, 2003).

9. At the same time, it is increasingly recognized that not all societies have, historically, been dichotomous when it comes to either sex or gender; see, e.g., Ifi Amadiume, *Male Daughters, Female Husbands: Gender and Sex in an African Society* (London: Zed Books, 1987).

10. I recognize that this is a problematic and opaque claim. Because of widespread explicit and implicit disparagement of the exhibition and practice of gender attributes not linked to biological sex, men are especially prone to deny attributions of nonmasculinity. Nonetheless, gender bending is a good deal more common than generally acknowledged.

11. Neil Jordan's 1992 film "The Crying Game" violates the norm in that the male protagonist, Fergus, falls in love with the transsexual Dil. Fergus is shocked to discover that Dil is biologically male, but he never completely abjures his attraction to her.

12. While it should be understood that I am contrasting binaries frequently associated with "men" and "women," throughout this chapter I prefer to use the binary that appears in the text—"masculine" and "nonmasculine," as opposed to "masculine" and "feminine." The latter, in particular, has multiple significations in language and popular culture and is commonly linked to women who fulfill these binaries—pretty, sexy, and so forth—rather than to individuals, whether male or female, who have been "demasculinized." As we shall see in the final section of this chapter, men can be presented as nonmasculine even if they engage in no obvious gender-bending activities or affectations.

13. Butler, *Gender Trouble*.

14. Chairman Alan Greenspan, "The Challenge of Central Banking in a Democratic Society," Board of Governors of the Federal Reserve System, December 5, 1996, www.federalreserve.gov/boarddocs/speeches/1996/19961205.htm (accessed March 19, 2009).

15. Russia, for example, is seeing a real decline in its population as a result of dropping birth rates and rising mortality rates; see Barbara A. Anderson, "Russia Faces Depopulation? Dynamics of Population Decline," *Population and Environment* 23, no. 5 (May 2002): 437–64; Nicholas Kulish, "In East Germany, a Decline as Stark as the Wall," *New York Times*, June 18, 2009, www.nytimes.com/2009/06/19/world/europe/19germany.html (accessed June 19, 2009).

16. Thomas Malthus expressed this fear in the eighteenth century, and it has been repeated ever since; see Eric Ross, *The Malthus Factor: Politics, Poverty and Population in Capitalist Development* (London: Zed, 1998).

17. Very few Olympic sports are, however, coed in terms of men and women competing directly; I have only been able to find reference to equestrian events. Ice dancing and pairs figure skating are not really coed in this sense.

18. One provocative notion is that "The Dark Knight" draws on commedia dell'arte, especially in its depiction of the Joker. I have not, however, been able to find a coherent discussion of this.

19. See, e.g., Manfred Weidhorn, "High Noon: Liberal Classic? Conservative Screed," *Bright Lights Film Journal* 47 (February 2005), www.brightlightsfilm.com/47/highnoon.htm (accessed March 19, 2009).

20. Max Weber, *The Protestant Ethic and the Spirit of Capitalism*, trans. Talcott Parsons (New York: Scribner's, 1958).

21. Contrast this with the plot of "High Plains Drifter," a 1973 spaghetti (and antiwar?) western, starring Clint Eastwood as the Man with No Name, which satirizes "High Noon" by "destroying the town in order to save it."

22. Leviathan has not, historically, been thought of as a "businessman" (although see Chicago mayor Richard Daley and others who have governed in Illinois; the 2009 NBC TV series "Kings" portrays the leader of the modern Kingdom of Shiloh as something of a gangster). When the police get into the business of selling protection and safety, they have crossed the ethical line into corruption. The growing privatization of security, á la Blackwater (recently renamed Xe), casts this issue in a rather odd light.

23. It is worth contrasting Kane's choices with Klaatu's parting threat: perhaps Old West marshals and planet-destroying robots are not that very different.

24. Michel Foucault, "Governmentality," in *The Foucault Effect: Studies in Governmentality*, ed. Graham Burchell, Colin Gordon, and Peter Miller, 87–104 (Chicago: University of Chicago Press, 1991).

25. See, e.g., Ben Wattenberg, *The Birth Dearth* (New York: Pharos, 1987); Kulish, "In East Germany."

26. This is the "right of the first night," the alleged right of a lord to take the virginity of the estate's women on the night of their marriage, a practice whose veracity remains in dispute. See also Gita Chowdhry and Sheila Nair, eds., *Power, Postcolonialism, and International Relations: Reading Race, Gender, and Class* (London: Routledge, 2002); and Anna Agathangelou, *The Global Political Economy of Sex: Sex, Violence and Reproductive Labor* (London: Palgrave Macmillan, 2004).

27. The primary problem here is that sex can be had at little or no monetary cost. Most other pleasurable pursuits require some outlay of funds.

28. Owen West, "An About-face on Gay Troops," *New York Times*, February 8, 2009, www.nytimes.com/2009/02/09/opinion/09west.html (accessed February 10, 2009). At this writing, however, the Obama administration has not yet moved to rescind "Don't Ask, Don't Tell."

29. Note that denial of heterosexual sex is not the issue here; rather, control of troops is the concern. Because women have, historically, been denied access to barracks and bases, sexual relations have been restricted to controlled zones. As women have become more and more integrated into military forces worldwide, and as homosexual relations have become more acceptable, such exclusion has become more and more difficult to maintain. See Cynthia Enloe, *Bananas, Beaches and Bases: Making Feminist Sense of International Relations* (Berkeley: University of California Press, 1990), ch. 4; Jan Jindy Pettman, *Worlding Women: A Feminist International Politics*

(New York: Routledge, 1996); Elaine Donnelly, "Constructing the Co-Ed Military," *Duke Journal of Gender Law and Policy* 14 (2007): 816–952; and Anne Gearan, "Military Rape Reports Rise, Prosecution Still Low," *San Francisco Chronicle*, March 17, 2009, www.sfgate.com/cgi-bin/article.cgi?f=/n/a/2009/03/17/national/w151908D57 .DTL (accessed March 20, 2009).

30. George Orwell, *Nineteen Eighty-Four: A Novel* (New York: New American Library, 1983), 57.

31. Orwell, *Nineteen Eighty-Four*, 12, 57.

32. Orwell, *Nineteen Eighty-Four*, 110–11. An interesting and provocative examination of this theme can be found in Joanna Burke, *An Intimate History of Killing: Face-to-Face Killing in Twentieth-Century Warfare* (New York: Basic, 2000), especially chapter 5.

33. Stephen Meyer III, *The Five Dollar Day: Labor Management and Social Control in the Ford Motor Company, 1908–1921* (Albany: State University of New York Press, 1981).

34. Orwell, *Nineteen Eighty-Four*, 60.

35. Note, for example, the social composition of the Iranian opposition movement following the disputed presidential election of June 2009.

36. Erich Lichtblau, "F.B.I., Using Patriot Act, Demands Library's Records," *New York Times*, August 26, 2005, www.nytimes.com/2005/08/26/politics/26patriot.html (accessed March 20, 2009). See also Ray Bradbury, *Fahrenheit 451* (New York: Ballantine, 1953).

37. This was the fate of the Shakers, who believed in strict celibacy and grew through the conversion and adoption of orphans. By 2006, there were only four Shakers still living, but all were quite old.

38. Edmund S. Morgan, "The Puritans and Sex," *New England Quarterly* 15, no. 4 (1942): 591–600.

39. There is one female cop, Detective Anna Ramirez, who betrays the state in order to pay her mother's hospital bills—there's that "othering" of women again!

40. This is in distinction to more recent graphic novels, such as *Watchmen* and its eponymous film (2009). On the history and politics of comic books, see, e.g., Bradford W. Wright, *Comic Book Nation: The Transformation of Youth Culture in America* (Baltimore: Johns Hopkins University Press, 2001); and Anne Rubenstein, *Bad Language, Naked Ladies, and Other Threats to the Nation: A Political History of Comic Books in Mexico* (Durham, NC: Duke University Press, 1998).

41. Michael Chabon's *The Amazing Adventures of Kavalier and Clay* (New York: Random House, 2000) provides a fictionalized version of how superheroes got their start.

42. On underground comics, see Charles Hatfield, *Alternative Comics: An Emerging Literature* (Jackson: University of Mississippi Press, 2005); on graphic novels, see Stephen Weiner, *Faster Than a Speeding Bullet: The Rise of the Graphic Novel* (New York: Nantier Beall Minoustchine, 2003). A recent survey of history of, and as reflected in, comics is Paul Buhle, "History and Comics," *Reviews in American History* 35 (2007): 315–23.

43. This quote is from "Sympathy for the Devil": "Just as every cop is a criminal and all the sinners saints."

44. Sasha Torres, "The Caped Crusader of Camp: Pop, Camp and the *Batman* Television Series," in *Camp: Queer Aesthetics and the Performing Subject: A Reader*, ed. Fabio Cleto, 330–43 (Ann Arbor: University of Michigan Press, 1999).

45. The line between hypermasculinity and cross-dressing parody is a thin one— witness the derision cast upon George Clooney's nippled Batman costume in "Batman and Robin" (1997).

46. Is Bruce Wayne, therefore, an androgyne? Would that explain his refusal to commit to Rachel Dawes?

47. Recall that Cosmo Kramer of "Seinfeld" exhibits an irrational fear of clowns— coulrophobia—which serves him well in "The Opera," an episode in which "crazy" Joe Davola dresses up as the clown from *Pagliacci* and spooks everyone.

48. See the image of Nicholson's joker at http://filmlinc.files.wordpress .com/2008/10/jack-nicholson_joker2.jpg (accessed June 19, 2009).

49. Heath Ledger's Joker can be viewed at http://techdivine.files.wordpress .com/2009/02/heath-ledger-joker-batman.png?w=379&h=400 (accessed June 19, 2009).

50. "Heath Ledger's Joker Is No Joke," *Orbis*, July 23, 2008, http://stickslip.word press.com/2008/07/23/heath-ledgers-joker-is-no-joke (accessed August 14, 2008).

51. Rebecca Hester, *Embodied Politics: Health Promotion in Indigenous Mexican Migrant Communities in California* (PhD diss., Department of Politics, University of California, Santa Cruz, 2009), ch. 3.

52. That is to say, the Joker is neither irrational nor nonrational; he is *without* rationality and simply acts. Note that terrorists are often said to act in this fashion.

53. The complete speech can be found in Dennis O'Neill, *The Dark Knight* (New York: Berkley, 2008), and at www.imsdb.com/scripts/Dark-Knight,-The.html (accessed June 27, 2009).

54. Andrew Klavan, "What Bush and Batman Have in Common," *Wall Street Journal*, July 25, 2008, http://online.wsj.com/public/article_print/SB121694247343482821 .html (accessed March 20, 2009); and Scott Mendelson, "Debunking the 'Dark Knight Endorses Bush/Cheney' Myth," *OpenSalon*, August 31, 2008, http://open.salon. com/blog/scott_mendelson/2008/08/13/debunking_the_dark_knight_endorses_bush cheney_myth (accessed March 20, 2009).

55. Markets can kill—see chapter 8—but they are not supposed to do that, and if they do, no one wants to know about it.

56. "Movie Censorship: A Brief History," The Picture Show Man, 2007, www.pic ture1showman.com/articles_genhist_censorship.cfm (accessed August 8, 2008).

57. Although this is not always so: "Watchmen" is certainly gendered—it even features a lesbian heroine from the 1940s—but it is also somewhat equivocal about who is gendered how.

Chapter 8: Capitalism and Disruption

1. Joseph Schumpeter, *Capitalism, Socialism and Democracy* (New York: Harper and Bros., 1942); Katherine Boo, "The Churn: Creative Destruction in a Border Town,"

The New Yorker, March 29, 2004, 62–73; Katherine Boo, "The Best Job in Town: The Americanization of Chennai," *The New Yorker*, July 5, 2004, 54–69; and W. Michael Cox and Richard Alm, "The Churn: The Paradox of Progress," reprint from *1992 Annual Report*, Federal Reserve Bank of Dallas, www.dallasfed.org/fed/annual/1999p/ar92.pdf (accessed December 6, 2005).

2. This is a theme of "Angels and Demons" (2009) as well as "The International" (2009); see also Ronnie D. Lipschutz, "From 'Culture Wars' to Shooting Wars: Cultural Conflict in the United States," in *The Myth of "Ethnic Conflict,"* ed. Beverly Crawford and Ronnie D. Lipschutz, 394–433 (Berkeley: University of California, Institute of Area Studies Press, 1998); and Ronnie D. Lipschutz, "Capitalism's Churn and Cultural Conflict: How Globalization Has Fractured American Society and Why It Will Be Difficult to Put the Pieces Back Together," in *The Impact of Globalization on the United States: Culture and Society*, ed. Michelle Bertho, vol. 1, 3–24 (Westport, CT: Praeger, 2008).

3. Peter Gowan, "Crisis in the Heartland: Consequences of the New Wall Street System," *New Left Review* 55 (January–February 2009): 5–29; and Maureen O'Hara, "Bubbles: Some Perspectives (and Loose Talk) from History," *Review of Financial Studies* 21, no. 1 (February 2008): 11–17.

4. Boo, "The Churn."

5. As Michel Foucault and others have pointed out, the origins of "public policy" are to be found in *police wissenschaft*, (i.e., the "science of police" having to do with order and discipline); see Michel Foucault et al., *Society Must Be Defended: Lectures at the Collège de France, 1975–76*, trans. David Macey (London: Macmillan, 2003), lectures 12, 13.

6. Rebecca Solnit, "Iceland Is Steamed," *Los Angeles Times*, February 8, 2009, www.latimes.com/news/opinion/la-oe-solnit8-2009feb08,0,5211860.story (accessed February 11, 2009).

7. In fact, this backstory is only too familiar to the citizens of Quebec; see Karen Fricker, "Philistines All," *Guardian*, February 14, 2004, www.guardian.co.uk/stage/2004/feb/14/theatre1 (accessed March 21, 2009).

8. Ronnie D. Lipschutz, "Imperial Warfare in the Naked City: Sociality as Critical Infrastructure," *International Political Sociology* 3, no. 3 (September 2008): 204–18.

9. Sigmund Freud, *Beyond the Pleasure Principle* (London: International Psycho-Analytical Press, 1922).

10. This is an argument at the heart of "Watchmen," in which New York is annihilated and Dr. Manhattan is exiled, all in the cause of "world peace."

11. My goal here is not to plumb the depths of the practice but to contemplate its relationship to capitalist economics. That there is no shortage of feature films depicting torture is evident from the listing at "Reel Torture: Torture in Mainstream Movies," at www.geocities.com/TimesSquare/Dungeon/9363/movies.htm (accessed January 25, 2009). See also "Torture on TV Rising and Copied in the Field," Human Rights First, www.humanrightsfirst.org/us_law/etn/primetime/index.asp (accessed February 3, 2009).

12. Karl Marx, *Capital*, vol. 1 (Moscow: Progress Publishers, 1954). This is discussed in Pranab Kanti Basu, "Political Economy of Land Grab," *Economic and Politi-*

cal Weekly, April 7, 2007, 1281–87, www.counterviews.org/Web_Doc/econ/Political
_Economy_of_Land_Grab.pdf (accessed February 11, 2009). For a lengthy screed on
the relationship between capitalism and violence, see Naomi Klein, *The Shock Doctrine: The Rise of Disaster Capitalism* (New York: Metropolitan Books, 2007); and Amy
Chua, *World on Fire—How Exporting Free Market Democracy Breeds Ethnic Hatred
and Global Instability* (New York: Random House, 2003).

13. The line comes from his Canto 56:

Who trusted God was love indeed
And love Creation's final law
Tho' Nature, red in tooth and claw
With ravine, shriek'd against his creed

14. On the relationship between Social Darwinism, development theory, and economics, see Ali A. Mazrui, "From Social Darwinism to Current Theories of Modern-
ization: A Tradition of Analysis," *World Politics* 21, no. 1 (October 1968): 69–83.

15. As noted earlier, behavioral economics tries to account for irrational behavior;
see Elizabeth Kolbert, "What Was I Thinking?" *The New Yorker*, February 25, 2008,
www.newyorker.com/arts/critics/books/2008/02/25/080225crbo_books_kolbert (accessed March 6, 2009).

16. A common expression for such behavior and consequences is "privatizing
gains, socializing risks."

17. GM's share price, for example, hit a peak of $93.63 on April 28, 2000, and
closed on March 9, 2009, at $1.45 (bankruptcy wiped out share value, of course).
"General Motors Corporation," BigCharts, http://bigcharts.marketwatch.com/quick
chart/quickchart.asp?symb=GM&sid=0&o_symb=GM&freq=2&time=13 (accessed
March 21, 2009).

18. David Hendrickson, "The Overall Idea," *Cause for Depression*, October 30,
2008, https://lodgeus.com/cgi-bin/nph-gowingo.cgi/000010A/http/pictorial-guide-
to-crisis.blogspot.com (accessed March 10, 2009).

19. Schumpeter, *Capitalism, Socialism and Democracy*; Cox and Alm, "The
Churn."

20. Steven Greenhouse, "Young and Old Are Facing Off for Jobs," *New York Times*,
March 20, 2009, www.nytimes.com/2009/03/21/business/21age.html (accessed March
20, 2009).

21. Boo, "The Churn"; Boo, "The Best Job in Town."

22. Note that under the economic regime in force from roughly 1975 to 2005,
redistribution went from the poor to the rich, rather than the reverse. See Paul Krugman, "Conscience of a Liberal: Even More Gilded," *New York Times*, August 13, 2009,
http://krugman.blogs.nytimes.com/2009/08/13/even-more-gilded/ (accessed August
20, 2009).

23. A supportive perspective on this general argument can be found in Jeffrey
Sachs, *The End of Poverty: Economic Possibilities for Our Time* (New York: Penguin,
2005); Joseph E. Stiglitz provides a critical analysis in *Globalization and Its Discontents*
(New York: Norton, 2002).

24. Gretchen Morgenson and Don van Natta Jr., "In Crisis, Banks Dig In for Fight against Rules," *New York Times,* May 31, 2009, www.nytimes.com/2009/06/01/business/01lobby.html (accessed June 1, 2009).

25. This is the story told by Katherine Boo in "The Churn."

26. Peter Schweizer, *Reagan's War: The Epic Story of His Forty-Year Struggle and Final Triumph over Communism* (New York: Doubleday, 2002).

27. See, e.g., Georgi Deluguian, *Bordieu's Secret Admirer in the Caucasus: A World Systems Biography* (Chicago: University of Chicago Press, 2005).

28. Mary Kaldor, *The Baroque Arsenal* (New York: HarperCollins, 1982).

29. David S. Sorensen, *Shutting Down the Cold War: The Politics of Military Base Closure* (London: Palgrave Macmillan, 1998).

30. But recall Lizzie Francke, "Deadbeat White Male," *New Statesman and Society* 6, no. 254 (May 29, 1993): 31–32.

31. N. Flynn and A. P. Taylor, "Inside the Rust Belt: An Analysis of the Decline of the West Midlands Economy. 1: International and National Economic Conditions," *Environment and Planning A* 18, no. 7 (1986): 865–900.

32. Christopher G. L. Hall, *Steel Phoenix: The Fall and Rise of the U.S. Steel Industry* (London: Macmillan, 1997).

33. Thomas Chippendale was an eighteenth-century cabinetmaker and furniture and interior designer, born near Leeds and based in London. See "Thomas Chippendale," Britain Express, 2000, www.britainexpress.com/History/bio/chippendale.htm (accessed March 21, 2009). Others have suggested that the name has to do with the Walt Disney cartoon chipmunks Chip and Dale. Go figure!

34. Agathangelou, *The Global Political Economy of Sex: Desire, Violence, and Insecurity in Mediterranean Nation States* (New York: Palgrave Macmillan, 2004).

35. Boo, "The Best Job in Town."

36. Globalization is a multifaceted phenomenon, with deep historical roots, a result of material, social, and cognitive changes over the past forty years. Globalization is material in the sense that it involves the rapid and largely unfettered movement of capital, technology, goods, and, to a limited degree, labor to areas with high returns on investment. Innovations in communications, transportation, and manufacturing practices facilitate the material dimension of globalization with social or political impacts on the communities and people to which capital moves and from which it leaves. Globalization is social in the sense that it fosters transformations in relations among people as well as disruption and reorganization in existing institutions, without much regard for the consequences for individuals, households, groups, and societies. And, globalization is cognitive in two senses: it is ideologically rationalized in the name of efficiency, competition, and profit, and its material and social effects change the way people both regard, and behave toward, themselves and others. In all three respects, even as globalization offers new possibilities to many and opens numerous political opportunities for social movements and other forms of collective organization and action, it also often disrupts existing forms of beliefs, values, and behaviors. This last effect is, perhaps, most germane here in the sense that the material and ideational processes associated with globalization affect and alter people's subjectivities. On globalization, see Paul Hirst and Grahame Thompson, *Globalization in Question,* 2nd ed.

(Oxford: Blackwell, 1999); Stiglitz, *Globalization and Its Discontents*; Jan A. Scholte, *Globalization: A Critical Introduction* (New York: St. Martin's, 2000); and Ronnie D. Lipschutz, with James K. Rowe, *Globalization, Governmentality and Global Politics: Regulation for the Rest of Us?* (London: Routledge, 2005).

37. Nationalism was especially in vogue in Quebec between about 1965 and 1985; see Richard Handler, *Nationalism and the Politics of Culture in Quebec* (Madison: University of Wisconsin Press, 1988).

38. Apparently, the party's first government was known as the "republic of teachers" because of the large number of college faculty involved in it.

39. Although Canada is officially bilingual and all Canadian citizens receive at least some instruction in French, my observation has been that those whose first language is English and who live outside of Quebec tend not to be very fluent in their second language.

40. Ronnie D. Lipschutz, *The Constitution of Imperium* (Boulder, CO: Paradigm, 2009), chapters 2 and 6.

41. Tourisme Quebec, "Tourism Figures 2007," April 2008, www.bonjourquebec .com/mto/publications/pdf/etudes/Tourism_%20figures2007.pdf (accessed January 25, 2009).

42. Alexander Hamilton, "Report on Manufactures Communicated to the U.S. House of Representatives," Union College, December 5, 1791, at www.constitution .org/ah/rpt_manufactures.doc (accessed August 20, 2009); Friedrich List, *National System of Political Economy*, trans., George-Auguste Matile and Henri Richelot (New York: Lippincott, 1856).

43. Lipschutz, *The Constitution of Imperium.*

44. Michael Slackman, "Young and Arab in Land of Mosques and Bars," *New York Times*, September 21, 2008, www.nytimes.com/2008/09/22/world/middleeast/ 22dubai.html?ei=5070&emc=eta1 (accessed January 25, 2009). More recent reports suggest that as the economy declined, many foreign workers fled Dubai. According to some reports, more than three thousand cars were abandoned at the airport by departing foreigners who could no longer afford to keep up payments on them; see Robert F. Worth, "Laid Off Foreigners Flee as Dubai Spirals Down," *New York Times*, February 11, 2009, www.nytimes.com/2009/02/12/world/middleeast/12dubai.html (accessed March 21, 2009).

45. This is so within limits, of course; see Zoi Constantine and Emmanuelle Landais, "Topless Woman at Beach Sparks 'Cover Up' Call," *Gulfnews.com*, May 8, 2007, http://archive.gulfnews.com/articles/07/05/08/10123731.html (accessed June 20, 2009).

46. Lipschutz, "Imperial Warfare."

47. Norman Angell, *The Great Illusion: A Study of the Relation of Military Power in Nations to Their Economic and Social Advantage* (London: W. Heinemann, 1912).

48. Foucault reminds us that the two are largely the same; see Foucault, *Society Must Be Defended.*

49. On the "electronic Pearl Harbor," see Michael Stohl, "Cyber Terrorism: A Clear and Present Danger, the Sum of All Fears, Breaking Point or Patriot Games?"

Crime, Law and Social Change 46, no. 4–5 (December 2006): 223–38; John Markoff, "Thieves Winning Online War, Maybe Even in Your Computer," *New York Times*, December 5, 2008, www.nytimes.com/2008/12/06/technology/internet/06security .htm (accessed March 21, 2009); and Ronnie D. Lipschutz, "Terror in the Suites: Narratives of Fear and the Political Economy of Danger," *Global Society* 13, no. 4 (October 1999): 411–39.

50. David E. Sanger and Thom Shanker, "Pentagon Plans New Arm to Wage Cyberspace Wars," *New York Times*, May 30, 2009, www.nytimes.com/2009/05/29/us/politics/29cyber.html (accessed June 1, 2009); David E. Sanger and John Markoff, "Obama Outlines Coordinated Cyber-Security Plan," *New York Times*, May 29, 2009, www.nytimes.com/2009/05/30/us/politics/30cyber.html (accessed June 1, 2009).

51. Clay Wilson, "Information Operations and Cyberwar: Capabilities and Related Policy Issues," Congressional Research Service RL31787, updated September 14, 2006, http://in-formation.re-configure.org/infw.pdf (accessed March 21, 2009).

52. National Security Agency/Central Security Service, "Defending Our Nation. Securing the Future," NSA, www.nsa.gov (accessed March 21, 2009).

53. U.S. Intelligence Community at www.intelligence.gov/1-members.shtml (accessed March 21, 2009).

54. Bobby Ray Inman, "Chinese Hacking Signals Age of Info Warfare," *New Perspectives Quarterly* 24, no. 4 (2007): 14–15.

55. A photo of Gabriel can be found at www.zuguide.com/image/Timothy-Olyphant-Live-Free-or-Die-Hard.2.jpg (accessed June 20, 2009).

56. Synopses of all seven seasons of "24" can be found at www.fox.com/24/episodes/7am.htm and www.fox.com/fod/play.php?sh=twentyfour.

57. On torture by U.S. agents, see Mark Danner, *Torture and Truth: America, Abu Ghraib, and the War on Terror* (New York: New York Review of Books, 2004); Mark Danner, "Tales from Torture's Dark World," *New York Times*, March 15, 2009, www.nytimes.com/2009/03/15/opinion/15danner.htm (accessed March 20, 2009); and Mark Danner, "US Torture: Voices from the Black Sites," *New York Review of Books* 56, no. 6 (April 9, 2009), www.nybooks.com/articles/22530 (accessed March 22, 2009). For a more general discussion of the subject, see Lipschutz, *The Constitution of Imperium*.

58. Mike Allen and Dana Priest, "Memo on Torture Draws Focus to Bush," *Washington Post*, June 9, 2004, www.washingtonpost.com/wp-dyn/articles/A26401-2004Jun8.html (accessed August 8, 2008).

59. Don Ross, "Game Theory," *Stanford Encyclopedia of Philosophy*, March 10, 2006, http://plato.stanford.edu/entries/game-theory (accessed March 21, 2009).

60. Karl Marx, *Capital: A Critique of Political Economy*, vol. 1 (New York: Penguin Books, 1976), 873, 915.

61. "Watchmen" again: is the sacrifice of New York a fair price for nuclear peace?

62. Kenneth Waltz, *Theory of International Politics* (New York: McGraw-Hill, 1979).

63. Although films such as "The 10th Victim" (*La decima vittima*, 1965), based on Robert Sheckley's short story "Seventh Victim" (1953), offer food for thought on this point.

64. Amartya Sen tells such a story in *Development as Freedom* (New York: Knopf, 1999).

65. Lawrence Freedman, *Deterrence* (Oxford: Polity Press, 2004); Lawrence Freedman, *The Evolution of Nuclear Strategy*, 2nd ed. (London: Palgrave Macmillan, 1989).

66. Herman Kahn's *On Thermonuclear War* (Princeton, NJ: Princeton University Press, 1960); *Thinking about the Unthinkable* (New York: Horizon, 1962), and *On Escalation: Metaphors and Scenarios* (New York: Praeger, 1965).

67. See also Clive Thompson, "Can Game Theory Predict When Iran Will Get the Bomb?" *New York Times Magazine*, August 16, 2009, www.nytimes.com/2009/08/16/magazine/16Bruce-t.html (accessed August 17, 2009).

Chapter 9: Through the Mirror, Darkly

1. Antonio Gramsci, *Selections from the Prison Notebooks of Antonio Gramsci*, ed. and trans. Q. Hoare and G. Nowell Smith (London: Lawrence and Wishart, 1971), 330n, 419.

2. For more on social regulation, see Ronnie D. Lipschutz, with James K. Rowe, *Globalization, Governmentality and Global Politics: Regulation for the Rest of Us?* (London: Routledge, 2005).

3. For a somewhat different view on this, however, see Adrian Parr, *Hijacking Sustainability* (Cambridge, MA: MIT Press, 2009).

4. But what about *The Anarchist Cookbook*, you might ask? As one website offering the complete text warns, "NOTICE: TO ALL CONCERNED Certain text files and messages contained on this site deal with activities and devices which would be in violation of various Federal, State, and local laws if actually carried out or constructed." See *The Anarchist Cookbook*, www.anarchistcookbookz.com/download-the-anarchist-cookbook-for-free (accessed February 24, 2009). Elsewhere, I have written about thinking and reading bad things without committing a crime; see Ronnie D. Lipschutz, "Imperial Warfare in the Naked City: Sociality as Critical Infrastructure," *International Political Sociology* 3, no. 3 (September 2008): 204–18. And, of course, Ray Bradbury has something to say about this, as well, in *Fahrenheit 451* (New York: Ballantine, 1953).

5. Who can have missed the irony, therefore, when the slum dwellings of two of the film's child stars were destroyed by Mumbai city authorities? See Vikas Bijaj, "Authorities Demolish 'Slumdog' Star's Home in Mumbai," *New York Times*, May 14, 2009, www.nytimes.com/2009/05/15/world/asia/15slumdog.html (accessed June 4, 2009); Dave Itzkoff, "'Slumdog' Star's Home Is Destroyed," *New York Times*, May 20, 2009, www.nytimes.com/2009/05/21/movies/21arts-SLUMDOGSTARS_BRF.html (accessed June 4, 2009).

6. Here I only note that although the United States might not have been the imperial master in colonial India, it has been deeply imbricated in the transnational

imperialist web of the twentieth century, which has enmeshed India as well as the rest of the global South.

7. Apparently, movie attendance is up in 2009 as a result of the recession; see Michael Cieply and Brooks Barns, "Despite Downturn, Americans Flock to the Movies," *New York Times*, February 28, 2009, www.nytimes.com/2009/03/01/movies/01films .html (accessed March 22, 2009).

Index

About the Author

Ronnie D. Lipschutz is a professor of politics and past codirector of the Center for Global, International and Regional Studies at the University of California, Santa Cruz, and during 2009 and 2010, a visiting professor of politics and international relations at Royal Holloway, University of London. His primary areas of research and teaching include international politics, global environmental affairs, U.S. foreign policy, globalization, international regulation, and film, fiction, and politics. His most recent books include *The Constitution of Imperium* (2008) and *Globalization, Governmentality and Global Politics: Regulation for the Rest of Us?* (2005).

Breinigsville, PA USA
08 August 2010
243135BV00002B/2/P

9 780742 556515